UNDER THE HAMMER

Jeremy Cooper

UNDER THE HAMMER

The Auctions and Auctioneers of London

Constable   London

First published in Great Britain 1977 by
Constable and Company Limited
10 Orange Street, London WC2H 7EG
Copyright © 1977 by Jeremy Cooper
Revised edition 1979

ISBN 0 09 461370 2

Set in Monotype Imprint 11pt.
Printed in Great Britain by
REDWOOD BURN LIMITED
Trowbridge & Esher

To my parents-in-law
and to o.c.

Contents

Illustrations

A picture sale at Christie's, from an engraving in the *Illustrated London News* of May 1856. *Frontispiece*

Acknowledgements

The early plans for this book were developed during a season of lecturing to different societies throughout the British Isles on various topics including 'The London Antique Market'. While most people at these luncheons and lectures had heard of Christie's and Sotheby's, and generally knew something about their important sales, remarkably few knew how the London auction rooms worked or ever thought of using them. This book is intended to encourage an active appreciation of the qualities of the London auction houses, as well as pointing out potential dangers in this competitive market. Naturally it is hoped that this account of the historical background and contemporary folklore will interest the auction room habitué, as well as the general reader.

For this book and much more I shall always be indebted to Sotheby's, where I worked for seven years until the summer of 1977; and particularly to Peregrine Pollen, then the Executive Deputy Chairman, and to the Chairman of Sotheby's, Peter Wilson, whose personal assistant I was for my last two seasons with the firm. I trust that my close involvement with Sotheby's has led in this book neither to the revelation of confidential information to Sotheby's undeserved disadvantage nor, on the other hand, to biased praise to their unfair advantage.

I am particularly grateful to Ben Glazebrook for his most essential critical attention to an initial draft and to Prudence Fay for being at once both highly professional and sympathetically personal in her editorial work.

All the photographs were kindly supplied by the auction houses themselves except plates 14, 26, 31 and 38 which were taken by Gunter de Graaff, with whom I look forward to working in the future.

I am also grateful to four anonymous 'critics' who read my manuscript at an early stage and pointed out areas of potential misinterpretation.

My wife, Helen, has been, as always, a source of continuous inspiration and encouragement.

Finally, my fullest thanks to Sue Bayley for her help with this book and with many other projects in recent years; I greatly enjoyed my time at Sotheby's and anything that may have been achieved there would have been impossible without her.

In the preparation of the second edition I am particularly grateful to Donald Wintersgill of the *Guardian* for his advice on some important issues and to Alannah Hopkin for her help with the guide section. Jon Baddeley and Victoria Cecil have been, and are, quite exceptionally helpful too.

JEREMY COOPER
48 Portland Road
London W11 4LG

1

Auctions and Auctioneers

For several years now the affairs of the London art market have commanded the willing attention of the national Press. All the major auctions are reported in detail in the newspapers, and feature articles regularly investigate the latest collecting fashion, argue the merits of art as investment, or marvel at the ingenuity of the latest fraud or theft. The tremendous increase of popular interest in collecting is also reflected in the proliferation of semi-professional magazines and books covering all aspects of the art market and of obscure fields in the decorative arts. The nation's taste has changed, so that quite a large section of the community now attaches some special value to all kinds of decorative objects which need not necessarily be 'antique', but must have that particular period quality which we seek to recapture in the possession of works of art.

Despite this advance in knowledge and interest in collecting, many people remain apprehensive about participating in the activities of the major London auction rooms. A surprising number of serious collectors, masterly competitors against the professional dealers at provincial sales, are over-awed by the international carnival of the London antique trade. Regardless of the popular publicity given to sales at Christie's and Sotheby's, the general fear remains that prices will be too high, the 'membership' too exclusive, and the ritual too complicated. And so the Christie and Sotheby mystique lingers on, when traditional attitudes to so many other hallowed national institutions have years ago been painlessly revised.

Mystique overwhelms reality partly because it is cultivated by television's bright lights and whirring cameras over-exposing the millionaires' playground of Impressionist picture sales. This selective attention to the big sales gives the false idea that every lot sells for tens of thousands of pounds. The misunderstanding is further compounded by the traditional image of the major London auction rooms as exclusive private clubs, entry into which is reserved for those alumni of Eton and Oxford who also possess six-figure accounts in Swiss banks. Even if a non-member succeeded in slipping past the uniformed doorman and scurried upstairs to the sale-room, he would, so the legend insists, be punished by an uncontrollable sneeze or the involuntary twitching of a catalogue, causing the fall of the hammer and the incontestable judgement of the auctioneer—'At fifteen thousand guineas, yours, sir.'

This nightmare reputation still haunts Christie's and Sotheby's in spite of the efforts of both houses to encourage everyone to take advantage of the free entry to the sale-rooms and to bring anything in for free valuation by their experts, and in spite of the emphasis laid in their press releases on the high percentage of lots that sell for under £200. The legend survives because, whatever the truth about today's business, at first experience the London auction scene does seem mysterious and even threatening, as habitués wander about the rooms smiling and nodding at each other, stopping to peer through magnifying-glasses at featureless oil paintings, stooping to inspect an upturned chair, always totally at ease as the auctioneer intones his sale-room liturgy of measured lot-numbers, whirlwind prices and half-heard buyers' names. At times the newcomer may feel as though he has fallen upon some bizarre religious ceremony, complete with secret signs and genuflections before graven images in response to the monotonous, hypnotic incantations of unworldly prices by the high-priest auctioneer.

An outsider seeking reassurance by eavesdropping on trade gossip is likely to have any misapprehensions confirmed, not dismissed. As in any close-knit community, the gossip of the London antique trade has a tradition and structure all of its own which can be as near or far from the truth as it may; and even the employees of the auction rooms themselves tend to embroider their own fables. Thus according to traditional caricature, Christie's reception counter is manned by a team of six-foot-six old Etonians in regimented blue pin-striped suits, all speaking an incomprehensible upper-class Esperanto; while Sotheby's female receptionists, draped in Hermès scarves, spend most of the day oiling their riding-whips before galloping off to tea at Fortnums. As for the experts, they are featured in these West End sketches as talented teenagers in short trousers offering venerable dealers bland assurances that their treasured Ming vases are all Victorian copies.

Many of these fables and popular misconceptions have clear origins in the history of the London auction rooms, and by discussing both the past and present principles of fine art auctioneering some of the ghosts may be laid to rest. At the same time, perhaps, the traditional qualities of the sale-room, with its necessary ritual and white magic, may be more widely appreciated. There are many classical references to auctions; indeed the word itself derives from the Latin word *auctio* meaning 'increase'. (Some of the first auctions to be held were of war loot held *sub hasta* or 'under the spear': the modern Italian word for an auction is *asta*.) The reference in Herodotus Book I to the Babylonian marriage market by auction was a well-known source in Victorian England, and it inspired a gigantic painting of the subject by Edwin Long, a picture (plate 1 and cover) which sold at Christie's in 1882 for 6,300 guineas, which was a record price at that time for a work by a living artist. Long's picture was bought by the pill king, Martin Holloway, and still hangs in the Royal Holloway College. The scene is portrayed in the picture as an elaborate caricature of Christie's, with a long line of maidens awaiting their turn to mount the stage where an attendant displays their attributes to potential husbands, who are staring quizzically like so many Old Master picture-dealers. The auctioneer stands in the rostrum above the crowd, gesticulating persuasively in the manner of the contemporary auction king, Thomas Woods (plate 7). Edwin Long even quoted from Swayne's translation of Herodotus, which described the maidens being sold 'in order of comeliness', and mentioned a system of averaging out the sale-proceeds which would hardly appeal to present owners—'by transferring to the sale of the ill-favoured the prices paid for the fair, beauty was made to endow ugliness, and the rich man's taste was the poor man's gain'.[1]

Fine art auctions of a recognizable form became a regular feature of London life in the late seventeenth century. Horace Walpole was one of the first to write in detail about the history of auction sales, and he researched at length into the Sir Peter Lely sale in 1688, eight years after the artist's death. Walpole gives us no source for the doubtful information that the sale extended over forty days and secured a total of £26,000. He went on, with greater accuracy, to describe the method, prevalent at the time, of selling 'by inch of candle'. By this method an inch-high candle was lit as a signal for the bidding to start, the lot being secured by the last offer made before the candle burnt out.

The professional auctioneer was an important figure in Dutch seventeenth-century commercial life, and the arrival of a Dutch King in London in 1688 had an encouraging effect on auctioneering in London. The earliest-known book-auction catalogue for London is dated 1676, and by the late 1680s Covent Garden was established as the centre of the auction business, with Edward Millington at its head. Within three decades several auctioneers had made reputations in the fine art auction business, the rival sales of Cock and Langford being particularly well known. Samuel Baker, the founder of Sotheby's, started his fixed-price book sales in the late 1720s and held his first open book-auction, according to oral tradition, on 7 January 1745, although the first auctioneer to become a society figure was the charming James Christie, founder in 1766 of the auction house that still bears his name.

The history of Christie's is described in the next chapter; and the general history of the whole London auction market is centred around the activities of this firm, which dominated London fine art auctions from the 1760s until after the Second World War. Here we will look briefly at the position which the auction rooms held within the overall art market. In these early years, auction rooms, according to Gerald Reitlinger, the leading authority in this field, played a relatively minor role in the exchange of works of art, it being inconceivable that the price of £3,500 which the Empress Catherine paid privately in 1779 for the Houghton Guido Reni could have been achieved in the auction rooms, where a price of over £1,000 was seldom recorded for anything in the eighteenth century. The haphazardness of the auction scene, indeed of collecting as a whole, is demonstrated in the 1795 sale catalogue of Sir Joshua Reynolds's collection, which claimed to present seventy Van Dycks, fifty-four Correggios, forty-four Michelangelos, twelve Leonardos and no less than twenty-four Raphaels. In all, there were 411 pictures in this auction, and the average price realized was less than £25 a canvas. Far more important than the auctioneers were artists and connoisseurs like Gavin Hamilton, who lived in Rome and supplied direct to the English aristocracy the real Raphaels and Correggios which were then at the height of fashion.

However, due to James Christie's charm and business acumen the London auction rooms gradually became more closely involved one way and another with the disposal of important collections, although the open auction remained very much a last resort. For example the Duc d'Orléans, in disposing of his grandfather's collection of pictures, first offered them to a private syndicate in England at an asking price of £100,000, but the deal fell through and the Duke was forced to sell the French and Italian pictures in the winter of 1791 to the Belgian banker, Walkuers, for 750,000 francs (then about £30,000). Walkuers sold them to Monsieur Laborde de Mereveille, who managed to escape to England from the Revolution with about 300 of the pictures in 1793. The Dutch and Flemish pictures from the Orléans collection were already in England, bought in June 1792 by a syndicate headed by Thomas Moore Slade. For the next eight or nine years, groups of paintings from these two sources appeared in various London auction rooms as the backers were obliged to realize money, but even then only after all other outlets had failed.

One of the largest single sales at this time, held by Christie's over four days in the summer of 1795, was the Calonne collection which Mereveille had again gambled on; but the auction prices were mostly below Calonne's original purchase prices, Reynolds's *Tragic Muse* falling from £735 to £320 and Poussin's *Triumph of David* from £800 to £600.

During the period 1800–1830 the fine art market was in the hands of dealers such as Michael Bryan and John Smith, who manipulated the fortunes of rich merchants like Thomas Maitland, influenced the tastes of enthusiasts like William Beckford, and cultivated the favours of aristocratic collectors like the Duke of Bridgewater. The little money there was to be made in Old Master pictures at the time came through complex wheeling and dealing within these circles, and a dull seventy-year period followed for the auction rooms; even in the late 1860s, only half a dozen Old Master paintings a season at Christie's sold at over £1,000.

As the nineteenth century progressed, the contemporary painter came more and more into his own, this favourable climate being created principally because of the commercial rewards of print copyright of the popular modern works. The Victorian professional classes were also put off buying Old Masters by the continuing insecurity in attribution. The sale-rooms participated in the contemporary art boom, recording enormous prices for the masterpieces of Millais and Landseer, and even of Rosa Bonheur, a painting of whose A. C. R. Carter, the sale-room critic of the *Daily Telegraph*, saw sold in 1888 for 4,200 guineas to W. H. Smith the stationer. Carter witnessed the sale of the same painting in 1929, again at Christie's, for 46 guineas.

The market for Old Master drawings was difficult in the nineteenth century, so much so that Sir Thomas Lawrence's collection of more than 2,000 drawings, which had cost him over £40,000 to buy, was refused by the nation at an asking price of £18,000, and was eventually sold to the dealer Woodburn for only £15,000. There was even less interest in Italian Renaissance painting, and at the Charles Greville sale in 1810, a fully-accepted Cimabue Madonna was sold for 12 guineas, and two heads of apostles attributed to Masaccio for 10 guineas. These last two predelli have been traced from that sale and, recatalogued correctly as part of Masolino's Santa Maria Maggiore altarpiece, were bought by the nation in 1950 for £15,750. Their present market value is towards £100,000.

Fortunately Sir Charles Locke Eastlake, the great nineteenth-century Director of the National Gallery, moved independently of fashion, making some marvellous purchases in this field, including the Piero della Francesco *Baptism of Christ* for only £241 10s, in Florence in 1861. The prices at English auctions were even lower, and at the Alexander Barker sale at Christie's in 1874, Benjamin Disraeli, as Chancellor of the Exchequer, obtained nine early Italian pictures for the nation, spending the same sum on all nine that Baron Grant had given for Landseer's *Otter Hunt*. In America it was just the same, for when James Jackson Jarvis (author of the marvellous comment: 'It has become the mode to have taste, private galleries in New York are becoming almost as common as private stables')[2] tried to raise collateral in 1871 on his collection of 191 Italian primitives, the most he was offered was £22,000.

Foreign buying of works of art from English collections was minimal in the first seventy years of the century, but this was changed by the Settled Lands Act of 1882 which coincided with an incredible decade of buying by the Rothschilds, as revealed to us recently in the gigantic disposal of Mentmore, Baron Mayer Amschel de Rothschild's home. The Settled Lands Act allowed for the disposal of land and chattels free of tax, providing the proceeds remained in Trusteeship; and the first large dispersal which resulted from the passing of the Act was the negotiated sale by the Duke of Marlborough of treasures from Blenheim Palace, between 1884 and 1886. It is interesting to note that still only the lesser pictures were sold at public auction in London, the major works being sold by private treaty. All the furniture and porcelain on the other hand was sold at auction in Paris, where the market was far stronger for the decorative arts. The prices secured for the Marlborough pictures marked the beginning of the modern art market, with Christie's negotiating a sum of £26,250 from Ferdinand de Rothschild for Rubens's *Garden of the Hesperides* and a record £70,000 from the British Government for Raphael's *Ansidei Madonna*.

The next watershed in the history of the London art market was the price of £103,000 which the American millionaire P. A. B. Widener paid the London dealer Knoedler for the Van Dyck portrait of *Marchesa Grimaldi-Cattaneo* in 1906. Only one other painting at that time is known to have sold for over £100,000— the Raphael *Colonna Altarpiece* bought in 1900 by Pierpont Morgan. The Van Dyck purchase heralded an unprecedented boom period in the sale of seventeenth- and eighteenth-century English portrait paintings. It also marked the first full impact on the European art market of the American industrialists. G. D. Hobson, the antiquarian book expert and Sotheby director, tells a story about this period, which concerned three Whistlers and two Puvis de Chavannes which Henry C. Freer desperately desired from Hobson's friend Arthur Studd. Eventually Freer gave the intractable Studd a blank cheque, on which Studd wrote himself £250,000—an immense amount of money before the First World War. The millionaire was unperturbed, and is supposed to have said, in legendary movie manner, 'I'm Freer of Detroit, I want those pictures'.[3] But Arthur Studd had already decided to present the pictures to the National Gallery, and tore the quarter-of-a-million-pound cheque to pieces.

These American collectors almost all became customers of that remarkable dealer, Joseph (later Lord) Duveen, who from the turn of the century till his death in 1938 dominated the whole European art market from his premises in New York. Duveen's influence on the taste of American collectors is given a lateral compliment in the introduction to H. Marillier's book on Christie's, published in 1926. 'In America there are still wealthy collectors of taste to be found, to whom price is practically no object. In England, what with taxation and death duties, the people who understand good pictures are readier as a rule to part with them than add to their number; and some of the new possessors of wealth (in England) since the War have hardly yet learned to distinguish between a Rembrandt and a Rolls Royce, a Ghirlandajo and a Gorgonzola.'[4] Although the important sales still tended to be negotiated privately, it was also a period of great prosperity for Christie's as Duveen led the way in the creation of an upward spiral of record prices for all things eighteenth-century. Duveen's position in the auction scene was so powerful that A. C. R. Carter, in commenting on the Holford sales in 1928 wrote: 'Let it be emphasized that the greatest bidder and buyer in the long chronicle of art sales stood down from competition in May 1928. It has therefore to be stressed that even without a Duveen participation in an auction contest, the momentum of the market nowadays is of such vigour that the record-breaking spirit shows no sign of abatement.'[5]

As we now know, Carter spoke too soon and the art market inevitably suffered from the American recession of the early

1930s. With the onset of war, the London art market did not recover till the 1950s. In New York in the mid-'40s, prices were already back near their previous heights and in a single sale, that of Mrs Henry Walters of Baltimore, a total of £180,000 was achieved. In London there were few sales of any merit, and those that did take place—such as the disposal of the Eumorphopoulos collection of Asiatic art at Sotheby's—were unmitigated disasters.

But the art market gradually improved and 'we now come to the study of a market which is totally different . . . a market created by inflated currency, topsy-turvy financial control and topsy-turvy systems of taxation, the market of the declining Roman Empire of Western man.'[6] As Western Europe struggled with a mid-1970s slump comparable in many ways with that of the '30s, it seemed possible that the London art market was indeed approaching the end of a historical cycle which had begun back in the mid-eighteenth century with the foundation of Christie's.

But there was no sign of these future dangers after the war, when the first signs of recovery in Europe appeared in Paris, at the Gabriel Cognacq sale in 1952, where the pictures of Cézanne and the post-Impressionists were the first works of art to show a price appreciation which did anything more than keep pace with war-time inflation. The strongest influence on the art market once again came from America, where a new tax law allowed for 30 per cent of the value of paintings presented to public collections to be offset against taxation. As the Duveen operations had succeeded in siphoning many of the best period pictures out of circulation, one of the few fields open to extravagant spending was Impressionist and modern pictures, and a flood of champagne prices was released when Stavros Niarchos paid over £100,000 for Gauguin's *Still Life with Apples* at the Paris sale, in June 1957, of the Mrs Thomas Biddle collection. With champagne prices, champagne sales—the first at Sotheby's in the following month, as the W. Weinberg collection from New York sold for £326,000. Almost more important, though, than the prices was the fact that the private view of the sale was attended by Queen Elizabeth, Prince Philip and Princess Margaret, to all of whom the awe-struck Weinberg executors were formally introduced. The headline 'Sell at Sotheby's and get to meet the Royal family'[7] was relayed across America by Mollie Panter-Downes of the *New Yorker*.

A stern battle had been raging between Paris, London and New York to take fullest advantage of the lifting of currency-exchange controls in America in 1954 and in England in 1956, but the Weinberg sale turned things firmly in London's favour. London boasted many natural advantages, such as established expertise in many fields, a still-massive residue of goods to sell, and, most important of all, the lowest sales commission in the world and the absence of any auction tax. The British Government has carefully preserved these advantages for the fine art trade, and this has been immensely important in establishing London as the world centre.

Even the Weinberg auction paled into insignificance beside the sale at Sotheby's on 15 October 1958 of seven Impressionist pictures belonging to the late Jacob Goldschmidt which were knocked down in a breathtaking nineteen minutes for a total of £781,000. This was a turning-point, not only in the history of Sotheby's, but also of the antique trade as a whole. Before the war, even in Christie's heyday at the beginning of the century, the majority of important collections to come on the market had been disposed of through the dealers. From 1958 onwards it was no longer the Agnews and the Wildensteins who hit the headlines with picture-sale records, but the auction rooms; and the point was proved once and for all when the Metropolitan Museum bid an astonishing $2,300,000 for Rembrandt's *Aristotle* at a Parke Bernet sale in New York in 1962.

Even dealers now accept the leadership of the London auction rooms as a fact of life. In an interview for the *Weekend Telegraph* in the summer of 1974, Joseph Vanderkar, who began dealing in London in 1913, admitted that, 'A collector used to work through the dealers much more . . . now the dealer takes the collector to a view at Sotheby's or Christie's, and the customer commissions him to buy . . . the dealer is often no more than a commission agent.'[8] In the same article Nicholas Ward-Jackson, ex-Sotheby's and ex-Managing Director of Colnaghi's, voiced the dealers' perennial criticism of the auction rooms' ability 'by glamorous publicity to persuade the public that the only way to buy or sell masterpieces is by auction'.[9]

But the art market is always in a state of change, and the auction rooms cannot expect never-ending supremacy. As already suggested, the whole art market was, in 1975, in danger of a recession, the first signs of which can in retrospect be seen to have appeared in 1969 with a certain pulling-back of their art-market commitments by the Americans when tax concessions on museum gifts were altered. For a year or two the Japanese filled the vacant space with some reckless buying of Impressionist pictures, and then the influx of investment money from the City created a buying balloon that is slowly deflating. In times of crisis the largest firms, with their heavy overheads, sometimes suffer most; and the auction giants show an occasional sign of feeling the pressure. Christie's presented to their shareholders in 1975 a 28 per cent reduction in profits, and Sotheby's announced a 19 per cent fall in turnover in the same year. On the other hand, Christie's and Sotheby's also have the international contacts and resources that enable them to take their business away from Europe to new markets, and the 1978 and 1979 figures show a complete recovery of profits and increase in turnover.

The London sale-rooms make a conscious effort to maintain many of the services and much of the style of the past, for it suits the outlook of many of their clients. All the same, the style of auctioneering itself has undergone considerable changes since the 1770s, when James Christie (plate 2), 'the King of Epithets', standing in his Chippendale rostrum, seduced bids from his audiences with phrases such as, 'Let me entreat—Ladies— Gentlemen—permit me to put this inestimable piece of elegance under your protection—only observe—the inexhaustible munificence of your superlatively candid generosity must harmonize with the refulgent brilliance of this little jewel.'[10] This caption to Mr Humphrey's contemporary caricature may be something of an exaggeration, but the scholarly diarist Dibdin was certainly serious when he described George Leigh, a Sotheby's partner from 1767, as 'the Raffaelle of auctioneers . . . his voice was soft, and he had a sort of jerk in his cadenza, somewhere between the affetuoso and the adagio.'[11]

Even in the nineteenth century the auctioneer was still inclined to ebullience, shouting at the end of the bidding, 'It is yours

Sir! I congratulate you, Sir! I wish you joy!'[12] As late as 1887 the *Graphic* described a Christie's sale in the following terms: 'The moment the picture comes upon the easel it is received with loud clapping of hands, repeated as often as the bidders outvie one another in their advances of perhaps a thousand guineas, and when the hammer falls at last to a lumping sum, there is a perfect uproar, just as the crowd roars its delight when the Derby is run, for the Christie audience revels in high prices simply for money's sake, though of course some of the applause is meant for the picture.'[13] In other London sales of the same period, modern pictures aroused such a furore of tasteful indignation that Whistler's paintings were actually booed from the rostrum. Not so for Turner who, at the de Tabley sale in 1827, bought back his own *Sun Rising Through Vapour* amidst wild cheering from the cognoscenti. Such receptions are seldom experienced now, although the sale in 1960 of the E. M. Forster and T. S. Eliot manuscripts was clapped enthusiastically, the elderly authors being seated together in the front row.

There is one fine art auctioneer left in London with some of the fire of his nineteenth-century forbears: Bill Brooks, Managing Director of Debenham and Coe before they were taken over by Christie's. Looking over the top of his gold-rimmed quarter-spectacles, Brooks used to announce the lots with the adjectival relish of a master of ceremonies at Collins' Music Hall, threatening to describe music stands as 'mellifluous' and Chinese vases as 'full of occidental promise'. The Debenham and Coe furniture and works of art sales were grand entertainment, as Brooks alternatively wooed and browbeat his audience into paying decent prices.

Modern auctioneering techniques are less theatrical than in the nineteenth century, principally due to the fact that the new high price-structure to works of art means that buyers need to feel a strong professional confidence in the auctioneer, and too much witty word-play destroys this. At major sales, more than 85 per cent of the successful bidders tend to be full-time dealers, and business is too serious and costly to enable the amateur auctioneer to survive.

All the same, despite the altered pitch of the art market, the job of the auctioneer has changed little in principle since the time of James Christie. The London auctioneer, both in and out of the rostrum, still needs to establish his reputation—first, in the correct identification and valuation of all manner of art objects; second, in his ability to bring together at a sale all the key potential buyers for a particular object; and third, in the conduct of scrupulously honest open auctions. These are the basic requirements, and above these the personal style, imagination and understanding of the art market of an individual auctioneer can only have a noticeable effect over a period of time.

The best-known post-war auctioneer is the Chairman of Sotheby's, Peter Wilson, described by *Vogue* as the 'sublime auctioneer', and dubbed 'art-gamesman No 1'[14] by Robert Wraight for terminating the 1958 sale of Cézanne's *Garçon au Gilet Rouge* for a then record-shattering £220,000, with a slightly pained, almost disappointed, 'Will nobody bid any more?' Over the years since the Goldschmidt sale of Impressionist pictures in 1958, Peter Wilson has created a reputation, both inside and outside Sotheby's, for being the only person who can really handle these gigantic international sales. And Wilson's auctions do have a special aura about them, from the moment this very tall, aristocratic figure steps up into the rostrum and smiles slowly at his gallery of tamed millionaire collectors and dealers. The experienced sale-room critic, Frank Davis, saw elements of innocence and surprise in the Wilson style, as 'amid the paraphernalia of television and ciné-cameras a calm, slightly sleepy voice, apparently doubtful that all this vast amount of filthy lucre is actually going to be handed over in exchange for a few square inches of canvas, registers the bidding as it soars upwards.'[15] Peter Wilson himself put it a little more boldly: 'You first have to get your audience's confidence, then dominate them—in the nicest possible way of course,'[16]—of course.

But the satisfaction of selling the only three paintings so far to be auctioned for over £1,000,000 fell to Patrick Lindsay and Ivan Chance at Christie's. Lindsay is an experienced and imposing auctioneer, noted for his sartorial elegance and for the intimidating way he raises his right eyebrow to prise another bid from a client. The most expensive of the three pictures was Velázquez's *Juan de*

Pareja and the hammer price on 27 November 1970 was a stunning £2,200,000. 'At two million two hundred thousand guineas, then—': it was the most dramatic line ever delivered on the auction stage, but Patrick Lindsay remained calm, clear and unhurried, in the best tradition of English phlegmatism.

While there are a number of women directors of the principal fine art auctioneers, only one of them takes sales regularly, Eve Bonham of W. and F. C. Bonham and Sons. The young Miss Bonham is a charming and commanding figure in the rostrum, but she is not quite as fiery as a stamp auctioneer at Robson Lowe's in the '50s. This lady was a stark disciplinarian and one morning she found it necessary to interrupt her sale twice to ask a certain Dr Barker, an old and respected collector, to stop talking. Finally she warned Dr Barker if he talked again she would throw her hammer at him—five minutes later he started up another con-versation with his neighbour at the table, and the auctioneer's hammer hit him very hard on the nose.

In the specialist smaller auction houses it is more common to find female auctioneers, and the doyenne of their profession, the remarkable Miss Dorothy Bagnall, used to perform to packed houses three or four times a year at Caxton Hall. Although Miss Bagnall, a regal grey-haired lady, takes her cigarette-card sales com-paratively fast, at about 100 lots an hour, she still finds time for friendly asides to an audience composed entirely of dedicated collectors, most of whom are known to her personally. When a lot sells at disappointingly less than the estimate, she terminates the bidding, 'Yours Mr Jones, yes, and I thought it would be more than that,' and if a particularly bulky lot is sold to a postal bid she announces with a sorry smile, 'Oh dear, another parcel to send abroad.'

All the best London auctioneers have developed certain mannerisms to suit their particular audiences and their own personalities. Various totally contrasting styles are equally successful—Richard Came of Sotheby's silver department, in his 1930s stiff collar, races through 140 lots an hour with incredible precision and politeness; whereas Alexander Meddowes of Bonham's picture department favours a leisurely pace laced with friendly asides to habitués in the front rows. Noel Annesley of

Christie's prints and drawings department has a donnish drawl and old-world charm very different from his opposite number at Sotheby's, Marc Rosen, a precise, soft-spoken American who commutes between London and New York

There are certain general principles of fine art auctioneering which it is important to understand. Auctioneers are frequently asked how they can even see, much less interpret, the diverse bids scattered through the crowded main rooms of Christie's and Sotheby's. In fact, it is surprisingly easy to spot the bids themselves, and difficulties usually arise in relating what happens in the sale-room to the complex instructions written in the auctioneer's catalogue from which the sale is conducted. Sotheby's auctioneers' catalogues contain a mass of hieroglyphics that would be totally incomprehensible to anyone else, and the auctioneer must act on them easily and clearly, without allowing any unnatural hiatus to occur in the sale of the standard 80–100 lots an hour. It is the auctioneer's job to put the bidders at their ease and to indicate clearly what is happening; and yet so much distrust of the auctioneer's 'guile' has developed that it might be helpful to describe exactly how a Sotheby auctioneer conducts a sale.

The most important figure in the auctioneer's catalogue is the reserve price, and this is inscribed in code beside each lot, together with the owner's name. The reserve is the price below which the object cannot be sold, and it is normally agreed between the owner and the expert several weeks before the sale. As the senior expert in each department is usually the auctioneer, he will have catalogued many of the lots and will know personally many of the owners, and this gives the auctioneer the confidence to respond immediately to any special problems that may arise during the sale. On calling each successive lot, the auctioneer makes sure that the porter is displaying the object described in the catalogue, and then, memorizing the reserve, he opens the bidding. As the reserve is usually somewhere below the lower estimate issued to the public with the catalogue, the auctioneer normally asks the room for an opening bid about 20–30 per cent below the reserve. If Sotheby's estimate of the value is correct, then the bidding will automatically rise above the reserve and the lot is simply knocked down to the last person bidding in the room. For the sake of clarity and politeness, the auctioneer will continue to take bids from the two first bidders until they have reached their limit, however many more people there are waving their catalogues. The regular rising bids, called out by the auctioneer, mount in increments of about 10 per cent.

However, because of an owner's excessive demands, a cataloguer's over-optimism, or simply because of temperamental lack of interest in the object on the day, the auctioneer is sometimes confronted with a high reserve against which there is only one person left bidding, at a price well below the reserve. It would be against the auctioneer's agreement with the owner to sell below the reserve, so he has to bid 'off the wall' until the bidder exceeds the reserve or until he drops out. In the latter case, the object is 'bought in' on behalf of the owner, who is then liable to a 'buying in' commission of 5 per cent before being allowed to collect his object. There is considerable misunderstanding about the auctioneer's concealed bidding 'off the wall', as the public assumes that this is merely a means of deceiving them into bidding more than they need. But there is no chance of this kind of malpractice in the major London auction rooms, and a bid 'off the wall' is, in this case, effectively a bid from the owner himself.

As well as the reserve, the auctioneer also has recorded in his catalogue all the bids that have been left by telephone, telex or letter from collectors who are unable to attend the auction in person. Thus on a lot with a modest reserve of £50, there may be one bid from America of £200 and another from a Scottish dealer of £300. If the bidding in the room takes the price beyond £300, then the commission bids remain superfluous; but if the last bidder at the sale drops out at £150, then the auctioneer takes the bidding automatically up to £210, when the lot is sold to the Scot who left the bid of up to £300 against the rival commission bid of £200. The third possibility in this particular example is that there may still be someone in the room bidding beyond £200, and then the auctioneer has to bid on behalf of the Scottish commission bidder, either 'off the wall' or looking down at his book, until £300 is exceeded or the room bidder drops out. Sometimes clients leave enormous commission bids, and the auctioneer must be trusted neither to tell the owner (who would wish to raise the reserve accordingly) nor to run the commission bid higher than is justified by genuine competitive under-bids.

In practice, well-known specialists often prefer to leave their bids with the auctioneer rather than appear in person, and thus avoid the danger of rivals competing with them just for the sake of it, or on the assumption that the specialists have spotted something that they have not. People often ask why there is so much secrecy about bidding 'off the wall' and wonder why it is not announced at the sale when a lot is 'bought in' on behalf of the owner, or sold to a commission bid. The answer is that all bids and reserves are matters of complete confidence between the client and the auction house, and anonymity, if required, will always be preserved on behalf of either buyer or seller. Whether the bid is on the auctioneer's catalogue, by prearranged signals in the room, by transatlantic telephone, or by normal bidding in the room, it is the auctioneer's job to maintain a regular pace and temperate atmosphere, so that everyone is able to bid freely to his desired limit and objects find their realistic price-level.

All this will be more or less familiar to sale-room regulars, but it is worth discussing a few more details as many people have no clear idea about London auction practice. It is important to remember that the fall of the hammer is not a final binding contract, and if an auctioneer suddenly sees someone bidding as the hammer sounds he will often call out 'with the hammer', and continue the bidding as though nothing had happened. Similarly, if a lot is knocked down by mistake to someone who really was not bidding, the auctioneer can reoffer the lot immediately, starting again at the beginning of the bidding; or, if the under-bidder wishes, selling the lot automatically to him at one bid below the hammer price. Another point—the phrase 'against you all' sometimes causes confusion, although it means simply that the lot is going to a commission bid and not to anyone who has been bidding in the room. Auctioneers will also be heard saying, 'Yes it is yours, sir', if a bidder mistakenly continues to bid when the last bid was his own; it may sound tempting for the auctioneer to take another bid from someone innocently bidding against himself, but this kind of dishonesty can only destroy the trust which the public must place in the auctioneer. The auctioneer is in an extremely powerful position, with endless scope for undetectable deception, and his personal integrity must be clearly established.

The professionalism of the London auctioneers and their good reputation is a valuable protection to both buyer and seller, and nowhere else in the world is there the same degree of expertise, experience, and integrity in the auction houses. All the same the art market is full of natural and man-made dangers, against which the auction houses can offer no ultimate protection. Ignoring the complexities of changing values—influenced as they are these days by external factors such as institutional investment policies and new taxation systems—there is still simply the constant natural change in fashion and taste that makes a particular period or style sought after one decade and valueless the next. In the same process, paintings, sculpture and even porcelain or musical instruments are also continuously reassessed and re-attributed by the next generation of scholars and connoisseurs. In that sense nothing is certain—even before one has taken into account the developed art of the forger.

Perhaps surprisingly, it is easier to detect the out-and-out fake of an earlier period than it is the genuine copy which, through the passage of time, has become almost indistinguishable from the original. As A. C. R. Carter used to say, 'Time and varnish are the two real Old Masters.'[17] So to the naked eye there often seems little 'wrong' with a large Stuart family portrait copied by a pupil of Kneller fifty years after the master painted the original, whereas the fake sixteenth-century drawings made by Peter Thompson in the mid-nineteenth century have long since ceased to deceive. Thompson, with considerable ingenuity, invented an amateur draughtsman whom he called Captain John Fyre, and to whom he gave a birth-date and lineage to satisfy the curious Victorian collectors. Thompson was not a good draughtsman himself, but this did not matter as Captain Fyre was only meant to be an amateur; and the drawings were enlivened by mouth-watering diary-like inscriptions in fake old English—'In ye next week to do Mister Shakespeare's house in ye Clink Street',[18] is a typical example.

Some of the supposedly documented stories of art frauds read so much like romantic novelettes that is is difficult to believe they really happened, and this is particularly true of the escapades of a confidence trickster who called himself the Marquis Eduardo de Valfierno. Valfierno began his career by persuading rich Argentinian widows that the noblest means of commemorating a recently dead husband was to place an important picture in a private chapel to his memory. The 'Old Master' chosen was normally a Murillo, and these were all produced by Valfierno's accomplice, a French painter called Yves Chaudron. From Buenos Aires Valfierno moved to Mexico City, and from there to Paris; by which time he had developed a sophisticated technique of supplying supposedly stolen masterpieces to unscrupulous collectors. Valfierno was able to provide spurious Press cuttings referring to the non-existent theft of the 'masterpiece', which was always a Chaudron fake; the new owners could never have their picture verified, and if they became suspicious of international silence on the subject of the theft, Valfierno would reassure them by saying that the French government was hushing up the matter and had hung a copy in its place.

But all of these operations were of small significance compared with a plan Valfierno hatched to steal the Mona Lisa, and thereafter to sell six of Chaudron's copies of the picture at vast sums to unscrupulous collectors throughout the world. This great theft from the Louvre was achieved with remarkable ease by Valfierno's agent, Vincenzo Perugia, on Monday 21 August 1911. The theft was not discovered till the next day, by which time the gang was on its way to New York to sell the six copies which had been smuggled into America weeks before the robbery. According to Carl Decker, the real Mona Lisa had remained in Valfierno's apartment in Paris. Perugia subsequently stole it back and in November 1913 wrote a letter to the Florentine dealer, Alfredo Geri, offering him the picture for sale. Geri at first thought it was a practical joke but fortunately checked into it—and a few weeks later the Mona Lisa was returned to its rightful place in the Louvre and Perugia went to prison. Perugia always maintained that he worked alone, none of the other members of the gang were ever found or convicted, and periodically stories are circulated indicating that the real Mona Lisa is still 'at large'. One such rumour originated in November 1926 when *L'Œuvre* published the reports of a certain Jack Dean who claimed to have been an accomplice of Perugia's and had 'proof' that the painting which Perugia showed to Geri, and which is now in the Louvre, was actually one of the copies.

Modern art frauds and fakes are ever more difficult to detect, and occasionally the artist himself is not quite certain whether a particular picture is his or not. If a modern masterpiece turns out not to be by Miró or Picasso or whoever it is signed by, it could well be the work of David Stein. He was sentenced in January 1969, by Judge Culkin of New York, to two and a half years in Sing Sing prison on three admitted charges of felony— forging a Chagall, a Picasso and a Matisse, a minute selection of his work. In the early '60s Stein had discovered an ability, through intensive study of an artist's works and personality, to produce highly convincing modern forgeries that seemed to fit perfectly into the particular artist's *oeuvre*. After testing his ability in London, Stein moved in 1965 to New York where he set up the Galerie Trianon, with a branch in Palm Beach. Stein had brought with him some genuine paintings and a store of his own, to which he regularly added as required; he claimed to have painted and sold over 200 fake Matisses, Dufys, Van Dongens, Miròs, Picassos, Derains and Chagalls.

The first Stein fake was discovered by New York attorney Joseph Stone, who specialized in art fraud, and it was confirmed by Chagall himself who was in New York at the time to paint two murals at the Lincoln centre. Apparently what angered Chagall most was that this and many other fakes were so bad, and yet had taken in many important collectors such as Irving Yamet and Abraham Lubin, who had both apparently purchased nine paintings from Stein. In September 1966 the Galerie Trianon was raided and photographs were found of Stein, stripped to the waist, painting another of his Chagalls. In January 1967, Stein was finally arrested in Los Angeles. He confessed, and while pending trial was lionized by the Press and celebrated by New York society. Stein even managed to organize a show for himself at the fashionable Ocean Side Surf Club in Seabright, which was

Plate 1

Edwin Long's picture of the Babylonian marriage market by auction – the text taken from Herodotus and the scene inspired by contemporary picture auctions in London. The painting was sold at Christie's in 1882 for 6,300 guineas – then a record price for a work by a living artist

Plate 2

A portrait of James
Christie by his friend,
Thomas Gainsborough,
done shortly after the
foundation of Christie's
in 1766

Plate 3

A less flattering portrayal
of James Christie as 'The
Specious Orator', executed
by Dighton in 1794

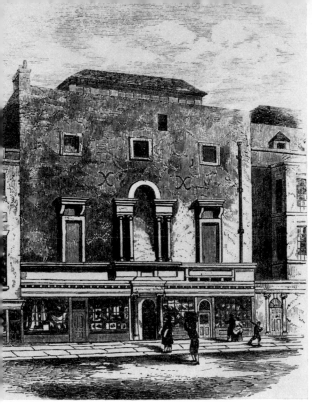

Plate 4

No 125 Pall Mall, early premises of Christie's, the first auction house to move from Covent Garden to the fashionable West End

Plate 5

Marquis of Bute
Paintings from the Country
144
68 Paintings [illegible]
Portland Place
Sale 7 June 1822
734
M B

Earl of Powlett
7 Paintings [illegible]
13 Do
Sale 15 June
4 Hors Load -12-0
735

Apsely Pellatt 31 May 1822
Saint Pauls Churchyard
A Painting in Case
736
Sale June 15
Delivered to Mr Pellett Order
14 July 1823 [illegible]
the Empty Case Sent to Bath
to Capt [illegible] Jany 27 - 182

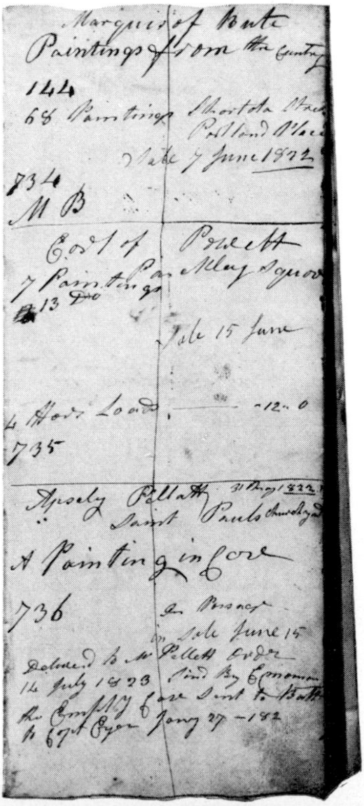

A page from the Christie's day-book for 31 May 1822, showing the receipt and subsequent sale of pictures from the Marquis of Bute, the Earl of Powett and Mr Apsley Pellett

Plate 6

A print taken from the painting by Gebaud of the sale at Christie's on
14 June 1828 of Reynolds's *The Snake in the Grass*, which fetched
£1,260

Engraving, published in the *Pictorial World*, October 1875, of a sale
in progress at Christie's. The legendary Thomas Woods is in the
rostrum

Plate 8

The Reverend Theodore Pitcairn with his Monet, *La Terrasse à Saint-Adresse*, shortly after it had sold at Christie's in 1976 for £588,000. He had bought the painting in 1926 for less than £4,000

Plate 9

The main viewing galleries at Christie's in June 1971, with a display
of furniture, tapestries and works of art removed from the Anna
Thompson Dodge mansion outside Detroit

Plate 10

The sale of Tiepolo's *Allegory of Venus Entrusting Eros to Chronos* at Christie's, June 1969. It sold for £409,500. The auctioneer is the ex-chairman of Christie's, Ivan Chance

followed in April 1969 by an exhibition, at the London gallery of David Hepburn, of over forty Stein fakes, this time signed with his own name as well. The only difference was the price. At the Galerie Trianon the forty paintings would have totalled over $800,000; at his own·show they were sold at an average of only $200 each.

The most recent art market scandal surrounds the work of Thomas Keating, the author of a number of pastiches of Samuel Palmer which were eventually sold in the London art market for record sums. Keating has now been acquitted in High Court of all accusations of fraud on the grounds that none of the paintings was executed on period canvas or paper, or with period pigments; and that across the underpaint of many canvases he had scrawled 'fake' or some other four-letter expletive. All these facts would have been revealed under careful scrutiny. Keating also claims that he was never involved in the selling of his 2,000–3,000 fakes, or 'Sexton Blakes' as he called them, as originals, although he claims to have evidence that certain dealers added signatures and provenances to his paintings and sold them for thousands of pounds in London. One or two experts had been suspicious about a growing group of so-called Palmers which first appeared on the market in 1969, and many more experts are now claiming that Keating's paintings are, as he says himself, so bad that it is an insult to Palmer that they were taken as originals. This retrospective claim by experts however is most unfair, for a number of the Keating 'Palmers' were included in a highly publicized and well-reviewed exhibition at the Bond Street gallery, Leger's, in 1971, and no one publicly challenged their authenticity then. One of the watercolours, *The Horse Chestnut Tree*, was bought by Lord Glenconner's son, the well-known collector Colin Tennant, who subsequently sold it in June 1973 through Sotheby's for a world-record price of £15,000. Geraldine Norman, the sales-room critic of *The Times* who uncovered the whole Keating saga and who later published a book on the artist, gamely admits that she was taken in by the 'Palmer' at Sotheby's and starred the lot three times, scribbling in the margin of her catalogue 'the real thing'. Geraldine Norman draws a useful lesson from all this—'All in all, the business of forming an art

2

collection is much more difficult than is generally allowed. If you
value a work of art for anything other than its visual qualities,
you lay yourself open to being rooked, deceived, subjected to the
vagaries of fashion or the machinations of the forger, and generally
taken for a ride. In a way this is quite salutary; art is thus capable
of defending its own purity from all the abuses of society, particularly the greed of the market place.'[19]

There are just as many forgeries in the field of furniture and
works of art, and in 1966 the *Sunday Times'* Insight team set out
to prove how unreliable the art market can be, publishing their
findings in August of that year. A master-framer, Vilmo Gilbello,
and a Maltese carver, Eduardo Pirotta, had found for many years
that the reproduction carved furniture that they supplied by
special order ended up all too soon at unworldly prices on the
antique market; and, angered by this kind of fraud, they willingly
lent their skills to the Insight campaign. The plan was to make a
pair of painted blackamoor torchères and pass them off around the
London trade as Venetian eighteenth-century. The first require-
ment was a large block of seasoned pine, and a telegraph pole
costing only £12 proved ideal for the job. (It was, incidentally,
no ordinary telegraph pole, for its previous function had been
to hold up the bookies' telephone at Ascot race-course, the
notorious 'blower line'.) Pirotta set to work and three weeks
later a magnificent pair of torchères emerged from his workshop,
suitably aged, intentionally broken and repaired, and with a
brilliant touch of deception—the trailing legs of the figures had
an exaggerated twist characteristic of the eighteenth-century
Venetian carver, Viani.

The auctioneers Knight Frank and Rutley[20] were the first
guinea-pigs, and having first suggested that the torchères were,
for some unknown reason, English of the Regency period, they
eventually catalogued them as Venetian eighteenth-century, 'in
the manner of Viani'. The torchères were illustrated and enthused
over in the *Guardian*'s forthcoming-sales column. As Insight did
not intend actually to perpetrate the fraud, the torchères were
withdrawn from the sale at a price of £650, and were carted
around the specialist West End dealers for their opinions. The
experts in the galleries were duped just as easily as those at the

sale, and no one even hinted that they might be modern. The comments were most entertaining. 'Of course the shells [which the blackamoors were holding] are recent. Believe me this type always held torches in their hands, look you can see where they have been altered,'—and from another expert, 'They are genuine, but made at different dates by the same hand.'[21]

Not that misinformation always works that way around. In 1933, Pierre Jannerat was a twenty-one-year-old reporter with a passionate interest in Renaissance Italy, and at a Christie's sale that season he bought a small bronze of a horse for eleven and a half guineas. Jannerat was absolutely convinced that he had removed from beneath the noses of the international art trade a bronze by Leonardo da Vinci, although even after the sale all the museum experts ridiculed the idea. Over the years Jannerat researched his bronze with the greatest thoroughness, and gradually people came around to his opinion. Eventually Sir John Pope-Hennessy included it in his exhibition of Italian bronzes, catalogued as one of only three extant bronzes by Leonardo, cast from a wax model for the Battle of Anghiari. With this attribution by one of the leading experts in the field, the auction value of Jannerat's eleven-and-a-half-guinea bronze could now be nearer £100,000.

The worst danger to owners, and the most-feared sale-room bogey is the 'ring'. Amidst the scandals and the denunciations it is often forgotten that a ring of some sort or another is absolutely inevitable and not necessarily illegal; for in its simplest form the ring arises from two or three friends attending the same auctions week after week and reaching a tacit understanding not to bid against each other, as much out of politeness as a desire to secure lots cheaply. According to the law, the Auctions (Bidding Agreements) Act of 1927, even this comparatively innocent agreement between friends becomes strictly illegal once money changes hands, especially if this takes the form of profit-sharing on the final sale, or indeed if any such non-bidding pact is reached in the sale-rooms themselves. What the Auctions Act is really aiming to curtail is the highly organized activity of a group of dealers, who give and take large bribes in order to secure lots at minimal prices. The full activities of a ring of this kind were revealed in a dramatic report published by the *Sunday Times* on 8 November 1964, and called 'The Curious Case of the Chippendale Commode'.

The remarkable thing about the *Sunday Times* exposé was the free naming of the culprits in a ring that succeeded in purchasing for £750, at a Leamington Spa auction, a Chippendale commode whose market value to the public was then about £7,000 and at present prices would be about £25,000. It seems that at the sale of the property of the late Sir Wathen Waller on 22 November 1962, a certain Major Michael Brett, at the time a council member of the British Antique Dealers Association, was the successful bidder for this commode at a price of only £750, although there were a number of other dealers present at the sale who remained silent while knowing that this was a ludicrously low price. After the sale, the bulk of Major Brett's account was settled by cheques from three other dealers, including precisely £750 from Roy Oliver; and it was Mr Oliver who later sold the commode to Frank Partridge's of Bond Street for an undisclosed sum, thought to have been in excess of £5,000. Although these occurrences are not illegal in themselves, they are highly suspicious; and on further investigation the reporter discovered that on the evening after the sale about forty dealers met at the Clarendon Hotel, Leamington, for a 'knock out' of the ring's purchases which resulted in the ownership of the Chippendale commode falling to Oliver against five major dealers at a price of £4,350, as a result of which each of the other five were paid by Oliver a share-out of about £600 for not bidding in the public auction.

In order to secure physical evidence of regular practice of this kind, another reporter, with a tape-recorder under his coat, found his way into the dealer's knock-out in the Swan Inn, Moreton-in-the-Marsh, after the Spencer-Churchill sale at Northwick Park on 28 September 1964. In fact the sale had not been particularly successful for the ring, as there had been many knowledgeable private collectors and outside dealers there, but the ring still held its own auction afterwards, chaired by the same Major Brett. A roll-call was taken of over fifty dealers, including three members of the BADA council and many rank-

and-file members of the BADA. It seems that in the mid-1960s there was a network of dealer's rings across the Home Counties, the West Midlands, the West Country and Wales, with acknowledged convenors in every locality who fixed the meeting-place and conducted the knock-out. Included in the ring at various levels of the pay-off were dealers, ranging from homeless runners paid out for their silence to top provincial shop-owners who shared the bulk of the profits.

The unveiling of this case caused a storm of protest across the country, and even engendered vitriolic debate in the House of Commons, at which the Member of Parliament for Cirencester was actually heard to say grandly, angrily, but slightly im-practically, 'The only way to kill these mosquitoes is to drain the swamp in which they breathe.'[22]

The rings no longer operate on such a large, organized scale, but there are inevitably numerous dealer-associations which, although strictly illegal, are extremely difficult to exterminate. The only way an honest auctioneer can combat the local ring is by arranging realistic reserves, and by encouraging as much activity as possible from private buyers, and from dealers outside the locality and therefore beyond the grasp of the ring. In London, of course, it is easier to defeat the ring as competition at the sales is international; although even in the major sale-rooms it is surpris-ing how few people in the world actually are interested in purchasing at auction, for example, a rare Louis XIV gold snuff-box at tens of thousands of pounds or an important Herez silk rug, and it is not unknown for the specialist dealers to divide a sale up, albeit in a most refined and genteel way, an hour or two before the London auctioneer steps into his rostrum. It is quite obvious that associations do exist; indeed it was admitted to me recently when one of 'the boys' approached me before the sale asking if, as the auctioneer, I would execute a substantial bid on a particular piece of furniture. To my seemingly innocent question, 'Would you like me to call out your name as the successful buyer?' the dealer replied, 'Yes—if you want to hear the rat-rat-tat of the machine-gun at the back of the sale-room.' When one of the members of the ring goes against his partners like that, or the ring falls out for one reason or another, then it works very much to the seller's advantage as vindictive competition leads to crazy prices.

The English auction system may be much slower than the Dutch flower auction, where the bidding goes in reverse, or the Japanese fish auction which is conducted on a show of hands, but it does allow the auctioneer to create a freer atmosphere, as well as giving the buyer a number of ways of registering his bid. While some buyers speak to the auctioneer before the sale and leave instructions on a coded bidding system, in the majority of cases the relationship between auctioneer and bidder is built up in the course of many sales. With regulars, the auctioneer soon learns the kind of lots they are interested in, and a smile can be enough to register a bid and a turn of the head enough to stop. But even with previously unknown bidders it is possible to build up an understanding in the course of one sale, at the end of which the auctioneer may simply look the client questioningly in the eye to learn whether he is bidding or not. As many dealers and collectors wish for one reason or another to conceal their interest from rivals, the ability of an auctioneer to read the signs with a minimum of fuss is greatly appreciated. Thus the price of a particular lot may rise at a tremendous rate without a visible nod from the room, and may eventually be sold to a gentleman sitting next to you who has no more than blinked. Perhaps it is experiences such as these which frighten the uninitiated.

Everyone has his own method of bidding. When the bidding is at £20 and is advancing in two's, some call out '£50!' in the hope that this will put off everyone else and prevent the bids proceeding steadily to the interjector's own £80 maximum. This trick sometimes succeeds, but there is danger of it backfiring as the auctioneer could have concealed a general lack of interest in the lot, and the impetuous bidder might actually have been successful at £22. Others sit with their backs to the auctioneer and bid with an index finger waggling at their ear, while regarding the rest of the room, and particularly rival dealers, with an expression of complete lack of interest in the proceedings. From an auctioneer's point of view, the most aggravating bidders are those who do their utmost to slow down the sale by offering each new bid just as the hammer is about to fall.

The dealer Jacques Helft tells an amusing story of a bidding trick that worked successfully at a Hotel Drouot auction in Paris in the early 1920s. Helft desperately wanted a rare ewer in this particular auction, and instead of attending himself and thus advertising his interest to the whole of Paris, he asked a diamond dealer called Alfred de Haan to go along and bid on his behalf. The first lot was a mixed collection of copper saucepans for which the auctioneer shyly asked an opening bid of about 20 francs. From that moment de Haan took sole charge of the auction, shouting out ever-increasing bids against himself and buying the saucepans at some ludicrous price. De Haan did exactly the same for the next twelve lots, before abruptly paying and leaving, no one having dared to compete against this seeming madman. The last of the twelve lots was Helft's ewer, which was thus purchased at a fraction of its value.

Specific bidding arrangements between auctioneer and client can be extremely complicated, and I well remember in my third sale as a Sotheby's auctioneer a dealer instructing me that he was bidding when his arms were folded, and at the same time the owner of a substantial section of the sale saying that when his pencil was in his mouth then I could sell that particular lot below the reserve. Such arrangements can land a client in difficulties—as on an occasion the musical-box expert Graham Webb describes when he had agreed that the sales-clerk would bid on his behalf on certain lots, until he placed a pencil in his top pocket. The inevitable happened—Webb dropped the pencil, and during his mad scramble to recover it from under the feet of rival dealers, the sales-clerk spent £200 more than Webb had intended.

At a fine French furniture sale at Parke Bernet in New York an agreement was made between a collector and the auctioneer that the gentleman was bidding on specified lots when his coat was undone, and had stopped when he buttoned his coat up. When one of the specified lots was called, the collector suddenly caught sight of a friend standing in the doorway and, with his coat still undone, rushed out of the room for a quiet word. A minute later the collector returned, still with his coat undone, to find he had bought a settee for some astronomical sum. After the sale a farcical argument ensued as to whether the bidder was right in claiming that an unbuttoned coat *outside* the sale-room should be considered the same as a buttoned-up coat *inside* the sale-room.

The best-known example of bidding-code chaos happened in the Christie's Old Master picture sale of 19 March 1965 (see also page 63). The star lot in this sale was Rembrandt's portrait of his son Titus, a painting which, because of its rarity on the open market, aroused the interest of many millionaire collectors. One of the best-tipped competitors was the multi-millionaire art collector from Los Angeles, Norton Simon, and as the bidding rose gradually to a European auction record of over 700,000 guineas, the crowd of art-punters in Christie's great room could not have been surprised to see Simon bidding eagerly and openly. But at 740,000 guineas the bid was with Marlborough Fine Art, at which point the auctioneer Ivan Chance looked very obviously in Norton Simon's direction, saying several times in a rather agitated way, 'Against you, sir, the bid is on my left, against you.' At this juncture Norton Simon also began to show signs of strain, and for fully thirty seconds Messrs Chance and Simon grimaced at each other, before Chance finally knocked down the Rembrandt to Marlborough Fine Art for the 740,000 guineas. At this, Simon leaped towards the rostrum, claimed to have been bidding, and read out, much to Chance's embarrassment, a bidding arrangement that had been confirmed in writing on Christie's headed paper—'When Mr Simon is sitting down he is bidding. If he bids openly he is bidding. When he stands up he has stopped bidding. If he sits down again he is not bidding until he raises his finger. Having raised his finger he is bidding until he stands up again.'[23] On the evidence of this extraordinarily confusing letter, the auctioneer had no choice but to put the picture up for sale again and it became Norton Simon's at a price of 760,000 guineas, in a tumultous blast of publicity—the very thing which the tortuous bidding agreement had been designed to avoid.

A casual visitor to a normal sale at Christie's or Sotheby's would scarcely believe that such theatrical events actually occurred. But even in the controlled atmosphere of an ordinary sale there are under-currents of tension and drama. It is this internal tension that draws the sale-room habitué back week after week, a prey to the pitfalls and a partaker of the pleasures peculiar to the auction scene.

Christie's. The Establishment Auctioneers

Christie's is the only art auction house in the world with an unbroken 200-year history of fine art auctioneering. From James Christie's first sale in 1766 till the present day, the firm has succeeded in presenting regular auctions of important pictures and works of art which have commanded international interest and respect. For generation after generation the foremost connoisseurs, specialist dealers and aristocratic collectors have attended the sale of masterpieces at Christie's, and Christie's power rests on continuing dedication to these historical traditions.

The other three London fine art auctioneers may be equally proud of their own eighteenth-century origins, but Sotheby's was only an antiquarian book-auction house until after 1900, while Phillips and Bonham's both failed to maintain their early impetus after 1875. This gives Christie's a tremendous advantage in the contemporary market, as it is the only auction house which can rely on long-standing contacts with the primary sources of supply for important sales—the aristocratic collections of England. Until 1870 aristocratic collectors dominated the international art market, but with modern changes in the country's financial structure they have become instead the most significant sellers of Old Master paintings. In today's market it is infinitely more difficult to acquire works of art for sale than it is actually to sell them, and Christie's are in the enviable position that the owners of England's inherited collections seldom see any reason to alter the family's traditional allegiance to 'the establishment auctioneers'. By preserving their expertise in this field and by developing professional services, Christie's continues to claim the loyalty of their leading clients.

Inevitably it is Christie's which has sold the only paintings to secure more than £1,000,000 at auction and, characteristically, all three of these pictures were consigned by English aristocratic families which had dealt with Christie's for generations. Indeed the three paintings, Velázquez's *Juan de Pareja*, Titian's *Death of Actaeon* and Duccio's *Crucifixion*, had all passed through Christie's at least once before in their history. To take the most expensive example, the second Earl of Radnor bought the *Juan de Pareja* portrait for £151 14s 6d in 1811 at Christie's, where it had already been sold ten years previously at a hammer price of only 39 guineas. In 1970 the painting was finally removed from Longford Castle to pay the death duties of the seventh Earl, and to become the most expensive work of art that has, to this date, ever been sold at auction. As has been said, it secured at Christie's the astonishing price of 2,200,000 guineas.

Awareness of the past and determination to maintain the advantages of their traditional relationships with leading dealers and collectors colours the character of present-day Christie's. That is not to imply that Christie's has remained drearily old-fashioned; quite the opposite. It is a public company answerable to whoever buys its shares on the London stock exchange; it has created a flourishing auction room in Geneva which does more business than any native Continental auction house; and amongst other ventures it has founded a company to publish modern prints. Christie's response to the conditions of the market even goes as far as the setting-up of a financial strategy division, which advises clients on the complexities of estate duty, capital gains and all the other taxes that complicate the disposal of works of art. The overall management structure and internal character of the company nevertheless maintains a traditional quality. At the time of its transformation into a public company in November 1973, it was characteristic of the Board to have rejected a strong recommendation by their accountants to engage an experienced Managing Director from the City to run the firm on rigid commercial lines. Instead, 'to the great relief of the Board'[1] Guy Hannen, an existing director and the third consecutive generation of his family to be senior partner at Christie's, agreed to become the new Managing Director. This quality of tradition is still carefully preserved amongst the younger generation of experts moving up within the firm, all of whom, whether Cambridge graduates in the History of Art or seventeen-year-old school leavers, started their careers in Christie's by months, and sometimes years, of learning the traditions of their profession as front-counter assistants.

In 1928 A. C. R. Carter, sale-room critic of the *Daily Telegraph*, described 'the lure of Christie's as one of the magnetic attractions of the world',[2] and even now, in a less romantic age, almost everyone attending his first sale at Christie's is still conscious of the sense of history in these great rooms. Every English connoisseur and collector of significance in the last 200 years has responded to the qualities that today draw us to number 8 King Street, St James's. The history of Christie's is therefore not just of antiquarian interest, for its past is an active part of the present.

Not a great deal is known about James Christie's childhood, and one of his ex-clerks, Harry Phillips, who founded the firm of London auctioneers still known by his name, may have been accurate rather than merely vindictive in pronouncing that the father of fashionable James Christie (plate 2) was actually a Scottish feather-bed beater. It is not even certain that the art critic Redford was correct in asserting that Christie had worked early on in his career for the Covent Garden auctioneer Annesley, but trade advertisements make it clear that Christie was mounting his own sales at various venues from 1764 onwards. St James's and fashionable London was his target, and in December 1766, at the age of thirty-six, James Christie held his first recorded sale in Pall Mall. 'Late the Property of a Noble PERSONAGE (deceas'd)',[3] the founding Christie's sale was advertised on the title-page of the catalogue as containing 'Household furniture, Fire-arms, China etc. And a large quantity of Madeira and high Flavour'd Claret—Large Pier Glasses, a curious Needlework Carpet—a Musical Spring Clock and Eight-day ditto'; and the first lot ever sold at Christie's was described as 'six breakfast pint basons and plates', bought by a certain Mr Shepherd for nineteen shillings. Having successfully disposed of these varied lots, including 'two hartychoaks', 'a fine india bandazeer' and 'a bird in a jessamy tree',[4] Christie proceeded to his first Old Master picture sale in March 1767. Despite his failure in this sale to secure bids of more than £4 18s for a 'Holbein' or 2 guineas for a

'Titian', Christie was entrusted the following year with the disposal of his first major collection, the pictures of the Duke of Leeds. From that moment his reputation was made.

This fashionable success encouraged Christie to risk obtaining the long lease of his own premises at 83 Pall Mall, and his limitless ambition is indicated by the polished style of his opening announcement in the *Public Advertiser*. 'To the Virtu and Public in general. Mr Christie begs leave to inform them that his new Auction Room in Pall Mall will be completed in a few days, and from its being mechanically constructed under the immediate direction of the first artists of the Kingdom with respect to justness of proportions, the repose of light, together with its magnitude and desireable situation, he hopes are motives sufficient to show the natural advantages that must accrue to those who shall favour him with their commands, which shall be faithfully attended to and executed with the utmost integrity. Money advanced on valuables in general intended for public sale.'[5] The Christie strategy was at once established in the general form that is still maintained today—the attractive appointment of fine rooms in the heart of fashionable London, the diligent search for important properties for sale, employing where necessary the extra inducement of 'money advanced on valuables', the careful cultivation of the Press, which Christie took seriously enough to become one of the original proprietors of the *Morning Chronicle* and, later, of its rival the *Morning Post*, and personal charm sufficient to bring the auction mart into the *beau monde*.

In the last task James Christie had natural advantages, for 'when waiting to take advances for bidding, the ladies would say he was irresistible'.[6] His popularity was also acknowledged in Charles Jenner's *Town Eclogues* which conducted the young lady of fashion through her rigorous daily routine.

In one continual hurry rolled her days
At routs, assemblies, auctions, op'ras, plays,
Subscription balls and visits without end,
And poor Cornelys knew no better friend.
From Loo she rises with the sun,
And Christie's sees her aking head at one.[7]

Christie was the first of many members of the firm to claim
familiarity with people in high, even Royal, places—a contemporary commentator describing him as 'courteous, friendly and
hospitable in private life—held in great esteem by his numerous
friends among whom there were many of high rank'.[8] To encourage the fashionable use of what had come to be known, as
they still are, as 'the great rooms', Christie also gave evening
receptions and private views, the natural antecedents to the
prestigious evening sales at Christie's which are now covered by
camera crews from three continents.

All the same, the Christie reputation did not rest entirely on
the founder's acquired social grace and tireless wooing of the
powerful; for the standard of expertise in James Christie's early
catalogues was widely admired at the time. Many contemporary
artists and historians were friends of Christie's and frequently
visited his rooms in Pall Mall, one of the most regular visitors
being Gainsborough who 'together with Garrick was often to be
found at Christie's'.[9] The same commentator noted that Christie
was well aware of the commercial benefit derived from the visible
support of successful artists, for he claimed 'their presence in the
rooms added fifteen per cent to his commission'.[10] Christie also
handled the disposal of a number of artists' properties, including
the probate valuations for the executors of Sir Joshua Reynolds,
Sir William Chambers and Johann Zoffany.

Full acknowledgement of Christie's accepted place in eighteenth-
century artistic circles is indicated by his close involvement in one
of the major private deals of the century, the sale of the Houghton
pictures to the Empress Catherine of Russia. In 1778 Lord
Orford asked Christie for a valuation, and the auctioneer as usual
called on the additional assistance of outside experts, in this case
Benjamin West, G. B. Cipriani, and the painter-dealer Philippe
Tassaert. Lord Orford was delighted with Christie, praising him
for 'the diligence and dispatch used in this business',[11] and
although Horace Walpole felt that the valuation of £40,455 for
the 178 pictures was far too high, most of the collection was
accepted by the Tsarina on the Christie valuations and
attributions.

Amongst early successful sales was that of the furniture and jewels of the Chevalier d'Eon de Beaumont, a transvestite adventurer whose intrigues in both male and female roles in the Imperial courts of Russia and France allowed Christie the pleasure of designating the property as belonging at one and the same time to 'a lady of fashion and officer of Dragoons'.[12] As happened quite frequently at this period, Christie's sent the Chevalier d'Eon's library to Sotheby's for sale. The frontispiece to this catalogue of 1791 is illustrated in plate 15.

As things became more unsettled in France, many valuable collections were smuggled out to England where their subsequent sale marked the beginning of London's supremacy over Paris in the world art market. It is also interesting to see the way in which the exhibition in London of large numbers of eighteenth-century French paintings influenced the style and taste of contemporary British painters, notably Turner and members of the Norwich School. James Christie involved himself in most of the important deals originating in France, and narrowly failed to negotiate the purchase, for £100,000 in 1788, of the Duc d'Orléans collection on behalf of an English syndicate. Christie agents in France succeeded in sending some sought-after consignments of Sèvres and Chantilly porcelain straight from the factories; and visitors to their auction, on 20 February 1790, of 'A Capital and Valuable Assortment of Beautiful Porcelaine of Monsieur's Manufactory' included the Dukes of York and Queensberry and the Lords Spencer, Shaftesbury and Camelford. Madame du Barry's singular collection of jewellery was offered under the hammer at Christie's 'on behalf of the Administrator', only a few weeks after the guillotine had removed her head. Things have changed little since then, except perhaps to become more circuitous, as Christie's and Sotheby's continue to try to outmanoeuvre each other for an opportunity of offering their services to the trustees of ailing collectors.

Not all the major sales proved profitable to Christie, the Reynolds Collection being particularly troublesome. The diarist Farington recorded that Lady Inchquin, Reynolds's heiress was dissatisfied with the reserves, no doubt influenced by Farington himself who never approved of James Christie and in February 1794 told Lady Inchquin that 'both last spring and at the present

time, Christie only consulted his own interests and convenience'.[13]
The auctions themselves, in March of the following year, produced
disappointing prices, as most critics believed that even those
pictures that were original had been heavily restored—possibly by
Reynolds himself, who frequently claimed to know better than
Correggio and Raphael anyway. The total achieved for 411
pictures was only £10,319 2s 6d, and Christie had difficulty in
paying off the overheads, as well as receiving criticism for a
defective catalogue. Nonetheless he managed to turn the auction
itself to his own and the firm's advantage, using the occasion to
display his auction artistry. Concerning Rubens's *Tigers in a
Landscape*—'the figures, as Mr Christie sublimely observed, were
perfectly vivified. It was knocked down for a hundred and ten
guineas and, as the auctioneer observed, the beasts looked exceed-
ingly sulky at not being sold for more money'.[14]

Christie carefully cultivated his reputation as an art expert
and man-about-town, but his business sense was acute. Monetary
comparisons between now and the eighteenth century are mean-
ingless, but the recorded income of £16,000 from commission on
sales during one year represents a substantial sum, when paintings
now worth a million pounds or more were then selling for a few
hundred. Some of the credit for this financial success must go to
Robert Ansell, a picture-dealer with an enviable talent for gathering important collections from abroad, whose services were so
crucial to Christie that he was forced to take him on as partner
in the firm between 1777 and 1784.

Christie's was also prepared to earn its income in many more
varied sales than it handles now, and the auctions included on
occasion out-dated lines in funeral dresses, the stock of an iron-
monger's shop, several fire-engines and 'seven bright nagtail
coach geldings'.[15] Even as late as the 1850s Christie's sold at auction
'a field of hay standing in Paddington',[16] more upright and
chauvinistic than today's sales of claret lying in Bordeaux. James
Christie also dealt in real estate, and near the end of the eighteenth century the firm had the distinction of selling at auction
the Borough of Gatton, which carried with it the right to a seat
in the House of Commons. Parliament was a profitable place to
be, so the Borough and its seat sold for £39,000, vastly more

than any other single lot had secured at Christie's by that time. Successful country-house sales were also organized, at which the proximity of many of these to London was a distinct advantage. In August 1772 Christie sold the contents of Zoffany's house 'near the six-mile stone at Brentford',[17] in those days a pleasant picnic-day away from London. In this case, the pleasure of the trip was dangerously diminished as Zoffany had died of the plague.

Rivalry amongst the London auctioneers was not then as intense as it is now, but all the same Christie was less than pleased to find the remnants of the Orléans collection turning up in Coxe's sale in 1800; especially as five years previously Skinner and Dyke had been entrusted with the Calonne collection, another important consignment from Paris. (The modern equivalent of this outrage was the successful removal by Christie's of the magnificent Helen Dodge collection from the perspiring grasp of Sotheby's; in 1970 Sotheby's claimed as much of a divine right to important collections coming from America as Christie's did to those coming from Paris in 1795.) Christie's suffered the further indignity of witnessing an American auctioneer, John Greenwood, persuading passers-by in Leicester Square to pay a shilling a head to see Prince Alexander of Lorraine's 'Dürer', prior to his disposing of it by auction to Mr Bryan, who sold it on to the Earl of Carlisle for 500 guineas. In 1911 it was bought by the nation for £40,000 and now hangs in the National Gallery, London, catalogued as by Mabuse. Greenwood's levy of a viewing charge may be seen as something of a precedent for the buyer's premium which Christie's and Sotheby's imposed in September 1975.

The founder died in 1803; but by 1794, when the younger James Christie took his first sale, the firm had consolidated its reputation. It was appropriate that the Christie heir, unlike his father, should have academic pretensions. As a leading member of the Dilettante Society he delivered a number of learned papers on subjects from Greek and Roman antiquity, including a 'dissertation on the Athenian Skirophoria'.[18] In 1807 Rembrandt's *The Woman taken in Adultery* came under the hammer at Christie's, after following a devious route from the Six Collection in Amsterdam through the blockade into the hands of a certain

M. Lafontaine in Soho. Scholars disagreed about its authenticity; but Sir Thomas Lawrence was convinced it was a masterpiece, and rushed off to Blackheath on the morning of the sale to persuade J. J. Angerstein to bid for the painting. According to Farington, Lawrence was delayed by a horse-drawn-traffic jam on Westminster Bridge, and arrived after the Rembrandt had already been knocked down for 5,000 guineas—considerably more than his authorized bid from Angerstein of 4,000 guineas. Lawrence later learnt that the painting had not really been sold, but had been bought back surreptitiously by the owner, who was threatening to risk the blockade again to take the painting back to the Continent in the hopes that the Louvre would show a more incisive acquisitive taste than the English authorities. In the event, the Lawrence–Angerstein partnership prevailed on the owner, and the Rembrandt was included in the Angerstein Bequest, which is the basis of the National Gallery Collection.

The auction market has always depended, to a large extent, on competition amongst the relatively small band of wealthy collectors who can afford to lock up enormous sums of money in the unproductive possession of works of art—unproductive, that is, in the commercial sense. The precarious nature of the art market was demonstrated recently in the way that early Chinese porcelain was devalued overnight in 1974, when the civil disorders in Portugal removed from the market one of the wealthiest and most competitive buyers in the field. Similarly, in the first decades of the nineteenth century, the auction market in London for eighteenth-century French furniture depended on the participation of the Prince of Wales and his court group. He continued collecting after becoming King, but did not attend the Phillips sale at Fonthill in 1823, as a direct consequence of which the wonderful 'Bureau de Roi Stanislas' was sold for only £178 10s. It is not known exactly what Beckford had paid for it, but there is a record of his having been offered the Bureau in Paris in 1792 for £760; and when it was made in the 1770s it would have cost as much as £2,000. When Christie's succeeded in enticing the King into the bidding arena at the Watson Taylor sale in 1825, the prices were transformed. George IV himself bought a pair of bronze and ormolu candelabra for £246 15s, and for £420 'a *chef d'œuvre* of the ingenious Riesener, sold by the Commissaries of the French Convention in the early period of the Republic.'[19]

Two years later James Christie the second discovered that royal connections were not all that mattered, for despite his elegant address from the rostrum at the sale of the old Duke of York's silver, the prices were disappointing. As the hammer fell on a fine sculptural candelabrum for only 6s an ounce, Christie politely rebuked the audience, saying that he felt 'sorry for the sacrifice which has been made in this article'. He admitted to even 'greater grief that the workmanship of the artist is valued so low'.[20] Perhaps the current incumbents of the rostrum at King Street could occasionally also enliven the proceedings at dull sales by experimenting with poetic homilies on the qualities of the principal lots. The surroundings themselves have changed little since the painter Gebaud recorded the scene at the 1828 Carysfort sale of Reynolds's *Snake in the Grass*. It was sold for £1,260 to Sir Robert Peel, standing to the left with his hands behind his back (plate 7). James Christie the second is in the rostrum, and collectors portrayed in the painting include the Marquis of Stafford, Lady Morgan, 'the bright Irishwoman with many friends and not a few enemies',[21] Disraeli's father, and Prince Paul Esterhazy.

The firm had moved from Pall Mall to King Street in 1823, and on the second James Christie's death in 1831, his son took the well-known book-seller William Manson as partner. When Thomas Woods came into the partnership in 1859, the firm assumed the name of Christie, Manson and Woods, as which it is still known—although the last member of the Christie family to work at Christie's retired in 1889.

The move to King Street came at a time when another London auctioneer, George Robins, had seduced a substantial amount of important business from the Christie circle, including the Wanstead House collection of 1822, Robert Heathcote's French furniture in 1823, Benjamin West's pictures in 1829, the second Watson Taylor sale in 1832, and the 'Cellini' dishes of Thomas Hamlet in 1834. Robins had established a reputation for rostrum oratory, and shortly before his death at the age of seventy in 1846, he turned down an invitation to travel to New York to conduct an important sale at a fee of 2,000 guineas with all expenses paid. Perhaps it was Christie's careful concern to avoid the disapproval of the fashionable which left Robins with the task of selling, in 1842, the contents of the unpopular Horace Walpole's 'Gothic mouse-trap',[22] Strawberry Hill. *The Times* described the house as containing 'nothing for which a good judge would have travelled a step out of his road'; but both *The Times* and Christie's miscalculated, for the furniture and works of art secured more than £33,000, and the prints and drawings nearly £30,000. Queen Victoria herself was amongst the buyers. Two of the Queen's recorded purchases were the historically dubious, but romantic-sounding, 'Anne Boleyn's Clock' and that wonderful Renaissance piece, the 'Lennox Jewel'. (The latter fetched only £132.) It is to be hoped that neither of these were pieces with which Robins had been accused of salting the sale.

The Stowe sale in the autumn of 1848 marked a turning-point in the history of Christie's, for throughout the forty consecutive days of auctions crowds of visitors 'flowed in an uninterrupted stream from room to room and floor to floor'.[23] After this popular success, Christie's position at the head of the London auctioneers remained unchallenged for over a century, until in the 1950s Sotheby's began to build its commercial power on the international sale of Impressionist and modern pictures. Although the Stowe sale gave Christie's excellent publicity and the sale total of £75,562 4s 6d sounded impressive, the prices were actually disappointing, often falling short of the Duke of Buckingham and Chandos's original purchase costs. Again the Queen participated, commissioning Gruner to buy a statue of the Venus Maritima in the Prince Consort's name; her birthday present to Albert was presented over the breakfast-table through the agency of the *Morning Post*'s report.

The Bernal sale in 1855 lasted a mere thirty-two days, but amongst the 4,294 lots there was much of lasting interest. Ralph Bernal was a complete connoisseur, who had formed his remarkable collection on modest expenditure with expert knowledge in virtually all fields. Many stories of Bernal's bargain-hunting are told, one—by Redford—of a day when Bernal 'had called at Colnaghi's the print-seller in Pall Mall, as he often did, and found

Dominic Colnaghi, the best expert in the line, looking over a heap of prints bought at sale. Bernal, glancing over his shoulder, spied one of Hogarth's *Midnight Modern Conversation* and said carelessly, 'I say, Dominic, you seem to have got a good impression there; what do you want for it?' Colnaghi, busy with his search for better things, and without examining the print, said, 'Oh, three guineas.'[24] Bernal walked out with that rare early state where 'Modern' is spelt 'Moddern', and at the sale of his books and prints at Sotheby's in 1855 the British Museum paid £81 18s for it.

Bernal's collection was particularly rich in medieval and Renaissance works of art, and amongst the 374 pieces of maiolica was one Caffaggiolo dish which Bernal had purchased privately at Stowe for £5 in 1848, after it had failed to sell at the auction. Because of Bernal's reputation in this field the competition for the maiolica at his Christie's sale was fierce, and Henry Cole had to pay £120 for this dish on behalf of the South Kensington Museum, now the Victoria and Albert Museum. Cole also bid £137 for the so-called 'Three Graces' Gubbio dish, but the Museum Board refused to ratify the purchase and the dish found its way to Paris, where it was sold two years later for the equivalent of £420. In 1861 Andrew Fountaine bought it from the dealer Roussel for £480, finally returning it to Christie's in 1885, where George Salting paid £819 for it before eventually presenting it to the Museum in 1910. It is interesting to note that already in the mid-nineteenth century, older collectors were despairing of the fact that the general level of knowledge and interest in antiques had developed so quickly that it was impossible to buy good things cheaply any more. Henry Bohm, cataloguer of the Bernal collection for the Christie's sale, wrote, 'These matters are better understood, and the day has passed when rarities of surpassing interest might be purchased for trifling sums.'[25] Every generation of dealers and collectors complains that it is no longer possible to buy good things, so people who now criticize the rise in prices of Chelsea porcelain and ridicule new interests such as Art Nouveau or Art Deco need not imagine that they are experiencing anything new.

The period 1860–1880 was most noticeable for the remarkable

prices of work by living artists. The reason for this development was partly the natural tendency of a newly-rich collecting public to display their status and taste by spending hugely on modern art; and partly the print-makers' desire to secure the copyright of popular contemporary pictures by purchasing the original. Many of the boldest prices were paid privately, such as the £10,000 Baron Grant is supposed to have given in 1874 for Landseer's *Otter Hunt*.

But the sale-room also played its part, and the first boom auction came with the disposal in 1872 of Joseph Gillot's collection of 525 paintings almost entirely of the English school of the period 1800–1850, which sold at Christie's for the exceptional total of £164,530. Gillot was the Sheffield mechanic who invented the steel fountain-pen, and went on to make a fortune for himself; so great was the interest in his sale that the *Daily News* reported traffic jams in King Street and crowds of people lining the street. The Turners were the chief interest, and Christie's did not disappoint the crowds for they succeeded in securing a bid of over £3,300 from Lord Dudley for *Bamburgh Castle*, which had been bought for only £525 twelve years previously. Dudley was a compulsive bidder at auction, and he also paid dearly at the dealers, buying Turner's *Grand Canal* from Agnew's in the early 1860s for £8,055. (This apparent extravagance was justified when Christie's sold the painting privately on behalf of Lord Dudley's heirs in 1885 to Cornelius Vanderbilt for £20,000.) Purchasers of paintings other than Turners fared less well at the Gillot sale, for specific comparisons can be made with prices secured in 1913 when many paintings that Lord Holden had bought in 1872 were again sold at Christie's. Thomas Webster's *Roast Pig* dropped from a stunning £3,727 10s to £262 10s, and this kind of Victorian painting only began to secure £3,000 at auction again in the last decade. (It is often forgotten that paintings must continously secure record prices just to maintain their real value against inflation.) Another dismal fall between 1872 and 1913 was Clarkson Stansfield's *Wooden Walls of England*, dropping from £2,835 to £168.

John Everett Millais was the most highly paid painter of his time, and his earning upwards of £20,000 a year in the 1870s amounts to immensely more than any living British artist earns in terms of post-tax purchasing power. Millais normally sold direct to clients, such as the iron-master Bolckow who bought *North-West Passage* in 1874 for £4,930. At Bolckow's death in 1888 Christie's auctioned the picture for £4,200, and apparently the fall of the hammer was greeted by cheers rippling through the fashionable crowd waiting all along King Street as far as St James's.

The William Graham sale of 1886 was another significant Christie event for collectors of contemporary art, as the paintings of Burne-Jones also sold for the first time, at auction for over £3,000 each. After the painter's death in 1898 the auction prices rose even higher; *Love and the Pilgrim* securing £5,775—the same painting auctioned at Christie's in 1942 failed to find a buyer at £21. Fred Walker, almost unknown today, was then well-liked, partly because of the rumour that he was the real-life model for 'little Billee' in du Maurier's *Trilby*: at the Graham sale his paintings sold for several thousand pounds, whereas the Whistler *Nocturne* secured only 60 guineas and 'when this lot came up, there was a slight attempt at an ironical cheer which, being mistaken for serious applause, was instantly suppressed by an angry hiss.'[26] Redford, who so described the scene above, thought that this Whistler was the same painting that Ruskin had called a 'pot of paint flung in the face of the public',[27] but in fact that was the well-known *Old Battersea Bridge*, which Graham had originally bought for £157 10s and the Tate purchased in 1905 for £2,000.

The last great sale of contemporary art at Christie's before the First World War was the collection of George McCulloch, whose 200 pictures made just short of £130,000—enough in 1913, as Reitlinger pointed out, to buy a new destroyer for the Royal Navy. It is purchasing-power comparisons such as these which give the clearest idea of real values. The two top prices at the sale were £8,190 for Millais' *Sir Isumbras at the Ford*, and £6,930 for Jacob Maris's *Dutch Landscape with Windmills*.

Throughout the second half of the nineteenth century, the London sale-room scene was dominated by Thomas Woods, who joined Christie's in 1846 as a seventeen-year-old clerk, first ascended the rostrum in 1854, and became a partner in 1859.

Even after retiring in 1903 he was still the centre of attention at the viewing of important sales, sitting there in his wheelchair as distinguished dealers and collectors queued for a word with 'Old Woods'. One of the sales-clerks told A. C. R. Carter that Woods was the son of a gamekeeper at Stowe, where he had once been wounded by a poacher. Whatever his background, Woods grew into a splendidly uncompromising character, proud of Christie's cosmopolitan atmosphere and reputation for professionalism, praising the firm because 'everyone seems to gravitate to this place, even if it is not so thick with Dukes as Newmarket Heath'.[28] Taciturn though he was, Woods, like all good Christie's men, was adroit enough when it came to putting together a good deal, and it was he who prised the £20,000 out of Vanderbilt for Lord Dudley's Turner. Woods's opinion about pictures was widely respected, and Carter recalled his recognition and recataloguing of two Frans Hals portraits which sold for £2,100 and £5,150 in 1899, as opposed to the 7 guineas and 10 guineas they had fetched on their previous appearance in the market at Stowe in 1848.

In the rostrum Woods (plate 7) was 'as masterful in his way as the first James Christie',[29] and was not above shaming his customers into bidding on a picture for which he had a particular liking; in 1882 he openly rebuked the National Gallery representatives from the rostrum, for allowing Sedelmeyer of Paris to outbid them for an Antonello da Messina. The best-known auction incident connected with Woods concerned the Doetsch sale of early pictures which most people, Woods included, believed were virtually destroyed by over-restoration. Against Woods's advice, Christie's had produced a special catalogue with academically-argued attributions by Professor Richter, and Carter claimed that Woods 'had unquestionably sniffed and snarled at the pictures'[30] at the public view in 1895. At the sale, after only 73 of the 448 lots, Woods summoned one of the porters to bring the ladder, climbed down from the rostrum and walked straight out of the building, leaving young Lance Hannen, grandfather of the present Managing Director, to take his first Saturday sale. The results of the sale were equally decisive, the whole collection only securing £12,970—although there had in fact been some good pictures, such as the Giorgione portrait now in the Washington Gallery, which had been catalogued as a Jacopo dei Barbari and was sold for 22 guineas.

Some of Christie's sales of modern pictures during this period have already been described, but the most important general sale was at Hamilton Palace in 1882. Reitlinger described it as 'unquestionably the most magnificent sale of a single collection that has ever been held anywhere'[31]—a description that is borne out by the illustrated price-catalogue that was published after the sale in several editions. In all areas there were objects of quality and eleven pictures were bought by the National Gallery. However, the most important historical fact about the sale was the establishment of a sensational new market for French furniture, as the Rothschilds chased the Royal pieces which had passed into the collection through William Beckford of Fonthill. Wertheimer bought a Riesener commode from Marie Antoinette's collection for Baron Ferdinand de Rothschild at 9,000 guineas, allowing the companion secretaires to go to F. Davis for the same amount. These were quite amazing prices for pieces of furniture not yet a hundred years old, and were not exceeded for over forty years, until 1926. The Hamiltons managed to sell all their possessions at the right time, as most of their English paintings were kept behind for the second sale in 1919, when American competition for pictures of this period was at its keenest and Duveen paid £54,600 for a Romney which he sold on to Huntington for £70,000.

The sale that attracted the most attention from the general public at this period was the Wynn Ellis sale of 1876, described by *The Times* as 'such a sensation as has never been experienced in the picture world of London. On the day preceding the sale, the interest came to a climax, and crowds filled the rooms of Messrs Christie Manson and Woods all day. Anyone passing the neighbourhood of St James's Square might have supposed that some great lady was holding a reception and this, in fact, was pretty much what was going on within the gallery in King Street. All the world had come to see a beautiful Duchess created by Gainsborough, and so far as we could observe, they all came, saw and were conquered by her fascinating beauty.'[32]

The auction of the *Duchess of Devonshire* was equally sensational, as Agnew's bought the painting in competition for 10,100 guineas, then a record price for any picture by any artist of any nationality. The authenticity of the painting was doubted by many, as it was known to have been bought in 1839 by a schoolmistress called Mrs Magennis for £50, and to have been subsequently cut down and restored for her by Bentley. A. C. R. Carter even claimed to know a man called Partington who had been employed by Bentley to 'paint the Duchess'.[33] Millais was just as positive on purely stylistic grounds, and stormed out of Christie's shouting to Redford, 'I don't believe Gainsborough ever saw it'.[34]

Despite the controversy, three weeks later Agnew announced the sale, presumably at a profit, of the *Duchess of Devonshire* to Junius Spencer Morgan as a present for his son James Pierpont Morgan. That evening the painting disappeared from Agnew's showrooms, and it was not heard of again for twenty-five years until, shortly before he died, the thief contacted them from America. The *Duchess* was finally returned to Agnew's in a Chicago hotel, and sold immediately to James Pierpont Morgan for a sum purported to have been between £32,000 and £35,000.

Rothschild competition again created unprecedented prices at the Fountaine sale at Christie's in 1886, for despite the formation of a British syndicate determined to buy the major works for the nation, most of the important pieces went to France. The most astonishing prices were paid for the work of Bernard Palissy and Henri Deux, as well as eighteenth-century works of art, but similarly heated competition for Old Master paintings was not seen at auction until the first decades of the twentieth century, when the new American collectors such as Frick, Widener, Altman and Morgan entered the market.

So in 1884 when the Duke of Marlborough began to disperse the Blenheim Palace Gallery, he had only the Rothschilds to play off against the European museums, and he rightly decided that his masterpieces would not secure their full value at auction. All the same, the Duke's decision to sell the best part of the collection privately still rankled at Christie's in the 1920s (to judge by Marillier's comments in his history of the firm, published in 1926) especially as most of the left-overs, which were included in a sale at Christie's in 1886, had failed to reach their high reserves. The Duke managed to negotiate some splendid sales, including the Raphael *Ansidei Madonna* to the National Gallery for £70,000; the two Rubens's *Helena Fourment and a Page* and *Family Rubens*, to Alphonse de Rothschild for £57,750; and a Holbein portrait of a young man and Rubens's *Andromeda* to the Kaiser Friedrich Museum for £5,000 and £15,000 respectively. Christie's can salvage some pride from their organization of the sale to Ferdinand de Rothschild, on behalf of Marlborough, of the *Garden of the Hesperides*, the Rubens now in Waddesdon Manor, for £26,250.

A. C. R. Carter's autobiographical *Let me Tell You* is full of sale-room anecdotes of the first three decades of this century. An excellent story is told about the Clapham bus-driver Will Jackson's discovery of the memorandum written by Nelson instructing his officers in their tactics for the battle of Trafalgar. According to Carter, Will was chatting one day to a man sitting beside him in a half-empty bus, and as Nelson somehow came up in the conversation Will revealed the fact that his father had been in service to an old Admiral, who had given him an old desk with a few letters in it, one from Nelson at Trafalgar. The man on the bus shrewdly offered then and there £10 and a suit of clothes for the desk and its contents. But the bus-driver was not to be deceived, and a year or two later he took it into Christie's for their opinion. It was sold in 1906 for £3,600. At the sale, the gallery was full of Japanese visitors, as the memorandum was well known in Japan due to Admiral Togo's habit of constantly reciting it by heart, in English.

During the First World War, Christie's found themselves doing a brisk trade in jewels but struggling to sell anything else, and so they were able to lend their energies to the great Red Cross sales of the war years. As Walter Agnew, one of the three senior partners, had died in 1916, the organization of these sales was left to Lance Hannen and W. B. Anderson, the only two directors who had not been called up. Carter was heavily involved in the promotion of the sales, he and Christie's giving their time free. The first sale began on 12 April 1916 and lasted for twelve days, during which time nearly 2,000 donated lots sold for £37,000. As the days of sales passed, emotions built up into a typically British display of patriotic generosity; Lord Newlands, for example, bought two Irish potato rings belonging to an airman killed in Egypt and returned them to the boy's parents who had donated them in the first place. Ten thousand pounds was paid to the Red Cross for Sargent's agreement to paint a chosen portrait; but the buyer, Sir Hugh Lane, died in the *Lusitania* immediately afterwards, and his executors decided that the portrait should be of President Woodrow Wilson. The fourth Red Cross sale alone fetched over £150,000, and Christie's continued for years afterwards to mark Alexandra Rose Day with the auctioning of garlands of roses presented for the occasion by the King.

When Christie's first Year Book was produced in 1928, Carter was naturally asked to write the introduction, and it is interesting to note that Carter's long experience had taught him to 'cease to marvel at auction results', as he remained 'fortified in my [his] determination to refrain from imposing any limitations on the acquisitive appetites of collectors'.[35] Again one is reminded that the 1970s are not unique in the expenditure of incredible sums on works of art, money that does not relate in any way to the real values of commercial life. But while marvelling at the single-day sale total of £364,000 for the Holford pictures on 17 May 1928, Carter also delighted in pointing out that he had seen just as many reversals of fortune in the art market (see page 18).

Between the wars many politicians frequented the great rooms at Christie's, and on several occasions Carter saw Balfour, Asquith and Rosebery all attending the same sale; Lord Lansdowne could often be seen closeted in the peace of the West Room, preparing his parliamentary speeches. In 1931 the Prime Minister himself, Ramsay Macdonald, turned up to purchase the Howard Grace Cup for the nation. It is hardly surprising that the quiet assurance of Christie's caused an American visitor to announce, within earshot of the ubiquitous Carter, 'Gee, this must be the House of Lords.'[36]

Lance Hannen was still active in the firm in 1930, but the younger directors such as his son Gordon, Sir Henry Floyd, and Alec Martin began to assume power. Of the three, Alec Martin, who was knighted in 1934, was the dominant figure, officially filling the post of Managing Director from 1940 until his retirement in 1958. At his memorial service in 1971 the address was read by the Rt Hon Edward Heath, then the Prime Minister. Sir Alec had joined Christie's in 1897 as a thirteen-year-old office-boy whose principal responsibility was to fetch pints of beer for the head porter. Later Woods recognized his potential and placed him in the picture department, where Sir Alec acquired his expertise in the traditional Christie's way—by daily experience in the handling of works of art. Sir Alec was described in *The Times* obituary columns as 'smallish, roundish, indefatigable and bright of eye', characteristics that could perhaps be expected in a man who rebuilt Christie's after the premises had been gutted by an incendiary bomb in 1941, and who wrote, 'As I watched the burning of our premises with many of its treasures, I was, in spite of my grief, determined not to be beaten by Hitler and his gang.'[37]

Arthur Grimwade, one of the most distinguished silver experts in the profession, joined the firm in 1932 on a two-year trial at £1 a week. At the time, only six secretaries and two office-boys worked at Christie's. The other office-boy, and Grimwade's immediate superior, was Ivan Chance, the retiring chairman in 1974. Jim Taylor, who retired as head porter in the same year with a staff of twenty, was also working at Christie's in the early 1930s when all the pictures were still brought up from the warehouse by the porters through a trapdoor in the centre of the main gallery. Jim, who was also an RSM, still goes in to Christie's regularly to help catalogue militaria. Chance remembers seeing collectors like Lord Portsea wearing morning-dress at all the sales, and arriving for the 1 o'clock start in a smart brougham. Chance and Grimwade joined Christie's during the aftermath of the great depression, and they can recall an art market the values and ethos of which were totally different from the present day. It was also a time when Christie's held total sway amongst the London auction rooms; it is significant that Chance in his article 'Eheu Fugaces', in Christie's *Review of the Season 1974*, reproduced a table originally printed in *The Times* in 1935, which recorded the highest-priced pictures sold at auction in London each year from 1910. Only one of these season's records was at

Sotheby's, one at Hampton and Sons, and one at Knight Frank and Rutley; the other twenty-two were at Christie's.

While Christie's premises were being rebuilt after the war, they operated in Derby House, then in Spencer House, before returning to King Street in 1953, sadly without James Christie's original Chippendale rostrum. The post-Second World War history of Christie's is easily traced through their own *Review of the Year*, which reappeared in 1956. Though prices and turnover cannot compare with the present day, the defensive mechanism of the auction rooms does not seem to have changed much in twenty years. In 1956 a robust art market was proudly noted 'in spite of, or perhaps because of the inflationary age in which we live,'[38] and the editor of the 1958 *Review* claimed that 'the past year has emphasized very strongly that London is once again the centre of the world's art market.'[39] This topic still dominates art market discussions, and even occasionally forces its way into the debating chamber of the House of Commons.

An art-market boom in the 1960s was forecast in Christie's annual figures with its remarkable increase in 1960 of over one million pounds to £3,700,000. Although buyers became more and more international in their outlook, the basis of Christie's successes in the '60s still rested on their traditional associations with the English aristocratic collections. From these sources came many wonderful sales, such as the Royal silver belonging to Lord Brownlow, sold in its own twenty-five-lot catalogue in 1962 for £141,300; it was viewed in the Duveen Gallery in New York prior to the London sale. The following year, Christie's negotiated the sale to the National Gallery of Lord Derby's Rembrandt, *Belshazzar's Feast*, at a tax-concessional price of £170,000; and the studio sale at the death of Augustus John continued an art-market tradition that had been established by the founder of the firm with his disposals of Reynolds's, Gainsborough's and other artists' studios.

The season 1964/5 saw the turnover almost double, to over £8,500,000 and this success was again built around the sale of important English estates, including those of Northwick Park and Harewood House. This was the year in which the Rembrandt *Portrait of Titus* came up for sale from the Cook Collection, and was bought by Norton Simon for 760,000 guineas (see page 40) a European record price at that time for a picture. The painting had originally been brought into England at the beginning of the nineteenth century by George Barker, a picture-restorer and dealer who missed his boat home from a particular trip to Holland and was forced to spend the night in a farmhouse near the Hague. On waking the next morning, he found himself facing a wonderful seventeenth-century portrait of a boy, which was hanging unpretentiously in one corner of the room. Barker studied the picture as he dressed, concluded that it really was Rembrandt, and on paying his bill of one shilling for bed and breakfast, asked casually if the farmer wanted the picture upstairs. He did not; neither did he want any money for it, so the story goes.

To mark the end of the bicentennial year, Christie's mounted an exhibition in 1967 of a wide selection of famous paintings that had passed through their hands in the past 200 years. Pictures were loaned from museums and private collections from Berlin to San Francisco, and this record of past sales inevitably showed the auction room to be a place of changing fortune. Denis Mahon, for example, had purchased Annibale Carracci's *Coronation* for 48 guineas in 1937, although the Earl of Lincoln had originally paid 400 guineas for it in 1856 at the Samuel Rogers sale, again at Christie's. Today it would be worth £150,000–£200,000 at auction. The descendants of Henry Hill of Marine Parade, Brighton, must have been most annoyed to discover from the bicentennial catalogue that their ancestor had sold Degas' *L'Absinthe*, now in the Louvre, for only 180 guineas in 1892. Later in the 1966 season, Christie's demonstrated how easily the art market can turn in the opposite direction and give a pleasurable surprise to unsuspecting heirs. Anthony du Boulay, the senior director in the Oriental ceramics department, was taken by friends to play tennis at a neighbouring country house, and as he was passing the dining-room window he spotted out of the corner of his eye an eighteen-inch Ming vase standing on the floor beneath the sideboard. Peering through the glass, he solemnly informed his host that this flask, which had mercifully survived the assaults of generations of maidservants and children, was

worth a considerable amount of money; and indeed it sold a few
months later for £25,200.

During the early '60s the auction rooms quickly increased in
size and power, as the centre of the art market shifted away from
the dealers; and the surest way of consolidating this power was by
increased specialization of sales, offering greater expertise in
different areas. So in 1966 Christie's decided to resurrect their
wine department by purchasing the City wine merchants,
Restell's, and by bringing in Michael Broadbent from Harvey's
of Bristol to head their operations. Due to Broadbent's ability and
enthusiasm, Christie's wine department soon established the
total ascendancy it still maintains in wine auctions. These were
described by the author and journalist John Russell as 'amongst
the most civilized scenes that the late-sixties have to show'.[40]

In the same season, the specialized costume sales were also
begun and these too are still mounted on a more expert and
serious level than those of any other auctioneers, with catalogues
that impose precise scholarship on a previously undisciplined
subject. The court dresses and whole wardrobes of period costume
often arrived with the most romantic provenances, and the mere
printing of the owners' names in the catalogues suggested
centuries of elegant luxury, images of the past that were substantiated by photographs of slightly self-conscious Christie's
secretaries, beautifully coiffured in the style appropriate to their
costumes. On a different, but no less eye-catching subject, the
first sales of historical steam-engine models were held around this
time, and on the day of the sale Jonathan Minns, the dealer
who produces these sales for Christie's, was generally to be seen
driving a model steam-locomotive up and down King Street to
the amazement of staid Old Master picture-dealers arriving to
view paintings for the following day's sale. *Time* magazine
reported of these sales that 'women were notably scarce, thus
avoiding the feeling of helplessness that swept over one young
wife when her husband, with the dazed look of one under
hypnosis, announced he was going to bid. "Darling you're joking,"
she said. "You are joking aren't you? Aren't you joking?" Then,
after a pause, "But where will we put it?"'[41]

In 1968 Ivan Chance had been chairman of Christie's for ten

years, and his 'disarming high spirits'[42] had raised the yearly turnover during this decade from £1,687,000 to £11,726,000— a fact he celebrated on 7 June 1968 by taking a Christie's sale in Geneva, the first to be held by a British firm on the mainland of Europe. Although Sotheby's quickly followed suit and is now more widely represented than Christie's on the Continent, with regular sales in Amsterdam, Monte Carlo, Zurich, Florence and Frankfurt, none of these offices quite matches the established cachet of Christie's in Geneva, where sales worth well over £9,000,000 were held during the 1975/76 season. The continuing success of this operation must largely be credited to Dr Geza von Hapsburg who works incessantly to bring important Continental collections to Christie's.

Christie's has never quite competed internationally with Sotheby's in the sale of Impressionist and Modern pictures, but it has nevertheless had some splendid sales, including the Rev Theodore Pitcairn's Monet, *La Terrasse à Sainte-Adresse* (plate 8), which merited a small hardback catalogue of its own, and sold for the record price of £588,000 on 1 December 1967. Theodore Pitcairn is a quite remarkable man. The wealthy son of one of the founders of the gigantic Pittsburg Glass Company, he was ordained minister of the Swedenborgian General Church of New Jerusalem in Bryn Athyn in 1918, before working as a missionary in Basutoland for several years. In 1926 he returned to the United States where he founded the Lord's New Church of Bryn Athyn, and remained its pastor until 1962. But before coming home he had already purchased his first Impressionist paintings, three Van Gogh's for $23,000 (which were also sold at Christie's, in 1966, for $660,000). The Monet had been bought direct from the artist by M Frat for the equivalent of £17 soon after it was painted in 1867, and from the Frat family it was sold in 1913 to the dealer Durand-Ruel for £1,700. Pitcairn described how he bought the Monet from Durand-Ruel's shop in New York in 1926: 'My wife and I were walking down 57th Street and saw it in a dealer's window. We bought it in ten minutes for about $11,000 (then about £3,800). I wasn't thinking of investment. We were both struck by its cheerful quality and thought this was the type of picture that would always give us a lift. At the time people

3

thought me rather odd. In those days Monet wasn't too well
known here.'[43] This is a salutary lesson on buying modern art as
investment; no need for intellectual justification or lengthy
market analysis, just buy something you like. Or as the Rev
Pitcairn put it, 'something that will give you a lift'!

The sale of the Monet was the major event at Christie's in the
1967/68 season but one of the attractions of the following season
was presented rather further away from home. In May 1969
Christie's again broke new ground by holding an auction in
Tokyo, which secured the magnificent sum of 695,000,000 yen
(although there is some precedent for sales in the Far East insofar
as James Christie, in 1792, sold fifty-five musical clocks from his
London rostrum while the clocks themselves were still in Canton).
The sale was held at the biggest Art Club in Tokyo, the Tokyo
Bijutsu, which was frequently used by Japanese auctioneers. The
Japanese method is for an auctioneer to hire the premises and
then, through advertisements, to encourage the dealers to bring
works of art to the sale. These are not catalogued but merely
brought along on the day and the sellers called in front of the
rostrum to parade their goods and give a short recitation of their
merits. The auctioneer then asks for bids from the floor, which
are all called out simultaneously. The highest bid is either
accepted or refused by the seller, and the auctioneer is paid his
commission. The best auctioneer in Tokyo can sell 200 lots an
hour by this method. The Christie's auction was a mixture of
Japanese and European styles, as bids were still shouted out but a
catalogue had been produced for the sale and, totally against the
tradition, the presence of non-dealers, and also ladies, was
allowed. The main hall was filled with chairs but everyone still
came in barefoot, even Christie's chairman who looked slightly
embarrassed in his immaculate dinner-jacket above stockinged
feet.

All Christie's off-premises sales and their foreign offices are
operated with a certain style and panache. The Rome office, for
example, is in the magnificent Palazzo Massimo Lancellotti in the
Piazza Navona; the Paris office is run by the Princesse de Broglie;
Düsseldorf by Baroness Olga von Furstenburg; and the Austrian
office by Baron Martin von Koblitz. Even in New York, where

until recently Christie's only ran a small office compared with Sotheby's at Parke Bernet, it seemed natural to take one of the few remaining town houses in Madison Avenue, the Rhinelander–Waldo mansion, where Messrs Richardson and Allsop installed themselves in the small oval ballroom. This office succeeded in maintaining an overwhelming period quality and invariably looked and felt as though Noël Coward was expected to tea at any moment, the atmosphere stylishly enervated. On Fridays the time difference meant that contact from London was unlikely after 1 o'clock and the office was then regularly transformed into an enormous luncheon party. This all changed in May 1977 with the move to Delmonico's at Park Avenue, where Christie's mounted their important opening series of auctions in the United States, and now intend to challenge Sotheby Parke Bernet in every field.

Even now, when the King Street premises is the centre of a vast international empire, an old-fashioned atmosphere remains at the heart of Christie's in London; and the coincidence of Christie's location in St James's and Sotheby's in New Bond Street happens to define an essential difference of attitude. The Christie's directors strive to preserve the traditional tempo of their business because that is how the majority of them prefer to live— the over-zealous application of modern commercial practice to auctioneering is considered not only undesirable but also unnecessary. This is a 'St James's' attitude compared with the relatively aggressive New Bond Street commercialism of Sotheby's, which may look old-fashioned enough but is aiming for a new professional efficiency.

In the past, the difference between Christie's and Sotheby's has often been described as one of social background, an inaccurate fable as both firms are dominated by old Etonians and old Harrovians, and the contrasts arise from divergent attitudes, not backgrounds. The choice of luncheon venues, for example, is symbolic of these attitudes. Sotheby's directors tend to remain cloistered in the tiny boardroom, endlessly discussing policy. If they are entertaining clients, they tend to choose either the Westbury for convenience or one of the fashionable Mayfair restaurants for pleasure. Christie's directors, on the other hand, can be found at lunch-time dotted around the St James's Street clubs in twos and threes, enjoying their own company and conversation about this and that—anything other than business. When Christie's does entertain, it is at large fortnightly lunches from which dealers are, in theory excluded, or at formal dinners in the delightful boardroom at Christie's, whence dinner-jacketed figures emerge to continue their conversations over brandy at the Athenaeum or chemin-de-fer at Crockfords.

'It must and it shall be spring in Pall Mall, When Bustopher Jones wears white spats.'[44] It is slightly surprising that T. S. Eliot did not encourage that 'Brummel of Cats' to visit 8 King Street on his rounds, although he might have been rather taken aback at the new entrance hall, redesigned in 1970. The well-dressed and well-meaning young men still receive enquiries there, but they now hover behind a modern reception-desk and glide about the 'foyer' on abrasively coloured pile-carpet. Instead of unpacking their parcels at antique counters, clients are now ushered into tiny cubicles to await the arrival from on high of the relevant expert, while typists tap away in the open hall. It all looks, and no doubt is, efficient but the atmosphere has become characterless. Even the ranks of catalogues in their pastel shades look less exciting than they used to, which is misleading as Christie's catalogues are outstanding in their design and in the quality of production. Until he retired in 1975, Ridley Leadbeater managed the front counter. Leadbeater had worked at Christie's for nearly thirty years, and on the morning of an important sale his was a familiar friendly figure standing virtually to attention at the foot of the great stairs, beaming benevolently at the visitors, half of whom he greeted by name. From time to time distinguished habitués of the sale-rooms would take Leadbeater by the arm and steer him into a quiet corner to impart confidential instructions before the sale. Others would receive a complimentary catalogue in exchange for some up-to-the-minute information about a particular lot which Leadbeater required for one of his clients. Now that Leadbeater has left, the reception area has lost its character and is the only part of Christie's which lacks style.

It is still a very special experience to view at Christie's before the major French furniture and Old Master picture sales, which normally take place on consecutive days three times a year. Apart from dress it feels as though nothing much has changed since the eighteenth century, as one strolls up the wide, shallow stairs, past couples halted half-way in unhurried discussion, into the main gallery with its lovely central daylight and view through to the octagonal sale-room. The furniture and works of art gain from their position in a natural setting in front of the Old Master pictures, and the elegant proportions of the three viewing galleries make some of the ornate Louis XV lacquer commodes or dark Italian mannerist paintings look considerably more attractive here at Christie's than perhaps they will do at the purchaser's home. As the sale-rooms necessarily sell whatever is offered at one particular time, it is impossible to hope for visual uniformity— even in a specialized French furniture sale. There are often revealing juxtapositions, and always stranger ones, than in a museum or even in a dealer's gallery where there is a natural tendency to uniform taste.

The combination of people to be seen at a Christie's view is also unique. In museums there is never the elegance, at West End dealers never the urgency. For everyone involved the urgency is real, as the view lasts for not much more than three days, during which time Christie's must find buyers, the dealers must reach their conclusions about age, authenticity and value, and the aesthetes and students enjoy seeing rarities that may never appear again on public exhibition in England during their lifetimes. Untidy grey-haired academics clamber up felt-padded ladders to peer through magnifying glasses at the backs of enormous canvases, while mothers and daughters wander below cooing and oohing at the estimated values of a sideboard or a long-case clock, 'identical' to the one at home in the dining-room. Leading dealers come and go continuously, frowning and smiling, solicitous in their attention to an accompanying client, and descending hawk-like on snippets of information or chance contacts.

The Christie's furniture department regularly produces superb sales, with impressive catalogues which are due to the research of Anthony Coleridge, author of a monograph on Chippendale, and the increasingly influential Hugh Roberts. But the rooms are never likely to look better than they did in June 1971, when the Dodge French furniture (plate 9) and Old Master pictures were on view together with Lord Harewood's Titian, *Death of Actaeon*. The most important piece of furniture of the sale is always placed in the centre of the main gallery, facing the visitor as he mounts the stairs; and the *pièce de résistance* of this sale was the porcelain-mounted *bureau plat* by Martin Carlin which was to be purchased by Habib Sabet, the Persian multi-millionaire, for 165,000 guineas—then a record price for any piece of furniture. The table had originally stood in the boudoir of the Grand Duchess Marie-Feodorovna, later the Tsarina of Paul I, in the Palace of Pavlosk; and at the Christie's auction it was in the balance as to whether it would end up in the Detroit Institute of Art, or in a reproduction of the Petit Trianon which stands in the hills at the northern extremity of Tehran. Before the sale the Christie's rooms looked really remarkable, with all the finest Boucher and Fragonard canvases, Van Risenburgh and Dubois commodes, sculpture by Lemoyne, Girardon and Vittoria, and large Beauvais tapestries, all of which Duveen had bought for Anna Thompson Dodge's vast mansion at Rose Terrace on the outskirts of Detroit.

When Anna had married Horace Elgin Dodge in 1896, they had had, according to the author John Parker, seventy-five cents between them, and sixty-five of these were spent on the honey-moon night. Just over twenty years later, in 1920, Dodge won a $40,000,000-court judgement against the Ford Motor Company, and went out to buy his first extravagant present for his wife Anna—five strands of 389 matched pearls, at a cost of $825,000. Six months later he died and in 1923, on marrying the failed actor Hugh Dillman, his widow went on her first spending spree. It lasted until she died in 1970, at the age of 103. One of her principal ambitions was to fill her eighteenth-century-style mansion at Grosse Pointe with legendary pieces of French furniture, and works of art of the period. The building of the house was largely completed by 1936, by which time many important pieces had already been purchased; and the sale of a selection of the contents by Christie's in London and Geneva in 1971 produced a total just short of £2,000,000.

The regular display of fine furniture and works of art in the Christie's galleries certainly adds to the attraction of visiting King Street. The expertise of Christie's furniture department, unrivalled by the other London auctioneers, is matched by that of an even more important department at Christie's, the Old Master picture department. However hard the Earl of Westmorland, Sir Philip Hay and the recently appointed the Hon. Angus Ogilvy of Sotheby's seek to persuade their many aristocratic friends and relations to dispose of the family treasures in Bond Street rather than King Street, year after year the finest pictures from the old English collections end up at Christie's. The reason for this, as has been said, is that for more than two centuries the English aristocratic collections have been bought and sold through Christie's, which is where the market has been established and the record prices necessarily made. If other auction houses could find the fine early paintings to sell regularly, they would no doubt be able to secure equally competitive prices; but such collections are rare and they almost automatically go to Christie's, thus confirming the tradition. And Christie's have been careful never to squander their birth-right, for they have always maintained a first-class team of Old Master picture experts and consultants.

David Carritt, a protégé of Bernard Berenson's, joined Christie's in 1962 and immediately endeared himself to the firm by making an important discovery. When Professor Morassi's catalogue raisonné of G. B. Tiepolo was published in 1962, three ceiling paintings were described as missing since the death of the collector Bischoffsheim's widow in 1922, when their house at 75 South Audley Street was sold to the Egyptian Government. Carritt, who specialized in tracing the whereabouts of lost masterpieces, decided that the first step was to go to the U.A.R. Embassy to look for some records as to when the paintings had been removed. Much to his surprise, the paintings were still in the ceiling, and one of them, *Allegory of Venus Entrusting Eros to Chronos* was eventually sold for £390,000 to the National Gallery (plate 10).

This was the most dramatic of Carritt's discoveries, but there were many others which required more determined detective work, such as the time when, after months of heavy research, he traced four lost Canalettos to a relatively small house in Dublin. When Carritt asked the owner if he could see the paintings he was regarded with incredulity, as no such pictures had ever been heard of: it was only as a last resort that Carritt thought of looking in the potting-shed, where he found the four canvases rolled up in a corner. Carritt was one of the last and youngest of the Berenson-school connoisseurs who succeeded in acquiring a massive general knowledge about Italy and Italian painting. The fashion has changed to the more literary, academic approach of the American universities—a complete waste of time, according to Carritt, who still insists that the only way for a young man really to learn anything about 'art' is to spend a minimum of five years travelling around Italy with a private tutor! He was greatly missed at Christie's when he left in 1970, to head the Banque Lambert-backed art-investment company Artemis.

But the Christie's Old Master picture department is still headed by Patrick Lindsay and William Mostyn-Owen, the incumbent private secretary at I Tatti when Berenson died. It has also been joined by the very able Gregory Martin, grandson of Sir Alec Martin, who had previously been working at the National Gallery. All the picture experts, including the cataloguers of English pictures and watercolours, still meet every week on 'the Hill', a particular room in Christie's basement where the floor begins to slope up to the back door, to discuss the previous week's cataloguing. Each expert normally presents every picture he has catalogued to his colleagues, and is obliged to argue its attribution. The knowledge of the whole department is thus pooled. After the early, tragic death of Hans Gronau in 1951, Sotheby's failed to produce comparable world-class experts in this field, despite the great experience and tremendous accumulation of academic contacts by his widow Carmen Gronau, and the appointment of the distinguished scholar Philip Pouncey to a directorship.

Attending an important Old Master picture sale at Christie's is a pleasure that should be denied no one who appreciates living history. There is a sense of occasion at any major auction at Christie's, but never more so than at a sale of important Old Masters. The night before the sale all the paintings are taken down from the walls of the viewing galleries, and stacked behind the rostrum and in the passage at the back of the sale-room. The red baize on the high walls of the octagonal sale-room shows pictures beautifully, beneath the filtered daylight from the cupola; and the two or three principal pictures normally hang immediately to the left and right of the auctioneer. Otherwise the largest pictures are hung in the auction room itself. The atmosphere begins to build up early, as distinguished foreigners, their fur-lined coats slung with precise casualness across their shoulders, wander down from the Mayfair or the Inn on the Park, and saunter around the galleries attended by an obedient porter, his service secured as much by the commanding presence of the foreigner as by any expectation of a tip. Meanwhile dealers who have just flown in from America or Germany hastily shuffle through the pictures piled in the passage, unable to see clearly in the half-light but hoping somehow that their instincts will tell them whether or not the pictures have been heavily restored. Surreptitiously one or two Christie's experts keep a look-out for important collectors or dealers, whose presence can make all the difference to the prices at the sale. Patrick Lindsay, the auctioneer, conceals his feelings beneath a bland exterior, but inwardly even he will be comforted to learn of the arrival of Professor So-and-so of a Berlin museum, or of Mr Such-and-such from an American private foundation.

By 10.40, twenty minutes before the sale begins, at least half the seats will be occupied, some by nervous owners who may have brought their children out on a specially requested day off school, the children blissfully unaware of the importance of the picture from home now hanging by the rostrum, or indeed of the contribution its really successful sale will make to their future security. The days have passed when *cognoscenti*, except for the very rich, can afford to indulge their taste for early Italian paintings at a Christie's auction, and the sale-room now lacks the extra dimension of the dedicated amateur nervously rolling and unrolling his catalogue, hoping no one else has spotted the grimy minor masterpiece by his favourite Ferrarese painter which has escaped with the nebulous catalogue description 'North Italian, sixteenth century'. Instead, today's 'outsiders' at an auction, buyers who are not part of the immediate circle of international dealers, professional advisers and well-known collectors, are the rich entrepreneurs who treat art principally as a comparatively inflation-proof capital investment for themselves or their companies. The rest of the large crowd, only a handful of whom will even contemplate participating in the bidding, will be composed of smaller dealers and collectors feeling their way in the dangerous waters of five-figure prices, together with perhaps a dozen Press people, topped by that cultivated crush of semi-aristocratic voyeurs who always manage to make their way to major sales at Christie's, and whose overheard conversation takes one back to an ill-defined period in the un-named Grand Duchy of Thomas Mann's *Königliche Hoheit*.

Patrick Lindsay, a striking figure in the elevated rostrum, assumes his place perfectly naturally in this ambience, maintaining the measured decorum of an institution that has been part of London's society life for two centuries. During the important part of the sale, most of the dealers sit quietly at the front facing the green baize table on which each picture is displayed as its lot-number is called. Occasionally a pin-striped figure may leap up from his seat to scrutinize the canvas hastily through a magnifying-glass, before replying, 'Yes, sir' to Lindsay's characteristic query, 'Another one? One more? No?' Beside the rostrum Ray Perman the chief sales-clerk follows events with a bright smile, frequently executing gigantic commission bids with total nonchalance. Leadbeater used to match Perman's colourful ties with the old-fashioned elegance of his waistcoats and his tangerine or pink rose buttonholes, standing as he used to in front of the rostrum directing the auctioneer's attention to discreet bidders, whose furtiveness was revealed to all by Leadbeater's loud call, 'Bidding fifth row from the back far left, sir'. At such a sale there is always a gently jostling crowd of Christie's staff behind the rostrum, their eyes following in unison the play of bids from one end of the gallery to the other like spectators in the stands at Wimbledon.

There is always a certain amount of movement in the room as people get up to greet each other or to leave, and disconnected murmurings intrude a little from the open door into the main gallery, where a further crowd gathers. At the back of the room a sinister-looking bearded man regards each picture through a pair of mini-binoculars; an Italian dealer begins to chew the end of his unlit cigarette; and a barrister from the nearby magistrates' courts rushes out in morning coat and wing-collar to resume his case.

No Old Master sale in recent years has enjoyed a build-up to compare with that of the Velázquez portrait of his mulatto servant *Juan de Pareja* on 27 November 1970. The only first-rate Velázquez that can be expected to appear on the market this century, it was sold by the executors of the seventh Earl of Radnor, and had been in the ancestral home, Longford Castle, since the second Earl had purchased it at Christie's, as has been said, for £151 14s 5d in 1811. The picture had originally been brought to England as part of the returning property of Sir William Hamilton, under escort from Naples by his wife's lover, Admiral Nelson.

Before the sale there had been wide disagreement as to the painting's value at auction, the older generation, according to the *Sunday Times* journalist Colin Simpson, both hoping for and predicting its purchase by the nation at a price of £800,000–£900,000. Agnew's also seemed to assume it their natural right to acquire the picture, and a television crew had been briefed to film the arrival of Agnew's dark-green van at a reserved spot near Christie's front door. As the appointed hour approached, two Agnew's porters positioned themselves at the foot of the stairs, ready to bear away the Velázquez with a ceremony fit for the occasion. The sale-room scene was a combination of an opening night at the National Theatre and an American presidential Press conference with a battery of lights, cameras and Press men, together with an impressive gathering of international dealers garnished with that essential ingredient of the modern sale, the millionaire's minion.

Patrick Lindsay started the bidding low, and the price rose steadily to over £1,000,000 through competition between a mysterious telephone bidder and the patriotic Hugh Leggatt. As the price spiralled into the kind of figures normally reserved for sales in lire or yen, Christie's Press-officer's fingers dug deeper and deeper into his neighbour's shoulder. Quickly the

field of play was left open to Alec Wildenstein and Geoffrey
Agnew, until the latter faltered at 2,100,000 guineas, threw in a
tentative 50,000 guineas, and after turning briefly to his colleagues for guidance was forced to leave the bid with Wildenstein
for 2,200,000 guineas (plate 11). There is a tendency to allow
such enormous sums to roll off the tongue with no more value
attachment than the national debt. Some sense of the reality of
the situation can be acquired by noting that at the latter stages of
the Velázquez bidding, the increments were a casual 100,000
guineas, and recalling that sense of indignation when the local
auctioneer suddenly raises the increments from five to ten guineas.
After the sale there was a momentary flutter of speculation as to
whether an export licence might be refused, but in fact there was
little hope of that, and Alec Wildenstein took the picture home to
the United States where it now hangs in the Metropolitan Museum
of New York. Perhaps Wildenstein already has a Velázquez
or two amongst his legendary stock of works of art, from which the
whole of the new museum of São Paulo was fitted out in the '60s.

The 'preservationists' were more successful with their campaign to 'save' the other million-pound picture of that conspicious
year at Christie's, the Harewood Titian, *Death of Actaeon*, which
was bought at the auction on 25 June 1971 by Julius Weitzner
for 1,600,000 guineas and was promptly sold to the late Paul
Getty for his Malibu Museum. Perhaps Weitzner's earlier
involvement in the sale of the Duccio *Madonna and Child with
Angels* to the National Gallery at £150,000, a few months after
the painting had been sold under suspicious circumstances at a
West Country auction for only £2,700, influenced the decision of
the Government to refuse the licence to export. In the event, the
National Gallery put up £1,000,000 to be paid across five years
of purchase grants, and the remainder of the money was gathered
by public subscription matched by a pound-for-pound Government donation.

The traditional strength of Christie's Old Master picture sales
is illustrated in almost every catalogue by reference time and
again to earlier sales in the firm's history. In November 1971
a magnificent view of the Ponte delle Navi in Verona by Bernardo
Bellotto was sold for 300,000 guineas, exactly 200 years after it

had first appeared at Christie's at what was, in real terms, the very similar price of £260 10s. It was then described as 'lately consigned from abroad', an evasive provenance indicating that James Christie may have had some financial interest in it himself, and was elegantly catalogued as 'Canaletti—A large and most capital picture, being a remarkable fine view of the city of Verona, on the banks of the Adige; this picture is finely coloured, the perspective, its light and shadow, fine, and uncommonly finish'd.'[45] The picture later passed into the collection of Lord Dover, who sold it again at Christie's in 1895 for 2,000 guineas to Agnew's, agents for the grandfather of the present seller.

Despite continual disposals over the last twenty years from important English collections, Christie's still comes up with stunning sales of what can justifiably be called 'Highly Important Old Master Pictures', such as the sale on 2 July 1976. The sale was full of masterpieces that had been continuously in the possession of one family or another for a century or more. From the Duke of Bridgewater's collection, sold on behalf of the Ellesmere 1939 Settlement, were the Pannini (which sold for double its estimate at £170,000), the Van Dyck and Paris Bordon; from the Page-Turners, a Pompeo Batoni portrait of Sir Gregory painted in Rome in 1768; and from Mary, Countess of Crawford and Balcarres, came the Duccio *Crucifixion*, which sold for exactly £1,000,000 and brought the morning's total for 95 lots up to £3,252,000. The twenty-sixth Earl, at the time still Lord Lindsay, had bought the Duccio at Christie's in 1863 for 250 guineas, having been the underbidder for it nine years previously when Walter Bromley-Davenport had paid 265 guineas for it. In the family records there is an amusing reference to this incident, as Mary Anne Lindsay Balcarres refused to accept a wedding gift of £100 from the future Earl because she said he could not afford it: 'Remember the Duccio that you could not buy for yourself the other day.'[46] All through the nineteenth century this marvellous little crucifixion panel was firmly attributed to Duccio, but due to some confusion over photographs it was later mistaken for another in the Crawford collection, and was therefore not included as Duccio in Bernard Berenson's lists of the 1930s. A year before he died in October 1959, Berenson received a full set of photographs

from Lord Crawford and replied, 'Only a word to tell you that I
have received the photos of your Sienese Crucifixion. Of course
it is by Duccio. Ever yours, B.B.'[47] Patrick Lindsay had the
extraordinary experience of dropping the hammer at £1,000,000 on
a painting that had hung in his own nursery when he was a child.

The wine auction is another area in which Christie's have led
the field since 1966, when W. and T. Restell were taken over. At
the moment the Christie's wine department inhabits the mezzanine
floor of 15 King Street, and on mounting the last flight of stairs on
wine-tasting days, the bouquet of fine wines draws on the
enthusiast. Wine-tastings are often thought of by young hopefuls
as free luncheon cocktail-parties, similar perhaps to those
boisterous quasi-tastings that the London wine merchants
generously offer to the undergraduate dining-clubs at Oxford and
Cambridge. While welcoming the inexperienced, whose eyes fall
gratefully on the liberal display of Michael Broadbent's books on
wine-tasting, Christie's see that the wine-tastings remain serious
affairs, particularly before the important sales when a few
treasured bottles are opened, their corks tied to their necks for
inspection by *cognoscenti*. On such occasions the silver department may even be persuaded to lend a regal pair of spittoons to
replace the clinical aluminium cones normally supplied. Wine-
tastings are surprisingly silent affairs. Apart from the noisy
gargling of the occasional Japanese taster, there is little to be
heard but the steady inhaling of bouquets and exhaling of satisfied
sighs, although some of the facial contortions necessarily produced
at a wine-tasting give a far less civilized impression. Michael
Broadbent, Master of Wine, publisher and publicist, presides over
the Christie's wine department, their auctions and tastings. Over
the last ten years he has not only produced some of the most
stunning cellars for auction at Christie's, but has also, often
against severe odds, managed to sell almost everything successfully, and has created a relatively stable climate in a notoriously
unstable field.

Early sales ranged from the incredible cellars of the Earl of
Rosebery, stocked as they were with pre-phylloxera clarets, to a
strange auction held in the Central Hotel, Glasgow, for which
Scottish cellars had been scoured for such oddities as late

eighteenth-century 'gean' whisky and a haul of genuine Kentucky moonshine from the prohibition days. In the 1968/69 season the wine department even ventured across the Atlantic to assist in the preparation and conduct of a sale for Heublein's of Chicago; the next season this was repeated, and wine-tastings were held in New York, Miami, Los Angeles and San Francisco. The wine department reports in Christie's *Review of the Year* tend to illustrate the imposing châteaux and enormous barrel-filled cellars of their major clients, together with photographs of bottles of wine over a hundred years old, 'complete with the original bin labels giving the price paid, the date binned, the name of the wine merchant and the cellarman who built the stacks which have stood the test of time'.[48] The sales also included 'collectors' pieces' such as 'A notable collection of miniatures, removed from a private address in South London and now lying at Christie's',[49] so described in the somewhat affected jargon of the vintner. Old corkscrews also command considerable interest, understandably so as the choice of the right corkscrew is more important in opening fine and rare old wines than playing with the correct club at golf.

In the season 1972/73 the turnover in the wine department doubled, to over £1,200,000, an increase which in part reflected the new fashionable interest shown in vintage wines and also the increasing speculation in wines as a hedge against inflation. Enormous individual sales followed at Quaglino's, where in July 1974 three days' tasting were allowed for the Bass Charrington sale at which more than 36,000 cases of vintage wines were disposed of. In the summer of the following year Broadbent orchestrated the vast combined sale from the cellars of Château Lafite and Château Mouton-Rothschild which made a total of £438,222, a success which did much to brighten up the drooping market. At the time of writing, Christie's sales of cheaper, less exotic wines have been transferred from the City of London to South Kensington, while Beaver Hall, the City venue, is extensively redecorated; this is a sad break in historical continuity, because Restell's had held regular City auctions there for many years before this.

Although Sotheby's have the bigger reputation both for

publicity and for Continental sales, Christie's were in fact the
first into both these fields. Early in 1958, John Herbert was
persuaded by the new chairman Ivan Chance to leave the *Daily
Express* to do a public relations study on Christie's, and the
following year he was made a director in order to set up the Press
office. Considering the number of Christie's and Sotheby's sales
now held abroad every year, it is astonishing to think that less
than ten years ago, on 7 June 1968, Christie's mounted in Geneva
the first fine art auction ever held by a British auction house on
the mainland of Europe. The Geneva office under the administration of Geza von Habsburg, and the tutelage of Anthony du
Boulay, immediately established itself as a leading auction centre,
particularly for jewellery, on which Swiss import duties are
particularly generous by comparison with England. Indeed in the
second season at Geneva a single jewel sale achieved a total of
over £1,200,000. This was for the jewellery collection of Nina
Dyer, the ex-wife of two of the richest men in the world—Baron
von Thyssen and Prince Sadruddin Khan, neither of whom were
amongst the 800 people attending the sale. The next year Christie's
expanded their horizons at Geneva by holding sales of Impressionist pictures and Continental porcelain, the last of which
was conducted in three languages by Hugo Morley-Fletcher with
his customary pomp and circumstance.

Auctions in other locations followed, sometimes with considerable local opposition—such as in Italy, where the licence
for the sale at the Villa Miani near Rome in October 1970 arrived
only just before the sale, after actual sabotage was suspected over
a fire in the grounds, and the British Ambassador had intervened.
Sales in Sydney, Australia, also developed successfully for
Christie's and their agent John Henshaw concentrated principally
on paintings by Australian artists. It is difficult to know exactly
what to expect in the future, as Christie's have always expressed
an unwillingness to do anything that may seem to threaten
London as the world centre of the antique trade; indeed, a season
seldom passes without Ivan Chance or Jo Floyd publicly express-
ing their loyalty and gratitude to the London antique trade. It
will be interesting to see how the new American venture influences
the traditional Christie's structure and policy.

Much depends on the attitudes of successive governments, for as long as both personal taxation and the tariff structure in Great Britain favour the free movement of works of art, then London will continue to dominate, whatever the state of the pound, simply because the private houses of England are still the foremost source of fine pictures and works of art for sale. Christie's, now a large modern public company responding to every challenge with determination and imagination, is nevertheless neither able nor willing to abandon the traditions of its 200-year history. The great muniments room at Christie's, which contains a priced catalogue of every sale that has taken place within the firm, is often considered the symbol of Christie's traditional power. In fact, the muniments room is not merely the symbol but the actual basis of Christie's greatness; a living, growing record of the firm's unrivalled knowledge of, and contact with, the finest private collections in the British Isles.

Sotheby's. Experts and Entrepreneurs

Sotheby's first auction in 1745 was of antiquarian books, a field
in which the firm continued to specialize almost exclusively until
earlier this century. In the 1920s Sotheby's was still described as
'that Rialto of books',[1] even though the move to Bond Street towards the end of the 1914–18 War was followed by the establishment of regular sales of pictures, furniture and other works of art.
Sotheby's still sells more books and manuscripts than any other
auction house in the world, and the book-rooms at both the Bond
Street and the Chancery Lane premises look today as though
little has changed in the bookman's world since Queen Victoria's
Diamond Jubilee. It merely requires Messrs Quaritch, Maggs
and other established dealers to don their grandfathers' top-hats
and frock-coats for the scene to be identical. To the casual
observer, Sotheby's, with its rambling premises, its staff of
connoisseurs and its outwardly archaic auction system, seems to
embody all the traditional attitudes of the fine art and antique
trade.

Within the trade, however, the modern Sotheby's has a very
different reputation, a reputation for aggressive salesmanship,
for extravagant innovation and for imaginative response to chal-
lenges in the market. This view is nearer the truth, for despite
antiquarian appearances Sotheby's has established itself as a
highly competitive modern business with an international turnover of over £150,000,000 a year. The Sotheby's Board of
Directors sees itself at the centre of a post-war art market in
which values and attitudes change so rapidly that not even the
experience of the previous season can necessarily be trusted. It is
Sotheby's adaptability to the frighteningly fast changes in the
modern art market which distinguishes the firm from all its

competitors. The historical perspective derived from nearly 250 years of auctioneering is only of use to Sotheby's forward-thinking directors insofar as it reassures them that today's mountainous prices and sudden changes in taste are nothing compared with certain earlier periods. There is extraordinary confidence, verging on arrogance, about the way Sotheby's straddles the art world and responds to the risks of its multi-million-pound business.

The first auction ever held at Sotheby's was of books, and the book department remains at the heart of the firm. In his introduction to the Sotheby annual review, 1965, Frank Davis wrote, 'In spite of many other spectacular happenings, to numerous people Sotheby's means books and manuscripts as it did in the days of the founder. I sometimes suspect that the book department, a trifle remote and immersed in its erudite cogitations, is tempted to look upon its comparatively upstart less sedate colleagues much as a Trollopian bishop would regard a newly hatched gaggle of curates.' The book department is still to a certain degree isolated from the rest of the firm, with its own sale-room by the back entrance and a larger, more respected band of experts than in any other department of Sotheby's. Books and manuscripts are also beginning again to command a larger share of the company's turnover, Sotheby's 1975/76 world-wide figure of £8,400,000 being over eight times Christie's turnover in books and manuscripts. This figure was helped by the remarkable £370,000, a record price for any manuscript, which was paid for a previously unknown Flemish *Hours of the Virgin* decorated in the early sixteenth century by Gerard Horenbout and Simon Beruz.

A disastrous fire at Sotheby's Wellington Street premises in 1865 destroyed most of the firm's records, and its early history is somewhat obscure. The firm was founded by the bookseller and publisher Samuel Baker, whose first extant fixed-price book catalogue is dated 19 February 1734. The sophisticated expertise and large size of this catalogue indicates that Baker must already have been in business for some time, and there can be no doubt that he was a leading and adventurous member of his profession. Baker's first auction is traditionally described as the sale of the

Thomas Pellet Library in January 1745;[2] and for the next decade
he continued to present regular public auctions at various venues
in and around Covent Garden, including that of Reverend Stuart's
library at St Paul's Coffee House in 1746, and of Reverend
Conyer Middleton's at the Great Room in the Rose and Crown.
In 1754 Samuel Baker moved into a permanent auction room in
York Street, Covent Garden, but the firm also continued well
into the nineteenth century to publish books under the Baker
imprint, on subjects ranging from scientific indices and the study
of birds, to sermons and poetry. George Leigh was taken in as a
partner in 1767, and at Baker's death in 1778 the founder's
estate was divided between his nephew John Sotheby and his
partner Leigh, though the first Sotheby probably never took an
auction. The next change was in 1800, when John's nephew Sam
Sotheby joined the partnership, two or three years after which it
moved premises to Wellington Street off the Strand.

George Leigh (plate 16) appears to have been a powerful
individual, and Nichols in his *Literary Anecdotes* describes him
in glowing terms. 'This genuine disciple of the elder Sam [Baker]
is still [1812] at the head of his profession . . . His pleasant dis-
position, his skill, and his integrity are as well known as his
famous snuff-box.'[3] The diarist Dibdin described the same snuff-
box as 'having no less an imposing air than the remarkable
periwig of Sir Fopling of old . . . When a high priced book is
balanced between £15 and £20 it is a fearful sign of its reaching
an additional sum if Mr Leigh should lay down his hammer and
delve into his said crumple-horn-shaped snuff-box.'[4] The ivory
hammer, which still hangs in Sotheby's general office, is also
mentioned by Dibdin, in his *Bibliograph: A Poem* of 1812: 'And
down th' important hammer drops (this instrument had wielded
been of old by Langford; he with dieing breath to Baker did
bequeath his sceptre of dominion which now decks the courteous
hand of Leigh)'.[5]

In the 1750s Baker had already begun to mount occasional
sales of works of art other than books, such as prints, coins, and
manuscripts from Dr Richard Mead, scientific instruments from
Joseph Harris, and coins and medals from Edward Townsend.
However all through the nineteenth century Sotheby's reputation

rested on book auctions, and the last member of the family to work with the firm, Samuel Leigh Sotheby (died 1861), was a bibliophile of note, his best-known work being *Ramblings on the Elucidation of the Autograph of Milton.*

In those early days the title pages were composed in Latin (plate 14) a guarantee was given on every lot, and the bidding started at six old pence and advanced up to ten shillings in threepences. The most expensive lot at Sotheby's first known auction in 1745 was *Mrs Blackwell's Herbal* at £14.

In the Victorian period Sotheby's sold coins, prints, antiquities and stamps as well as books, and there was an unwritten agreement with Christie's that they would pass all pictures, furniture and other works of art to King Street, on the understanding that Christie's reciprocated with the introduction of libraries. John Wilkinson was taken into the partnership in 1842, and Edward Grose Hodge in 1864. Tom Hodge, the latter's son, joined the firm in 1878 and by 1896 was the sole active partner. Apart from the occasional reference in A. C. R. Carter's memoirs, the principal sources of information on the history of Sotheby's from 1900 to 1930 are two articles by Tim Wilder (plate 22) in *Art at Auction*, 1968 and 1969. Wilder joined Sotheby's in 1911, and his writing about the personalities of the firm at this time is full of life and warmth.

The overriding impression of Sotheby's given by these articles is of a firm which inspired the total involvement of all the staff in its triumphs and disappointments, despite the autocratic attitudes of the partners. The loyalty of the staff was clearly expressed by the clerk Kendall, who continued to receive the catalogues after his retirement and whose last words are reported to have been, 'Well, do you know, I think we shall have a good sale today.'[6] Most of the porters in those days came from the Guards Employment Bureau, and many of them retained their ranks 'below stairs'. Carpenter, a large moustachioed foreman who can be seen in the background of most of the sale-room photos of the '20s, was known as 'Corp' to his under-porters.

Tom Hodge was an uncompromising man who refused till the last to make use of the telephone or typewriter; and when the young partners, Montagu Barlow, Felix Warre, and Geoffrey

Hobson, whom he had taken on in 1909, introduced female staff into Sotheby's he promptly retired to keep bees in the country. As Edith Bourne, one of the guilty female intruders, later wrote, 'The hegemony of the hive, unaltered since creation, must have been pleasing to his intransigent spirit.'[7] But Hodge was an acknowledged expert in numerous fields and presided over many distinguished sales of books and manuscripts, not least that of the *Psalmorum Codex* sold on behalf of Sir Hayford Thorold for £4,950 in 1884; of the grand Ashburnham Library in 1901; and that of the Robert Burns Bible for £1,560, at the sale of 10 December 1904, which was still held at the traditional time of 2 o'clock on a Saturday afternoon.

Hodge enjoyed an excellent relationship with the book trade, although like all good auctioneers he kept them all in order. Cohen, of the Charing Cross Road dealers Marks and Co, remembered attending a Saturday sale when a run of lots, just before a fine illuminated manuscript, sold for tiny sums, no more than a shilling or two each. Bertram Dobell then waspishly offered an opening bid of a shilling for the illuminated manuscript, and Hodge said, 'Come, come Mr Dobell, you ought to know better than that.' 'No, I'll give a shilling for any lot, sir,' replied Dobell in mock seriousness. The manuscript easily sold for over £1,000; but a few lots later a nondescript bundle of books was offered without producing a single bid from the room; and Hodge promptly dropped the hammer, calling out, 'A shilling to Mr Dobell'. Dobell indignantly denied bidding, at which Hodge replied, smiling but firm, 'Just now you said you would give me a shilling for any lot,'—and for the rest of the afternoon all unwanted lots were knocked down to the unfortunate wit.[8]

Tom Hodge's most important discovery was at Queensferry, where he had been called to make an inventory of the Hopetoun Library. The carriage had been called and he was just about to leave, when he instinctively insisted on diving into a dusty kitchen cupboard, emerging from it with the two-volume *Mazarin Bible* which sold for £2,000 in 1889.

Tim Wilder had been engaged as a clerk in the main book-room, where he was 'in charge of the only typewriter, a small telephone exchange with three or four extensions, an arrival book in which to enter properties coming up for sale, and, of course, masses of letters to type.'[9] He was also employed as personal clerk to Montague Barlow, who was already a member of the House of Commons and had only recently left his practice as a barrister. Sir Anderson Montague Barlow, Bt, Minister of Labour (as he was to become), was ambitious for Sotheby's and quickly altered the practice of sending pictures to Christie's by selling Lord Glausk's Frans Hals portrait for the excellent price—in 1913—of £9,000. He was also a masterly entrepreneur, in 1914 negotiating the private sale to Henry Huntingdon of the Chatsworth Caxtons and Shakespeare Quartos, for £300,000. When the Wellington Street lease ran out, Barlow was determined to move into the fashionable West End and purchased numbers 34 and 35 New Bond Street on the site of the Black Horse Inn, the outgoing occupants of which were the wine merchants Basil Wood and the Gustave Doré Gallery.

The move to Bond Street in 1917 marked the beginning of a new era for Sotheby's, which was celebrated by the first disposal of an important general property, the Earl of Pembroke's collections of armour, pictures, drawings and prints. Tim Wilder regretted 'that the family should have been forced to sell two magnificent suits of armour, now in the Metropolitan Museum, New York, after they had stood in the main hall at Wilton ever since their capture at the battle of Saint Quentin in 1557.'[10] Proper celebration of the move to Bond Street was postponed till the end of the war, when Barlow gave a Victory Dinner for all the staff and a few chosen guests such as the journalists A. C. R. Carter of the *Daily Telegraph*, William Roberts of *The Times* and Tom Grieg of the *Morning Post*. Barlow, like the present chairman Peter Wilson, knew the value of good relationships with the Press. He also attached importance to the social graces, and apparently reprimanded Wilder for not dancing at the party. But Wilder wrote that he was 'content to bask in the reflected glory of Mark Hall, a young assistant at the British Museum Print Room. He was our guest and, resplendent in military uniform, busied himself bowing over neglected ladies and escorting them on to the floor.'[11]

Barlow was a tyrant in the rostrum, regularly denouncing

fidgety dealers with the roundly delivered remark, 'Was that a bid, sir, or merely a salutation?' and threatening to 'name one of you gentlemen if the chatter does not cease immediately.'[12] G. D. Hobson, one of the new partners with Barlow in 1909, was unable to take sales due to his very poor hearing, but he still exerted a strong influence on the development of the firm, particularly with regard to maintaining the standard of cataloguing in the book department. Hobson, known as 'Il Magnifico' by some of the staff, was a fine scholar with a passionate desire for accuracy in all things academic. In the early days at Bond Street he always proof-read the sales catalogues, but occasional inaccuracies slipped through. One such mistake was discovered by Hobson when he was escorting a client around a picture sale, and was confronted by a picture of a child standing beside a large conical hat described in the catalogue as *Boy with a Dog*. The client looked a little puzzled and asked where the dog was. 'Under the hat, I expect,' replied Hobson, and made a mental note to reprimand the unfortunate cataloguer.[13]

The number of Sotheby's cataloguers increased, but none of the newcomers could match old Will Edmunds who catalogued most of the Oriental works of art. Edmunds was also a poet and had a number of verses published, in addition to the private distribution of his Christmas poem around the Sotheby staff. He lived and dressed with a mildly eccentric extravagance, wearing instead of the regulation bowler in winter and straw boater in summer an expensive broad-rimmed felt hat and an equally large panama. According to Wilder, he lived to a great age, 'was seen running for a bus at eighty-four, and was heard to say at the sight of a particularly alluring female client, "I wish I was seventy again" long before this witticism came into general use.'[14]

Barlow also brought in some of the leading dealers as part-time consultants; by scaling their fees to the auction prices, he made sure that it was in their interests for consignments to secure reasonable prices and thus to a certain extent he curtailed the activities of the dealers' ring which was particularly strong in London in the '20s. Charles Francis of the Ashmolean was succeeded as picture consultant by Tancred Borenius, who made numerous discoveries which benefited Sotheby's clients; but having established the right to an introductory commission on every lot he catalogued, Borenius kept a sharp eye out to see that no one else trespassed on his ground. There was also a female expert, Millicent Sowerby, known as 'the Girton girl', who joined Sotheby's just before the move to Bond Street. All the female staff were kept in order by Barlow's sister, the formidable Evelyn, who insisted that she and all the other women wore large blue overalls at work so as not to distract the men; Miss Barlow is known to have taken auctions but it is not recorded whether or not she wore her overalls in the rostrum. Miss Sowerby subsequently went to work for the Rosenbach Company of Philadelphia, who were the major foreign book-buyers at Sotheby's in the 1920s.

In 1928, just before the American crash, Barlow left Sotheby's to take a more active part in politics, and sold his controlling interest in the firm to Charles Vere Pilkington and Charles des Graz. The two became successive chairmen, Vere Pilkington retiring in 1958, leaving the firm in the capable hands of Peter Wilson.

Peter Wilson has been a dominant figure within the firm since he became a partner in 1938 at the age of twenty-six. From the late '50s he is also considered to have been a major influence on the whole international art market, an opinion which is not merely the creation of Sotheby's own publicity machine but has been endorsed by many collectors and dealers who, as clients or as rivals, have long admired this Tamburlaine of the modern art market.

Wilson's impact is clearly demonstrated in Sotheby's trading figures. In 1938 when he joined the Board, the gross turnover at Sotheby's was no more than £350,000 in the season, whereas their rivals in King Street had already produced a morning sale's total of £364,000 in 1928. In 1950/51 the Sotheby turnover exceeded Christie's for the first time in their 200-year history of competition; in 1958, the year Wilson became chairman, Sotheby's turnover was £3,077,526 as opposed to Christie's at £1,687,373; and in the 1977/78 season, the Sotheby Parke Bernet net turnover at auction was over £160,000,000, nearly double Christie's total.

Although members of both houses, like the thoroughbred show-jumpers that they are, haughtily deny the existence of coarse commercial rivalry, in reality they compete at every fence in every major event. The rivalry is outwardly friendly but many of the experts hide with difficulty their jealousy of the other's sales and clients, and the mere thought of moving into the opposing camp at anything but the most junior level is an unforgivable crime. The only clients that are exchanged willingly by the losers are the difficult ones. Quite recently the head of Sotheby's furniture department was observed at the counter responding with admirable self-control to the angrier and angrier insults of a client concerning the estimated value of his Edwardian bureau. The owner finally rounded on the director with the fist-shaking threat that in future he would take all his business to Christie's. The director replied with perfect decorum, 'Sir, I can recommend our esteemed rivals to you with the clearest conscience; and, fortunately for my conscience, they are most unlikely to ask me whether I can recommend you to them.'

Sotheby's achieved their new financial supremacy by being first to develop, under Peter Wilson's leadership, two new aspects of the auction business. In 1954 Sotheby's took immediate advantage of America's de-restriction of its wartime currency regulations, by opening an office in New York and offering a direct service to the new breed of American collector. This process was completed in 1964 by the outright purchase of the biggest American auctioneers, Parke Bernet. The other central development at Sotheby's was the decision in 1955 to mount specialized sales of Impressionist and later paintings, thus establishing ascendancy in a new multi-million-dollar market. Both these elements, the creation of an international market based on London and the rocketing public demand for modern paintings, gave Sotheby's auction rooms a newsworthiness that the company was determined to exploit. These Sotheby developments changed the whole balance of the art market, which had previously favoured imaginative international dealers like the Duveens, the Kugels, the Partridges and the Wildensteins, and which now allowed the auctioneer to assume a natural right to many of the major deals. The vast publicity received by these record-breaking sales made it progressively easier in a competitive market to prove that the auction room was the best place to dispose of major works of art, and the auctioneer's argument became irresistible as major paintings at auction proceeded to secure two or three times the price that even the most ambitious dealer would have thought of asking in his gallery.

None of this would have been possible without the selfless and occasionally ruthless determination of Peter Wilson to ensure that Sotheby's triumphed. Wilson has devoted his life's ambition to Sotheby's, and seldom ceases from work for the company. At the shortest notice he will fly any distance across the world and back, if there is a chance of securing a major collection for sale; indeed he can be expected on the doorstep of a palace in Italy, a castle in Norway or a ranch in Texas on Christmas Day, if he has heard of the possible defection of a customer and his property to a rival auctioneer. Wilson's particular strength is the way he combines an encyclopaedic knowledge of the whereabouts of the remaining major collections in private hands, with the maintenance of a direct line of communication to the people most likely to buy these works of art at record prices. These are the skills of the salesman, but Wilson's eye for quality and rarity in virtually all fields of the fine and decorative arts has also made him the favourite aesthetic guru of many important collectors. This combination of qualifications gives him an unassailable dominance over all his rivals in the international art market, and the chairman's personal power naturally passes to Sotheby's.

Described in such terms, Wilson begins to sound like a humourless art-market machine. As anyone who has worked with him will know, this is far from the truth, for he seldom remains completely serious for more than five minutes and even the most vital discussions are studded with witticisms and iconoclastic comments. Wilson is as determined to enjoy himself as he is to see Sotheby's successful, and he particularly enjoys the company of rich and eccentric collectors; he adores looking at and assessing works of art of all kinds; and he revels in the challenge of competition. Wilson has no intention of retiring for many years, but when he does Sotheby's will change and, at least to begin with, will suffer.

Sotheby's internationalism is, as has been pointed out, an important feature of the firm's structure and character. Christie's were the first on to the Continent of Europe, with a representative in Geneva many years before Sotheby's made a move in that direction. This early development in Geneva is reflected in the considerable present strength of Christie's there, which Sotheby's struggles to emulate in Zurich. It was only by weight of numbers that Sotheby's eventually built up a wider base than Christie's on the Continent, and these new activities often placed a considerable financial burden on the firm—as with the purchase of the Amsterdam auctioneers Mak van Waay in 1974 at a price in excess of its real value. The Sotheby flair and commercial instinct expresses itself most successfully in the Monte Carlo operation, for which an exclusive contract with the Société des Bains de Mer was quietly negotiated by the chairman during summer holidays at his château near Grasse. The Monte Carlo sales placed Sotheby's in direct competition with the State-owned Paris auctioneers, as works of art passed freely into Monaco from France; and the project was unveiled at the successful *beau-monde* auction in spring 1975 of contents from the Hotel Lambert and Château de Ferrières. There is no one in the whole international art market to match Peter Wilson in this kind of operation, involving the patronage of princes, the partnership of casinos and the seduction of the international jet-set.

Sotheby's really established their international dominance in the United States, so much so that every year now the auction turnover in America approaches nearer and nearer the combined total of England and the Continent. The first Sotheby office in the United States was opened by John Carter in October 1955, in a borrowed room with a part-time secretary in a friendly lawyer's office in Manhattan. John Carter was a tremendous asset to Sotheby's. A considerable scholar in the field of antiquarian books, he combined a keen desire to meet, converse with and convert the rich or the great, with an unexpected commercial awareness of the intricacies of the art market. He was particularly aware of the potential gain for London in the re-establishment of free trade with the United States in 1954. Having already visited forty-four of the forty-eight states when he was Personal Assistant to the British Ambassador, Carter soon set out again with a different mission; persuading American collectors that London was the most important centre of the international art market and explaining that the commission and tax structure there was particularly favourable to buyers and sellers. One medium he used was the English-Speaking Union lecture tour, through which the aesthetes of Chicago and Detroit, Memphis and St Louis, Palm Beach and Charleston were served up with a Sotheby's advertising campaign, thinly disguised under such lecture titles as 'Bull Market in Bond Street', 'Going, Going Gone', and 'Renoir is a girl's best friend—or is it?'[15]

The New York office immediately produced two important consignments; the Arnold Schoenlicht collection of Chinese porcelain, which sold in December 1955 in London for £27,400, and the De Coppet library which, over ten sales, secured the sum of £196,454, more than twice the appraisal of John Carter's New York rivals. Carter, despite his wide general knowledge, refused to make expert assessments on his own and therefore relied for advice on the London heads of department. Carter had known Cyril Butterwick in England as an Eton schoolmaster; as well as Butterwick there was Jimmy Kiddell, for whom he 'formed a lifelong affection at first sight',[16] Anthony Hobson whom he 'knew and warmly respected',[17] and Peter Wilson, Tim Clarke, Carmen Gronau and Richard Timewell.

The second important innovation for which Peter Wilson and John Carter were responsible was the first sale ever held in London totally devoted to Impressionist paintings. This was held on 4 July 1955, and the following season consignments from America rose to 20 per cent of the record £3,168,476 turnover. They included the Weinberg collection, the essential preface to the second Goldschmidt sale of 1958 (see page 25), whose £781,000 total exceeded for the first time the 1928 single-sale total achieved by Christie's for the Holford pictures. This Impressionist boom is fully discussed later.

Another innovation of Carter and Wilson's was the publication in 1957 of a small volume called *Sotheby's 213th Season*, which grew into the weighty *Art at Auction* and remains as a memorial to John Carter, whose death in 1975 removed from Sotheby's one of the three most influential figures in the establishment of its present dominant position.

The third member of this trio, Peregrine Pollen, heir apparent to the Wilson chair, chooses to keep a low profile in London, but in the United States he was permanently in the public eye from the moment he went over in 1960, at the age of twenty-nine, to set up with Carter a registered trading company in New York and subsequently to purchase the leading US auctioneers Parke Bernet in 1964. He was President of the new company until returning to London in 1972. Parke Bernet was the creation of Hiram H. Parke and Otto Bernet, who had left the American Art Association-Anderson Gallery monopoly in 1937, just before it was torn apart by the new owners John T. Geery (who committed suicide in 1940) and Milton Logan (who was convicted for grand larceny). Mitchell Kennerley, who had been the cause of Major Parke's rift with the AAA-AG and had negotiated its sale in 1938, himself committed suicide in 1950. The newly created Parke Bernet quickly established itself in the vacuum, benefiting from the leadership of this highly respected and greatly experienced pair, and after Parke retired in 1949 (Bernet had died in 1945) the firm was left in the capable hands of Louis Marion, Leslie Hyam and Mary Vandergrift. In 1950 Parke Bernet moved into its present premises at 980 Madison Avenue, where there were numerous important sales before the Sotheby takeover in 1964, including the Lurcy collection in 1957 and the Foy sale in 1959, each at over $2,000,000; and the Erickson sale in 1961, which totalled more than $4,500,000 in just less than an hour.

Sotheby Parke Bernet in New York is now back under the control of the American partners with, appropriately, the son of Louis Marion—John—as the energetic President of a subsidiary which, with a turnover in 1976 of £39,000,000, had overtaken London. New York has become infinitely more than a Sotheby outpost, but the other smaller foreign offices in eighteen different countries also contribute essentially to the success of modern Sotheby's which relies on the cultivation of personal contacts with millionaire collectors throughout the world. With the European and American economies apparently in a permanent state of crisis, it becomes more and more difficult to find buyers from traditional sources for the six-figure works of art, and therefore the introduction of only half a dozen rich new buyers from Dubai can have a life-saving effect; just as the steady growth in turnover of properties from the Far East in their Hong Kong auctions looks particularly healthy on the company accounts.

It is foolish to suggest, as some commentators do, that Peter Wilson as Sotheby's mastermind is almost entirely responsible for 'internationalizing' the antique trade and for creating the ambience for today's continuous escalation of prices. By going international Sotheby's and Peter Wilson did not transform the art market, they merely assumed the same kind of advantages that the most successful international dealers had always enjoyed—the purchase of business-getting premises in as many places as they could afford. Certainly, immense Press coverage was given to the new structure of values seen publicly in the auction rooms, but this did not necessarily mean that such prices had never been secured before in the private dealer trade—quite the contrary. Giuseppe Bellini, the Florentine dealer and master-chef, described how works of art have always had a special value in the hands of particular dealers. 'My father', he tells, 'once called on a lady at her house and bought a picture for £1,000. He had it cleaned and then offered it in his gallery for £20,000. The lady heard of this and taxed him with it. He replied, "Madam, in my gallery your picture is worth £20,000. If you wish I will return it at once to your house. There it will again be worth £1,000." '[18] Peter Wilson was potentially the greatest dealer of his generation, but he chose to become an auctioneer instead and has worked hard to make sure that almost every category of work of art also has this 'special' value at Sotheby's, just as it did at Duveen's or Bellini's galleries. Once this had been established in the public's mind, the reputation was rather easier to maintain at an auction house, as high prices benefit the sellers more than Sotheby's. The insistence with which Sotheby's emphasizes this inescapable fact is perhaps the characteristic that most antagonizes the West End dealers.

Lot 52. A genuine Turner, painted during the artist's lifetime[19] ran the caption to Gardy's Punch cartoon, caricaturing the naïvety of fashionable collectors at the beginning of the century. Sotheby's has always known that much depends on the quality of its expertise, and in 1828 Joseph Halewood drew up for his friend Samuel Sotheby a set of 'Hints for a young auctioneer of books', in which the first rule was, 'Consider your catalogue as the foundation of your eminence and make its perfection of character an important study.'[20] While mistakes may occasionally appear in the catalogues, and pressure of time may prevent the experts from completing all the research they might like to, Sotheby's catalogues of major collections are invaluable works of academic reference, and confidence in their own expertise is now displayed in the five-year guarantee of authenticity which was introduced for London sales in September 1975. Sotheby's can also be credited with leading the field in departmental specialization, beginning in the late '50s when the picture department divided into four separate units: European Old Masters, English Paintings and Watercolours, Impressionist and later painting, and Old Master Prints and Drawings. Since then there have been more and more departmental divisions, and highly specialized experts can now be found dotted about the premises in tiny offices surrounded by their esoteric treasures (plate 24). The result is that magnificent catalogues are produced on such narrow fields as Japanese metalwork and early photographs, and specialist dealers and collectors from all over the world fly into London to compete at the auctions.

The distinguished nature of Sotheby's expertise in so many fields was emphasized in an advertising campaign in the summer and autumn of 1976, called 'Capitalise on our Expertise', which told of some of the discoveries that had been made by Sotheby's experts. Perhaps the most sensational discovery of recent years was a painting for which an Edinburgh schoolteacher called in the Sotheby Scottish office. The story has been told before but is worth repeating. The painting had been in her family for three generations but the owner, Mrs Cattrell, had always disliked the rather macabre figures, and it had therefore been allowed to languish in the dining-room behind a thickening layer of candle-black. Mrs Cattrell told the Sotheby representative that she hoped to buy a better second-hand car with the proceeds, and was encouraged in her hope by the fact that the painting was considered worth sending down to London for inspection. Initially the Sotheby Old Master picture experts found it difficult to assess

Plate 11

The most valuable painting ever sold at auction, Velázquez's portrait of his mulatto servant, *Juan de Pareja*. It was auctioned at Christie's on 27 November 1970 for 2,200,000 guineas

Plate 12

Christie's hold highly
successful sales in Geneva,
the most important of
which are taken by the
chairman of Christie
Manson and Woods,
J. A. Floyd

Plate 13

Wine-tasting at Christie's,
the centre of the wine
auction trade

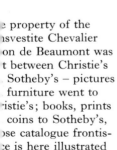

MVSEVM MEADIANVM,

SIVE,

CATALOGVS NVMMORVM,

VETERIS AEVI

MONVMENTORVM, ac GEMMARVM,

Cum aliis quibufdam

Artis recentioris et Naturae OPERIBVS;

Quae Vir Clariffimus

RICHARDVS MEAD, M. D.

Nuper defunctus comparaverat.

Relliquias, veterumque vides monumenta virorum. Virg.

LONDINI,

Catalogus proftat apud A. Langford in area dicta Covent-Garden;
et S. Baker in vico dicto York-ftreet.

[Pret. 1s. 6d.]

Plate 14

The title-pages of early Sotheby's catalogues were in Latin – like this sale in 1754 of Dr Richard Mead's coin and manuscript collection

Plate 15

The property of the transvestite Chevalier d'Eon de Beaumont was split between Christie's and Sotheby's – pictures and furniture went to Christie's; books, prints and coins to Sotheby's, whose catalogue frontispiece is here illustrated

Plate 16

George Leigh, an
influential partner at
Sotheby's from 1767
to 1816

Plate 17

A drawing by James
Gillray, March 1807, of
the Marquis of Stafford
and two other famous
collectors, Caleb White-
forde and Julius Anger-
stein, on their way to a
sale at Christie's

Thomas Rowlandson's drawing of a book-sale in progress at Sotheby's at the turn of the century

Plate 18

(*Opposite above*) The sale of books and manuscripts was still Sotheby's   *Plate 19*
principal activity in 1928 when the manuscript of *Alice in Wonderland*
sold for £15,400

(*Opposite below*) The sale of the Goldschmidt collection of   *Plate 20*
Impressionist paintings on 15 October 1958 was a turning-point in the
history of Sotheby's. Peter Wilson, seen in the rostrum, sold Cézanne's
Garçon au Gilet Rouge for £220,000

(*Above*) A crowded sale-room at Sotheby's in November 1963 for the   *Plate 21*
sale of the Crown of the Andes

James Kiddell (*right*) and Tim Wilder (*left*), who joined Sotheby's in

Plate 22

the condition or quality of the painting behind the years of grime, but it was provisionally identified as being by a German or Flemish mannerist painter, and worth 'several thousand pounds'. As cleaning progressed a most extraordinary scene of the *Temptation of Eve* was revealed, and detailed research showed the sixteenth-century painting to be by a rare German master called Hans Baldung Grien. Mrs Cattrell's panel suddenly became a museum picture, and about three weeks before the sale she was told that a price of £50,000 was expected. As the day of the sale approached, the picture department learnt that there was immense interest from all over the world and a really high price was predicted for this little masterpiece. No one, however, imagined that it was going to secure the amazing sum of £224,000 (3 December 1969), which, even after the deduction of capital gains and all the other taxes, still left the Edinburgh schoolteacher with a small fortune.

More recently, in October 1975, the wife of a civil servant brought in a small silver bowl to Sotheby's, which the local jeweller had suggested might be worth £100 or so. The owner was extremely excited at the thought, for she had bought the bowl at a Girl Guide's jumble sale several years before, together with an Edwardian velvet cape, an old army jacket and a pair of second-hand rugby boots, for the combined total of 80p. Sotheby's experts discovered that the bowl was marked with the maker's insignia of Claude Payne and was dated 1686. A little cleaning and restoration also revealed that the bowl was silver-gilt, and it sold at auction for £9,000.

In the construction of their powerful platform Sotheby's naturally acquired some critics, notably the French government anxiously protecting the state-owned Paris auctioneers, and the sale-room critic of *The Times*, who objected to Sotheby's monolithic mastery of the contemporary art market. The main criticism of Sotheby's concerned some of its special innovations in the practice of auctioneering, other than obvious beneficial changes such as the publication of pre-sale estimates which had previously been guarded like the Holy Grail, or approved publicity stunts such as conducting satellite sales simultaneously in London and New York. The really contentious issue surrounded the growing

4

tendency of Sotheby's to become the owner in its own right of works of art, instead of merely agents for their sale. In New York, Sotheby's had for some years offered a guarantee contract for certain major properties where an agreed sum, normally 20 or 30 per cent below the estimated value, was guaranteed as sale-proceeds—regardless of whether this total was achieved or not. The selling-commission received by Sotheby Parke Bernet under the guarantee system was rather different from the standard terms. This did not in itself materially affect the situation, but Parke Bernet inevitably began to acquire in this way a certain amount of property, even though, the company's general policy was to sell at a trading loss below the guarantee, rather than take property to house. Many people would argue that, however infrequently purchases are made in this way, the policy is dangerous because in the resale of 'house' properties Sotheby Parke Bernet has a personal interest which makes it impossible for the company to act as a truly independent agent and adviser to the buyer, despite acknowledgement of ownership in the catalogue.

The first public indication that this practice had quietly slipped over to London was the insertion in April 1973 of an extra sentence in paragraph 3 of the Sotheby conditions of sale: 'In some cases Sotheby and Co or their associates may have an interest in lots put up for sale.' The evident contradiction in condition 1 as it then stood, 'Sotheby and Co act as agents only . . .', was strongly denied on the grounds that the company was merely acting as its own agent and that, anyway, it would continue to do business with customary probity as agent of both buyer and seller.

This sudden change in the sale conditions and the guarantee system were publicized by journalists in the argument that surrounded the sale of the Mr and Mrs Jack Dick collection of English sporting pictures, the first part of which was sold in October 1973 and the last in April 1976. Even though this was not strictly sold under a guarantee system, all the journalists treated it as though it were and it did indeed mark the beginnings of an art-market row that still continues. The way in which Sotheby's secured this vast collection for auction demonstrates the sophistication of its methods of negotiating deals, and indicates the complex risks that Sotheby's was then prepared to take in order to win major consignments from competitors. The Jack Dick sale was especially complicated, for he was selling his paintings under indictment in America for forgery and grand larceny, and Sotheby's presumably took on responsibility for repayments to the various creditors including the US taxman, despite the fact that the majority of the pictures had been bought comparatively recently—and at the top prices fanned by personal rivalry with Paul Mellon. The situation was further complicated by the sudden death of Dick soon after the first sale. In the event, with the falling picture market of 1973 to 1975, Sotheby's struggled to sell the collection at a profit to the Estate.

The anomalies in the conditions of sale have now been removed, and the Sotheby's Board always indicates clearly in the catalogue when a particular lot is owned by them or sold against a guarantee. But this does nothing to allay the fears of those who have always mistrusted the major auction rooms, refusing to believe that any commercial organization can be expected always to resist the temptation to push the price just a little bit when receiving vast commission bids on lots which they own themselves, or at the very least from which they gain both added prestige and a bigger commission on achieving a high price. There is also the less tangible benefit of pleasing an important owner, who then continues to sell through the firm and persuades his wealthy friends to do the same. The danger of corruption of power in the auction rooms is clear, and, when it comes to the point, the only security both vendors and buyers have is the knowledge that Sotheby's and Christie's business depends totally on the maintenance of an unsullied reputation.

The guarantee system is seldom brought into operation any more, not because of adverse public opinion, but because the unsteady art market and sudden fluctuations in international currency regulations now make it dangerous to offer guarantees. Meanwhile a more serious criticism of Sotheby's policy has arisen. Sotheby's are accused of offering to buy works of art on their own account, direct from collectors who come to their premises for advice about the disposal of their possessions. If it were true that Sotheby's actually volunteered to purchase works of art direct, then this would contradict the basic principles of auctioneering, for it poses the question of how much profit the firm would make on the resale of the purchase, this profit being at the expense of an inexperienced private client. Although Sotheby's openly admits that it occasionally does buy on its own account from the collector, this certainly only happens at the specific request of the vendor, and even then only as a last resort when all other means of securing the business have been explored and rejected by the client. Sotheby's critics again would argue that the business should be turned away rather than resorting to an outright purchase agreement.

In the autumn of 1975 both Christie's and Sotheby's announced a fundamental alteration in their commission structure: a new buyer's premium of 10 per cent. The dealers were incensed by the premium because, even with the reduction of the vendor's commission from 15 to 10 per cent, this still produced a total commission of 20 per cent for the auctioneer. The beginning of the September 1975 season was a dramatic period at both houses, with groups of London dealers staging boycotts of the auctions; there were also questions in Parliament and considerable internal deliberations. Many dealers wrongly believe that Sotheby's makes vast profits at their expense, despite enormous overheads including an estimated £500,000 p.a. in unrecovered advertising costs, and the vast printing bill for the 900 catalogues a season.

Another bone of contention is the British Rail Pension Fund, to which the Sotheby experts give academic advice on the investment of considerable sums in works of art. Some critics not only think it wrong that a nationalized pension fund should invest even a small percentage of its funds in an unproductive luxury, but also object to Sotheby's involvement. No doubt there is a potential conflict of interest in many of these cases; again Sotheby's directors, for the sake of their reputation, can be expected to act fairly.

These developments in the conduct of its business are a reflection of radical changes over the last decade in Sotheby's internal organization and atmosphere. The most obvious, and in a sense the most far-reaching, development is the increase in the size of the Sotheby Board. In 1964 there were only ten directors, Wilson, Butterwick, Hobson, Kiddell, Clarke, Rose, Timewell, Gronau,

Rickett and Pollen; and one Associate, John Carter. At the last count, the London Board was composed of forty-eight directors, sixteen assistant directors and four Associates—far too many to decide policies or to discipline the firm in the old style, through informal gatherings at lunch and by relying on daily contact in handling different parts of the same properties. Nowadays the senior director of a department may not even see the members of his own department every week, as he and they fly about the world chasing after collections; and he is also unlikely to handle personally more than a small percentage of the works of art passing through his department. Many argue that the demise of old-style Sotheby's was completed by the installation of a centralized accounting computer in 1968, and the senior members now tend to spend more time solving the technical problems of keeping a gigantic auction machine on the road than they do in producing catalogues and keeping in touch with important collectors. This inevitable increase in the administrative responsibility of departmental heads has led to a number of directorial defections to the trade, where experts can concentrate on their own favourite fields without continuous interruption.

An answer to this dilemma is slowly emerging, and the most important contributor to its solution is Peter Spira, who joined the firm as Group Finance Director in 1974 and soon after became Managing Director. Spira's departure at the age of forty from Warburg's, where he was one of the two Vice-chairman, caused a stir in banking circles—as it did in the art market when one of his first actions was to cancel the staff Christmas party on the grounds of Sotheby's poverty. Peter Spira and Andrew Alers-Hankey, the new Company Finance Director, have a difficult task ahead of them because some directors who are primarily art experts are in two minds about the problem; neither willing nor able to take on the financial responsibilities of running such a large international company, the art experts nevertheless fear that the managerial specialists might fail to allow sufficiently in their calculations for Sotheby's key intangible assets. The preservation of Sotheby's mystique and of long-established personal relationships between expert and collector might not, the connoisseurs fear, feature sufficiently prominently in the financier's desire for speedy payment and accountable assets. The crucial rôle of mediator between the new administrative hub, called the Office of Chairman, and the expert departments, fortunately falls on a senior director well-suited to maintaining the balance between efficiency and instinct—Marcus Linell, who joined Sotheby's in 1957 at the age of sixteen, is now Joint Managing Director and has considerable personal influence within the firm. At the moment 'traditional Sotheby's' is conducting a lengthy courtship with its administrative *alter ego*, and once the marriage is consummated then Sotheby's will be in a position to continue its rapid growth.

In view of Peter Spira's previous reputation in the City for successful public issues, including that of the powerful Sainsbury Group, the announcement in May 1977 that Sotheby's was 'going public' came as no surprise and in the summer, on the crest of the wave of Mentmore successes (see page 110), Sotheby's joined Christie's as a publicly quoted company. Future plans at Sotheby's no doubt include the opening of another London auction house to deal at speed with the less valuable properties and thus to contest the ambitions of Phillips. But whatever happens in future reorganizations, Sotheby's will remain the same satisfying place in which to work so long as the majority of people are there primarily because they prefer to handle works of art rather than money; indeed, its commercial success also depends to a large degree on this distinctive quality.

Traditional Sotheby's is protected to a certain extent from the harmful aspects of total modernization by the physical nature of its building, which periodically reduces visiting time-and-motion analysts to despair. From the Bond Street façade, Sotheby's looks comparatively straightforward, until one realizes that 400 people work somewhere on the premises; looking on the back from St George Street, it can be seen that this was made possible by piecemeal expansion into five adjoining blocks. Because this expansion occurred over a comparatively short period in the '60s, few of the adjoining buildings have yet been fully converted or incorporated into the main structure, and some of Sotheby's staff find themselves cosily ensconced in small, private rooms off the narrow staircases of several eighteenth-century houses. It must be rather like living in a rabbit warren, with secretaries forever scurrying up and down passages and staircases until they locate the room they are looking for; with experts at the extremities of the building studiously cataloguing in cellars and attics, and porters burying works of art in corners and cupboards until they are resurrected for the auction—all this, and much more, leading off from the large, noisy, communal galleries of the sale-room itself. Protected from surprise attack by the complexity of connecting doors and changing levels, one can picture the Sotheby expert sitting in his office, cocooned in his favourite works of art, pondering on the infinite variety of human expression. With the Sotheby network giving him a direct line across the world to the collectors and dealers in his field; with the back-up staff of porters and travel agents, accountants and Press officers, warehouses and foreign offices; with a leading rôle in the drama of the auction room; and with the security of working in an old-fashioned firm that seldom seriously criticizes any employee; it is not surprising that so many spend the whole of their working lives in the comfort of the Sotheby warren.

The most glamorous department in Sotheby's is the Impressionist and Contemporary picture department. In the space of three years in the late '50s, Sotheby's captured for itself this sensational new market, a fateful blow not only to the Paris auctioneers who had been building up a highly competitive trade with such sales as the Cognacq Collection in 1952; but also to the Parisian dealers who had controlled the market from its inception, during the last decade of the nineteenth century. The original supporters of these contemporary painters were relatively obscure enthusiasts such as Victor Chocquet, a poorly paid customs official in Paris who sacrificed everything for the sake of his collection, and whose tiny apartment gradually filled through the 1870s and '80s with treasures ranging from Gothic ivories to Rodin bronzes, Louis Quatorze clocks to Japanese woodcuts, Fragonard sketches to Gauguin oils. If collecting should be described as an incurable addiction or, as Princesse Marie Bonaparte always insisted, as a direct form of anal eroticism, then Chocquet was a chronic case, frequently returning home late in the evening, so it is told, with a parcel tucked under his arm and the excited explanation to his wife, 'No chicken this Sunday, dear, I've found a little Daumier.'[21]

One of Chocquet's distinctions was the way he supported the best of the modern school against the virulent opposition of fashionable cognoscenti. In the 1870s in Paris there were already occasional auctions of the recently dubbed and popularly depised 'Impressionists'. One of these sales at the Hotel Drouot on 24 March 1875 aroused such passions that buyers were assaulted, canvases slashed and the *gendarmerie* called in to protect the auctioneer. Chocquet bought Manet's *Paysage d'Argenteuil* for 100 old francs at this very auction, and had the good fortune to meet the artist later that evening. The shy Chocquet subsequently became friendly with most of the Impressionists working in Paris, and was even farsighted enough to recognize the qualities of Cézanne, to whom he gave very necessary material support out of his own meagre salary. In 1897 the Chocquet Collection came under the hammer in Paris. Included in the sale were eighty-nine paintings attributed to Delacroix, thirty-two by Cézanne, and a fairy-tale treasure of other pictures, furniture and works of art, of a variety and quality inconceivable to the modern collector.

The most expensive of Chocquet's Cézannes in 1897 was the *Maison du Pendu* at £248; and the splendid *Mardi Gras* now in the Hermitage was sold for only £184; but even these prices showed an enormous increase from the few pounds he had paid for them, and remind one that a fine picture by Cézanne has the distinction of being consistently one of the best long and short term speculative investments anyone could make. Regular Impressionist auctions continued in Paris, and there were even one or two in New York in the '20s, such as the Kelekian sales in 1922, well before the first Cézanne was sold at auction in London— a watercolour of Mont St Victoire, for £400, at the Bernard d'Hondecourt sale at Sotheby's in 1929. From the start, the major buyers from Parisian dealers were the Americans, who preferred the kudos of importing their culture privately rather than supporting a more accessible New York-based market in contemporary French paintings. The fundamental change in attitude to collecting Impressionist pictures came largely as a result of a change in US tax legislation, which allowed those who donated works of art to museums to deduct from their taxes 30 per cent of the declared value, while maintaining possession of the works of art for the rest of their lives. As the museum which was to benefit from the donation had the sole responsibility of making the valuation, there appeared a whole crop of 'mushroom museums', as Reitlinger put it, the principal purpose of which was to act as favourable valuers for the most easily obtainable 'museum quality' works of art—Impressionist paintings. If the valuations for tax purposes were far enough above the original purchase price, rich men actually earned money by spending thousands of dollars a year on Impressionist paintings.

Sotheby's were the first to test the concept of multi-million-dollar public disposals of Impressionist paintings; at the same time they were also the first to cultivate the Americans as both buyers and sellers in London, for at their first big test sales of paintings from New York, the Weinberg Collection in summer 1957 and the initial Goldschmidt sale of spring 1958, the paintings were almost exclusively bought by Americans. The first Gold-schmidt sale was a success, and this gave Peter Wilson the opportunity to persuade the executors of the late Jacob Goldschmidt to take an imaginative gamble with him. They agreed to mount the first evening sale ever held at Sotheby's, a sale which consisted simply of seven Impressionist paintings.

It turned out to be a magical evening for everyone but most of all for Peter Wilson who, by knocking down those seven paintings for a total of £781,000, established himself as the master impresario of the international art market—the only man of his generation who has succeeded in keeping an ever-expanding stable of trained buyers and sellers equally happy in the purchase and sale of masterpieces at record prices. Cézanne's *Garçon au Gilet Rouge*, which had already caused an auction sensation when it was sold for £3,600 at the Count Mariczell de Nèmes sale in 1913, was bought at the Goldschmidt sale by Paul Mellon for £220,000 (plate 20). A week later when Mellon was lunching in Washington with John Carter, the Sotheby representative, he proved himself to be a buyer with style and courage to match Wilson's as a salesman. Mellon asked Carter, 'Did I pay too much?' and immediately replied to his own rhetorical question, 'No. When you stand in front of a painting like that, what is money?'[22] If the *Garçon au Gilet Rouge* were put up for auction now, it would probably secure over $2,000,000, so Mellon had not wasted his money anyway.

The 1957/58 season was the real turning-point in the history of Sotheby's, for the year's two major events, the Goldschmidt sale and the sale of the Rubens *Adoration of the Magi* at £275,000 (a world-record price at the time for any picture) sent Sotheby's turnover up to nearly double Christie's at £5,750,000. Sotheby's have maintained this lead to the present day. Their supremacy depends to a large degree on keeping up an unbeatable brand of sophisticated showmanship, displayed in events such as the conduct of an auction simultaneously in London and New York, via the Early-Bird satellite. This screened the Parke Bernet audience on to the back wall of the London gallery, and allowed Peter Wilson to take bids direct from New York. This was adventurous enough in itself, but the supreme Sotheby publicity touch was to invite Richard Dimbleby and his 'Panorama' cameras to film all this for European television, so that potential sellers in Europe, as well as buyers in America, were impressed by Sotheby's omnipotence. The subject of the sale was Audubon's *Birds of America*, strangely interleaved with two Impressionist paintings and an oil by Sir Winston Churchill, the latter securing the chauvinistically satisfying price of £14,000.

In New York in 1970 a painting by Sir Winston Churchill topped this 1964 price by securing just over £16,000; but this record was shattered by Christie's disposal in March 1977 of five of his paintings sold by Lady Spencer-Churchill. The ninety-two-year-old widow of Sir Winston was said to have been forced into the sale of these paintings due to pressing debts, and the price of £48,000 (six times the estimate) paid by the Tryon Gallery of London on behalf of an American client for 'Mimizan', reflects the strength of feeling engendered by this report. One of the minor works in the sale, but nevertheless a favourite of Lady Spencer-Churchill's, was bought by the London picture-dealer Roy Miles for over £3,000, and was promptly returned to her as a gift.

Sotheby's could be relied on to sell with flair any collection of distinction, occasionally to the company's own financial loss, but invariably to the enhancement of its reputation. Thus as a result of an experimental sale of Ballet material in Bond Street, in June 1967, the chairman of the Diaghilev and de Basil Foundation approached Thilo von Watzdorf of Sotheby's Impressionist picture department to see if he could undertake the sale of all the surviving decors and costumes of these companies. So in September of that year von Watzdorf, a Sotheby colleague David Ellis-Jones, and their mentor Richard Buckle, the ballet critic and historian, found themselves rummaging through an enormous hoard of battered boxes and ancient trunks in a warehouse in the southern suburbs of Paris. Out of these emerged, in clouds of dust, amazing records of the most definitively *avante-garde* ballet of all time. These three balletomanes suddenly found in their arms such treasures as the Chinese robes for *Le Chant du Rossignol*, hand-painted by Matisse himself, and at least half the costumes from the most lavish spectacle of them all, Bakst's *The Sleeping Beauty*. These costumes were previously thought to have been seized from the Alhambra in 1921 by Sir Oswald Stoll for non-payment of debts, and subsequently to have been ruined by a leaky swimming-pool installed for a music-hall act at the Coliseum, where he had them stored below the stage.

Sotheby's responded to the challenge and produced a wonderful catalogue, including many photographs of the original productions together with colour photographs of the costumes modelled by dancers of the Royal Ballet School. The master-stroke was to hold the sale in the Scala Theatre, where the auction could be unmasked as pure theatre, performed as it was against a variety of dramatic backdrops which included Picasso's design for Cocteau's *Le Train Bleu* (plate 23) executed by Prince Schervachidze—a vision of two monumental women dancing wildly across the beach, which must have made a strange contrast to the acrobatic Dolin who starred in the original ballet. The next Diaghilev and de Basil ballet sale was held at the Theatre Royal, Drury Lane, and was even more of a theatrical performance. As almost every lot was called, members of the Royal Ballet School danced out of the wings in the original costumes to give a short imitative offering of respect to their earlier masters, to the delight of a large audience ranged through this enormous theatre. Wilson was perched in his rostrum at the side of the stage, and Sotheby's staff were placed throughout the auditorium to help identify the bidders, calling out at the tops of their voices, 'Bidding here, sir'.

The next logical step for the picture department in London was to follow New York in holding specialized sales of contemporary art, and the first sale of paintings, drawings, prints and sculpture of the period 1945 to the present day, was held on 5 July 1973. These sales created some unusual problems, not least for the porters, one of whom was apparently discovered beginning to unpack a complex parcel covered in sacking and tied with rope in all sorts of strange knots, but was stopped before he completely destroyed an 'original work of art' by Christo, entitled *Wrapped Stand*. On another occasion a porter unpacked a Lucio Fontana canvas to find a large hole in it, and immediately rushed upstairs to the expert to disclaim all responsibility, waving the receipt on which he had written 'damaged on arrival'; not unnaturally it never occurred to the porter that the artist might have defaced his own canvas. The regular buyers of antiques at Sotheby's also found the viewing of these sales rather confusing, sometimes mistaking the electrified sculpture and ceiling-hung mobiles for part of a new Sotheby decor, and wandering around shaking their heads at such a lapse in taste.

Of a more serious nature is the embarrassment caused by these contemporary art auctions to London dealers in this field, who find their careful marketing of a particular modern artist's work can be shattered when a painting or a print recently bought from them secures half its purchase price at a gala international sale at Sotheby's. Modern galleries have always had, to a certain degree, to protect the prices for their contracted artists, but this was easier before the large international auctioneers began sales in this category, as most collectors previously had little alternative but to return to the source of supply for resale. All the same, at first the market held up relatively well, until by the time of the December 1974 auction at Sotheby's the whole modern art market was in a difficult state, and beneath the chic trappings at the evening auction there was considerable tension. The red carpet and frilly canopy projecting into Bond Street may have reassured some of the visitors, as they were helped from their limousines by the uniformed doorman; the secretaries issuing tickets at the foot of the stairs looked relaxed enough; and there was still the flattering attention of handsome young men and women in evening dress showing the 'guests' to their seats. It is part of the Sotheby style to treat collectors and dealers like honoured guests at a private party reserved for the cultured rich.

Strangely, the first sign of nerves came from the Sotheby's directors jostling for position behind the rostrum, as they peered intently at the audience, rushing up with thinly disguised anxiety to certain individuals, presumably the owners in many cases. Only the chairman remained outwardly calm as he prepared to ascend the rostrum. Minions rushed in and out through the side-door with essential props, the stage-lights were adjusted for the last time, and the more attentive members of the audience who had been watching these preparations began to feel decidedly nervous, almost embarrassed, as though they were backstage before curtain-up on the first night of a play that was badly constructed and under-rehearsed, doomed to be a flop. The New York sale of contemporary art the week before had been dismal, and Christie's auction the day before a disaster, so the large gathering of all the same people suddenly seemed more like a flock of circling vultures than potential buyers.

As always, Peter Wilson succeeded in concealing the worst, and although not many pictures sold well, the evening passed off with a certain amount of style and humour which comforted the fashionable, appeased the dealers and ensured that Sotheby's emerged unscathed. When the Ellsworth Kelly composition *Loop* was held up a different way from the illustration in the catalogue, a chorus of voices in the front row pointed out the error, which gave Wilson the excuse for a courteous correction of his clients, 'I am sorry to disagree but actually it is the right way up here— believe it or not, the Sotheby catalogue is at fault.' A little earlier in the evening, when the porter held up in his gloved hand Lot 31, a small tin inscribed in three languages *Produced by Piero Manzoni, Artist's Shit*, Wilson hastily removed the handkerchief from his top pocket, held it to his nose, and sniffed deprecatingly, before catching the eye of a friend in the audience and collapsing into disarming giggles. Everyone else immediately joined in and the proceedings were held up for several minutes. The bidding for Manzoni's Dada-esque comment finally went up to £400, but it failed to reach its reserve.

Impressionist picture sales have recently become equally nerve-racking for those involved. Perhaps there is some justice in this, for to many people there is something distasteful, during a time of economic hardship and of shortage of funds for productive investment, in the spending of such enormous sums on such an unadventurous area of the fine arts as Impressionist paintings.

It is characteristic of Sotheby's directors that, just when the Impressionist picture market seemed to be slipping back, they managed to produce a sale in another field which received more publicity than any art market event since the war—the Earl of Rosebery's disposal of the entire contents of Mentmore Towers, 18–27 May 1977. Such crowds of people attended the private view that cars were kept waiting at the gates for hours on end, and the whole event recalled to mind the great sales of the nineteenth century such as Stowe and Hamilton Palace, where the Rothschilds had in fact purchased many of the pieces for their two Buckinghamshire palaces, Mentmore and Waddesdon. The first of the ten days of sales produced a total of just less than £1,500,000, setting Sotheby's on their way to the extraordinary total of £6,389,933 for the whole sale. It is a sad indictment of government policy, from a commercial as well as a preservationist point of view, that the contents, the house itself and 600 acres of prime farming-land were turned down by the nation six weeks before, at a price of £2,000,000 (plus the cancellation of death duties, rumoured to be about £3,500,000). Another interesting point about the sale is that it was mounted by Sotheby's and not by Christie's, who had a far longer-standing relationship with this, as with many other aristocratic collections. All that was entrusted to Christie's were the wine cellars, a reversal of recent rôles that must have delighted Peter Wilson, especially as it turned out that Sotheby's sale at Mentmore coincided with, and completely overshadowed, the opening sales of Christie's in New York.

Sotheby's continues to handle the outstanding libraries of the world, the most notable of which, still being sold in lengthy series, are Major Abbey's and Sir Thomas Phillips' collections. The bibliophile Munby worked out that on his death in 1872 Phillips possessed approximately 60,000 manuscripts and 50,000 printed books, all of which he was determined to keep from his eldest son-in-law, James Halliwell. The library therefore passed to John Fenwick, his second son-in-law, but, lacking the funds to house the books, Fenwick began to sell the incredible library through Sotheby's from 1885 onwards. Then in 1945 the residue of the Phillips library was sold privately to the dealers Lionel and Philip Robinson, whose executors in their turn consigned the books and manuscripts to Sotheby's in 1965. It is this second series of sales that continued till 1978.

Three of the other great post-war disposals in Sotheby's book-room were the Dyson Perrins, which totalled £888,370 for its three sessions between 1957 and 1959; the Chester Beatty Library in 1968 and 1969; and the Harrison D. Horblit collection of scientific books which began in June 1974. The Horblit catalogue is not only in the best tradition of English scholarship, with the minutest descriptive detail matched by original interpretation; it is also printed and bound to a standard rarely seen in modern commercial production. The attitude of Sotheby's book experts is clearly illustrated in their Preface to the first Horblit catalogue: 'We hope that this series of catalogues will bear adequate witness to the contribution which one individual can make to the history of this aspect of man's search for truth about his environment. In the manner of its disposal, Mr Horblit joins such distinguished company as Mr Boise Penrose and the late Thomas W. Streeter, and other collectors of this and previous centuries, who have chosen to dispose of their libraries for the benefit of other collectors, but whose catalogues remain as a monument to their taste and skill.'[23]

Arguably the finest piece of original research and scholastic dissertation in any Sotheby's catalogue in recent years is John Collins' work on the three-volume catalogue of the magnificent botanical library of the Siftung für Botanik, collected by the late Arpad Plesch (1890–1974). In producing this catalogue, Collins responded to the unique qualities of the collection which was formed, not only with a bibliographer's eye, but also to serve as the working library for a serious botanical garden. The Sotheby catalogue contains a great deal of new information, particularly in collation of the rare editions, as well as helpful and witty interpretation. In the introduction, buyers are encouraged to follow the advice given by W. S. Gilbert in *Patience*:,

> 'Come, walk up, and purchase with avidity,
> Overcome your diffidence and natural timidity,
> Tickets for the raffle should be purchased with avidity—
> Such an opportunity may not occur again.'[24]

Almost all the book sales are taken by the head of the book department, Lord John Kerr, whose benign manner contrasts with the fierceness of his wide, white side-whiskers. A book auction is a quiet intimate affair, with seldom more than eighty to a hundred people in the room. The auctioneer knows the names of practically every buyer, and the dealers look totally at home, as though they had occupied the same seat once a week for generations past, as indeed some of them have. Amongst the dealers sit a number of distinguished-looking private collectors, some of them no doubt in the process of forming their own magnificent libraries. There is also a sprinkling of tousled, tweed-coated gentlemen, whom the romantic may choose to see as eccentric German professors bidding on behalf of their rival museums.

The only violent change in the book world in the last decade has been in the field of Oriental miniatures and manuscripts, which are also handled by this department. A few Iranian collectors and dealers have regularly attended sales at Sotheby's for years, but recently there has been a vast new influx of buyers, many of whom are influenced by the Empress of Iran's encouragement. Prices for Persian miniatures have risen sharply, but they are still no higher in real terms than in the 1920s when the American collectors were last in the market in force. However, the field of nineteenth-century Qajar painting was totally ignored until the recent wild developments, and the art market gasped when a large canvas of the *Fifteen Sons and Grandsons of Fath Ali Shah* sold for £200,000 in December 1974. Basil Robinson, now Sotheby's consultant, had been the underbidder when the painting had last been sold at Sotheby's thirteen years before, for only £380.

Further weight was added to Sotheby's dominance of international book-auctioneering by the purchase in 1968 of Hodgson's Rooms in Chancery Lane, but its activities there are described in the chapter on the specialist auction rooms.

The clearest way of describing the working day at Sotheby's is to follow an object on its way from consignment by the owner to collection by the buyer.

It is not generally appreciated that anyone can bring anything into Christie's or Sotheby's, or for that matter to Phillips or Bonham's as well, for free advice on its saleable value. It is strange that many more people do not take advantage of this service, for the curious owner can simply walk in any time with his porcelain vase, silver coffee-pot, enamel snuff-box or whatever—although it is safest to telephone in advance to make sure that the relevant expert will be at Bond Street on the required day. At the front entrance either George, the grey-moustached doorman, or Fred Hughes at the catalogue counter will direct the client with, for example, his enamel snuff-box, to the works of art counter at the back of the building. Fred Hughes has worked at Sotheby's for nearly thirty years and knows all the regulars, whom he looks after by guarding their dogs while they view the sales upstairs, by supplying catalogues when they have forgotten their own, and, where appropriate, by exchanging his latest line in tap-room stories. At Sotheby's there are four separate reception counters, each serving a particular group of expert departments in the different areas of the building, and the works of art counter is one of the busiest. There is a continuous stream of people unpacking potential treasures from cardboard boxes, or sitting at the side in earnest conversation with the Sotheby expert, clutching possessively at Gothic woodcarvings or seventeenth-century violins.

While waiting for the girl at the desk to call down the expert, there is plenty to watch and listen to. A particular dealer comes almost every week to unload his recent discoveries, which have been purchased at local sales and private house-calls up and down the country. This dealer has no premises and works out of his van, supplying certain shops and disposing of the rest through the auction rooms. An incredible variety of objects is always produced from a series of ancient Gladstone bags which can, on bad days, be worth rather more than the things they contain. Too many of his goods are damaged or over-restored, but everything has a particular quality which the dealer has clearly recognized. As yet another object emerges from its newspaper package, he apologetically prefaces its inspection with remarks like, 'Well, I shouldn't really have bothered you with this bit of nonsense, but I haven't seen this mark before and thought the shape of the handle was unusual.' At least once a year he produces some rarity for which he has paid a few pounds, and which Sotheby's sells for several thousand. Once it was an early English pottery figure which sold for over £2,000, and another year it was a Ming porcelain vase which secured over £10,000. The dealer initially thought he had paid too much for the vase, £32.

Naturally a number of clients are disappointed about the real value of some long-treasured possession, and Sotheby's staff must develop a talent for breaking such news gently. One of the ceramics experts has a particular way of coping with the modern Chinese porcelain figures of the fat-tummied God Puttei, which owners have often been led to believe are 'Ming' and worth thousands of pounds. Other clients can be disarmed by the brazen charm of some of the self-confident young experts who are called to see them. Two or three years ago a friend witnessed the following theatrical vignette. A murky Dutch flower painting was being shown to an Old Master picture-expert by a regal-looking lady who obviously expected, almost demanded, that the picture be a masterpiece. The picture and the lady might have stepped straight from the pages of Katherine Mansfield, indeed so might the expert in his gold-rimmed spectacles and long-jacketed grey suit, with large spotted handkerchief in the top pocket. The expert delighted his client with an admiring analysis of the 'quality of the brushstroke' and other aesthetic points, impressively produced a few obscure names as possible painters, and concluded intimately, 'But, your ladyship, which way up does it go?'

Our client's snuff-box which is being shadowed on its journey through Sotheby's, will be inspected at the counter by John Winter, son of the late Fitzwilliam Museum Director, or by Julia Clarke, daughter of Tim Clarke, an ex-director (who remains a master in the rostrum, when he can spare the time from study of his favourite subject, the history of the rhinoceros in art). The expert will tell the owner all the technical and historical details about his snuff-box, before estimating its value and agreeing to a suitable protective reserve below which price it will not on any account be sold. The counter girl then fills out a detailed receipt, including an insurance figure for which there is a small charge to the owner from the sale-proceeds. After the reception areas have closed to the public, at 4.30 p.m., the department porter collects all the works of art which have arrived during the day, checks the receipt number on each label, and takes the pieces upstairs to the department. Normally within two or three weeks, depending on the proximity of the sale and on the number of previous consignments, the expert will catalogue the snuff-box, researching all the relevant information in Sotheby's records library and typing the description out on to a catalogue sheet, which remains in the file while the used receipt or 'property card' is dispatched to the departmental administrator.

The next step is the putting together of the right kind of specialist catalogue from amongst the varied works of art awaiting sale in the department; a catalogue which must attract international dealers and collectors. This naturally requires experience; and each sale must also fit into Sotheby's whole sale calendar which is planned between six and nine months in advance. This ensures that there will be enough space in the viewing galleries for complementary sales; that sales likely to attract the same collectors do not clash; that there will be no conflict of interest with events such as the opening of Grosvenor House Antiques Fair or major sales at Christie's; and that sales are not scheduled for public holidays or relevant religious festivals. The placing of a particular work of art in the right position in the appropriate sale can make a great deal of difference to the auction price. The senior expert in each department is responsible for the formation and design of each catalogue, the copy-sheets and photographs for which are delivered to the printer exactly two calendar months before the sale date. Over the following four weeks galley-proofs and block pulls are produced, checked and altered, before the final paste-up of the catalogue is approved for the printers. All this planning in advance is undertaken so that Sotheby's catalogues have at least three weeks to be sent all over the world, first to the paid-up subscribers in that particular category, normally more than a thousand people; and then to all the collectors and dealers who write in for the catalogues after seeing the special advertising and sales announcements in international art journals and newspapers. For some sales, an additional hundred or so catalogues may be sold at the door to yet more people who come independently to view the sale.

Meanwhile an important administrative process is following its course, and although this is purely technical it is important to know something about the administration in order to understand how Sotheby's works. As soon as the lot-numbered copy-sheets are handed to the printer, the carbon set of these, with details of the owner's name and address, property number, estimates and suggested reserves, is passed to the department's administrator who begins to 'edit' the sale. This basically involves extracting from the files each owner's master property card, on which is listed all the works of art that were brought in at the time, together with any special instructions the owner may have given. The administrator then marks off on the master card the sale date of the particular items being sold, and takes note on the copy-sheets of any special instructions. The 'edited' carbon set is then sent off to the computer programmers for processing into account cards and alphabetical and numerical property lists. In yet another corner of the department, the porter will have been collecting together in a particular location all the items for that particular sale and tying on labels with lot-numbers and sale dates, before taking them down to the public gallery for the minimum three days' view before the sale. The owner will also meanwhile have received a copy of the catalogue confirming an agreed reserve, or asking for instructions on this.

The public view is a crucial event in the sale-room life of our client's enamel snuff-box, for during these three to five days it is inspected in the minutest detail by interested collectors and dealers who note in their catalogues the exact condition and quality of each piece they are considering buying, and also mark the price they intend to bid up to in the auction. If the snuff-box is illustrated in the catalogue, then dealers from abroad may feel confident enough to leave commission bids, or at least to contact the department for more detailed information than is given in the catalogue. It is impossible to publish condition reports in the catalogue, due to the inevitable disagreements that arise in the interpretation of phrases such as 'slightly damaged'; but the experts are always delighted to give this information on personal request. The porter François, who retired in 1976, used to be master of ceremonies on viewing days in the New Gallery, for he spoke five languages including Arabic and was known and respected by all the regulars. Some dealers left him to do all their condition reports on the lots they were thinking of buying, and on one famous occasion a dealer spent over $1,000,000 in one porcelain auction on the strength of François' detailed reports. The view of an important *objets de vertu* sale is generally smooth and sophisticated. Swiss dealers, their slender hands bronzed and manicured, are brisk and efficient in the handling of these luxurious bibelots, which they occasionally regard through a complex system of magnifying lenses hinged to their own spectacles. A beautiful Iranian may stand at one side applying Renaissance pendants to her breast, and regarding her reflection in the display case. An estimate of £10,000–£15,000 does not worry such sophisticated beauties, long accustomed to gift-storms of diamonds and emeralds.

On the evening before the auction, the sale-room porters collect all the lots from the viewing gallery and place them in lot-number order in cabinets behind the rostrum. As well as the main sale-room, there are three others in the Bond Street premises, the book-room at the back entrance, the George Street Gallery on the lower ground floor (which is often used for the more movable sales such as prints and drawings), and the Royal Water Colour Society gallery which is leased to Sotheby's during certain months of the year. By 10.30 on the morning of the sale the auctioneer's catalogue will have been completed, with all the reserves and commission bids written in code; and the auctioneer goes carefully through the sale with the cataloguer, checking that there are no mistakes in the reserves and trying to anticipate any difficulties that might occur. Meanwhile collectors who have arrived at the last minute from America or the Continent will be anxiously waiting for the busy porters to show them a particular lot for inspection before the auction commences. Herman Baer, Ernie Graus and others from the set of established London dealers, wander about the room greeting their friends and clients, changing effortlessly from one middle-European dialect to another. The atmosphere at such a sale is calm and professional, and as the objects are all relatively costly, the trade is controlled by three or four specialists in each field, with the occasional intrusion of one of the large furniture dealers buying on commission from a client, or acquiring some exotic object to enhance the appearance of a particular table or cabinet.

Descriptions of the sale itself, of the auctioneer's job and of the attitudes of the buyers can be found in the first chapter; here we are more concerned with the technical aspects of the auction. When each lot is called, it is held up beside the auctioneer before being shown to the dealers seated at the horseshoe of green baize tables in front of the rostrum. No one has official right to a place at the unfortunately named 'ring', but these seats are invariably occupied by regulars who watch each other like hawks throughout the sale. Assisting the auctioneer and seated at his side at a lower rostrum is the sales-clerk, whose job is to take down all the prices and buyers' names and to make out individual bills for each buyer. Whenever neither the auctioneer nor the sales-clerk knows the name of the purchaser, then a 'runner' is sent into the room to secure the stranger's address and signature. In theory a deposit is required from new buyers, but in practice the whole business is surprisingly easy and casual, and no real pressure to settle the account is exerted until several weeks after the sale. On the other hand, quick payment is obviously encouraged and buyers may pay their bills at the sales-clerk's desk during the sale, and can often also collect their purchases from behind the rostrum while the sale is in progress, if the porters have the time. Our client's snuff-box could even be paid for and collected by midday, and be in the new owner's pocket on a lunchtime flight to Geneva. If the account is not settled immediately after the sale, then all the uncollected purchases will be taken down that evening to a different location beside the packing-room, and the buyer must settle his account at the cashier's desk before collecting his purchase from the packing-room.

From then on the computer takes over, feeding information on to the buyers' and sellers' account cards, sending off sale results to each, and, exactly one month after the sale, sending a cheque to the owner for the hammer price less 10 per cent sales commission and sundry charges such as insurance, illustration in the catalogue and special advertising.

With each property following this complicated routine on its journey through Sotheby's, it is somewhat bewildering to think that, with a sale every day for eleven months of the year, there must be over 140,000 lots sold on the Bond Street premises every year. There can even be as many as four different sessions of sales in one day amounting to more than 700 lots, owned by 300–400 different people, and bought by 200–300 different collectors and dealers. During the height of the season, when an Impressionist picture sale coincides with Chinese Ceramics or Important Jewellery, Sotheby's can produce a turnover of more than £3,000,000 in one day.

The people we have seen to be involved directly with the sale of the snuff-box, the receptionists, experts, porters, secretaries, auctioneer, sales-clerks, cashiers and accountants, are backed up by numerous other departments which the public seldom meets. For instance, Sotheby's employs a full-time insurance broker who continuously negotiates through Minets with the other insurance companies that cover the Sotheby risk. By his close attention to departmental disciplines, and with the assistance of the ex-CID security officer and his team of guards, Sotheby's manages to keep breakages and theft of works of art down to a minimum. Then there is Clark Nelson the P.R. company, with thirteen permanent staff, the advertising office with five staff, the photographic department with thirteen, shipping with five, the valuations department with ten people, the international office with a staff of four, the post-room with four to five people, four telephonists and a telex girl, four porters at the furniture warehouse, six specialists in catalogue production, a fluctuating staff at catalogue dispatch, a permanent house-staff of electricians, painters and cleaners and of course the vast accounts and company administration departments.

But although Sotheby's has become a large and amorphous place, it would be wrong to allow its contemporary reputation for aggressive business techniques to blind observers to the traditional qualities that remain. Old-fashioned satisfaction in length of service is still most clearly seen amongst the porters, and now that George Brown has semi-retired perhaps he will have time to finish his memoirs of 'below-stairs at Sotheby's since the war'. George joined straight from the navy at the end of the war, and first worked in the arrivals room 'unloading goods coming in—I call them goods now, but my first impression was what a load of junk.'[25] The longest serving porter is Charlie Donaldson, who now works at Sotheby's Belgravia but originally joined Sotheby's as a message boy in 1929. His letter of employment from Felix Warre described his job as 'taking messages, parcels, catalogues etc for us by means of box tricycle or otherwise . . . salary twenty-five shillings a week, but if good work is done and the tricycle kept clean and in good condition, five shillings extra will be paid at the end of each week following.'[26] There are also two long-serving porters in the book-room, Frankie Greville who joined in 1946 and Jock Campbell who has worked at Sotheby's for twenty-five years; Jock still works on average fourteen hours a day and knows more about books than many a successful dealer. Len Parkinson, the chief cashier, joined Sotheby's in 1946. Everyone joining Sotheby's even now is bound to acquire from these characters some sense of the atmosphere of the past; and indeed many of the directors also seek to preserve these traditional attitudes to life in the art market. No computer is capable of assessing the value of the real feeling of shared purpose and interests that has grown up over the years between the firm and its clients, the experts and the porters, the auctioneers and the trade.

At the moment the spirit of Sotheby's resides in the figure of

Jimmy Kiddell (plate 22), who came to work for the firm in 1920 in a post called 'manager of the porters'. Kiddell brought to this position a warm understanding of human nature that has enabled him to be the true guardian of the firm's integrity. Kiddell took his first auction in 1922, and in the years since has catalogued and auctioned almost every category of work of art that Sotheby's handles, although his international reputation is founded on his knowledge of Chinese ceramics. During these years he formed his well-known 'Black Museum' which contained nothing but fakes and later reproductions. These were often used to test young experts, and a few years ago they also deceived a thief who stole almost every piece from Kiddell's home. When objects from the Black Museum begin to reappear on the market in ten years' time or so, it is to be hoped that the younger generation recognizes them as Kiddell's fakes.

More important, however, than any narrow specialist expertise is Jimmy Kiddell's desire to learn about the varied works of art that confront him, and from the moment he joined Sotheby's he attached himself as a voluntary helper to every expert in the company. Now there are two or three generations of experts at Sotheby's who have themselves been educated by Kiddell's enthusiasm for works of art. It is a great comfort to watch Kiddell walking briskly through the viewing galleries to his office in the morning, and to see him stop and kick up the corner of a carpet to make sure that a rare early piece has not been passed over. At another corner of the gallery he may pick up a porcelain vase, collaring the first person in sight, secretary, picture expert or messenger boy, to explain some special point about the glaze or the shape. This, then, is Sotheby's best insurance for the future— the continuous education of a new generation of experts in the pleasures of discovering works of art.

[4]

'Phillips the Auction People'

Of the four major London auction houses, Phillips has been by far the fastest-growing over the last five years. The yearly turnover has risen from an uncompetitive £4,000,000 in 1971 to an aggressive £27,462,907 in 1978, during which time the company has opened up or taken thirteen new auction rooms and offices. While consistently disclaiming any hope, or even any intention, of rivalling the international empires of Christie's and Sotheby's, the partners at Phillips have laid down a clear challenge for supremacy in fine art auctioneering in the United Kingdom. Phillips now has three different auction rooms in London, with sales in their main premises off New Bond Street assuming ever more imposing proportions and appearing in increasingly sophisticated catalogues. Phillips's dominance in the rest of the country is already unrivalled, more especially since the takeover in 1976 of the leading Yorkshire auctioneers, Heppers of Leeds, and of one of the largest West Country auctioneers, Jollys of Bath, which complemented their existing permanent auction rooms in Edinburgh and in Knowle, Warwickshire. Add to all this activity the popular country-house sales in which they have also overtaken Christie's and Sotheby's, and, as far as the British public is concerned, Phillips has become the most competitive auction house in Britain.

For the sake of appearances, the senior partners at Christie's, Sotheby's, Phillips and Bonham's remain in gentlemanly communication, refusing to admit publicly that considerable increase in activity at one auction house inevitably leads to loss of business and prestige at one of the others. Whatever Phillips's energetic young chairman, Christopher Weston, may say in answer to direct questioning, there can be no doubt that he understands

competitive realities and as head of a smaller, more disciplined
organization he can react with far greater speed and efficiency to a
market that constantly changes. If Christie's and Sotheby's are
unable to see the danger of Phillips, it is because Weston refuses
to be drawn into a trial of strength on his rivals' terms and instead
constantly emphasizes the different qualities of his firm, directly
advertising its independent attitudes. Christie's and Sotheby's
may yet discover that the most successful form of rival development is to do things differently.

Because Phillips is developing so rapidly and has such an
impressive contemporary history, mention is seldom made of its
distinguished past, which includes the only public auction known
to have been held in Buckingham Palace. It was a great honour
for the founder Harry Phillips in his old age that the firm should
have been summoned by Queen Victoria to sell off the 'ten costly
Gothic lanterns', 'a magnificent glass dome by the celebrated
artist Doyle', 'an electrifying machine'[1] and all the furniture and
brocades which the young Queen threw out of the Palace on her
accession in 1836. There were four days of sales in all, the auctions
being held in the detached offices of the Palace 'at 1 o'clock for 2
precisely, entrance in Pimlico',[2] rather like a cocktail party for
minor civil servants.

In 1796 at the age of thirty, Harry Phillips (plate 28) had
resigned his position as chief clerk to James Christie, determined
to emulate his polished master in mounting fashionable auctions
in the West End. The first sale was of 'neat and elegant' household furniture, held at the vendor's house in Crown Street, Westminster; but by late the following year Phillips was able to move
into his own premises at number 67 Bond Street. The Christie's
sales-clerk had taken with him a good reputation, a number of
important clients, and a natural style, for he was soon giving
elaborate evening receptions in residential Bond Street and
establishing himself as a reliable auctioneer and an agreeable man
of fashion, the *Morning Chronicle* noting that it was 'perfectly
delightful to see Mr Phillips play the amiable in the rostrum'.[3]
Only two years after starting his new career Harry Phillips
produced the catalogue of a 'collection of twenty-five capital
pictures recently removed from the gallery of the late Queen

Mary Antoinette at St Cloud's near Paris',[4] which sold in February 1798 for remarkably good prices considering that the London market was flooded with collections brought in from France by brave speculators. The deposed Queen had been beheaded five years previously, and her possessions dispersed at the time, but ambitious auctioneers of Bond Street were no less skilled at international intrigue than they are now. Phillips was equally successful some years later in securing for sale Napoleon's effects on his death in St Helena.

In those early years Harry Phillips secured so many important properties for auction that the ailing James Christie must have regretted not offering his clerk a partnership. There were the King of Poland's pictures and Queen Caroline's furniture as further infringement of Christie's monopoly of Royal collections; and then Sir Godfrey Kneller's studio sale, which was a threat to the Christie connections in 'artistic circles'. Harry Phillips's greatest auction was the Fonthill sale of 1823, a particular embarrassment to Christie's who the previous year had tirelessly produced endless revisions of their Beckford catalogue, as the owner changed his mind about certain lots and sold privately many of the most important pieces. Eventually Beckford solved his financial problems by selling the whole of Fonthill Tower and its remaining contents to the gunpowder magnate John Farquhar for £350,000; Farquhar then, despite a reputed income of £40,000 a year, decided to recoup some of the cost by getting Phillips to sell the contents. Reitlinger cites a number of contemporary records which indicate that Harry Phillips was guilty of 'salting' the sale with other properties, and Beckford and his son-in-law the Duke of Hamilton bought back some of their favourite objects, so it is difficult to assess the sale. It was certainly popular, with 'Fonthill fever' raging in London for most of its thirty-day duration. The most expensive single lot other than a picture was the Hungarian topaz, supposedly carved by Cellini for Caterina Cornaro, which sold for 600 guineas. On the other hand, the Bureau du Roi Stanislas now in the Wallace Collection only secured £178 10s, and Beckford was happy to buy back his two Fiammingo-style ivory tankards at £294, considerably less than the £497 which he had paid for the pair only four years earlier.

Harry Phillips died in 1840, but his son William Augustus took over the business, which continued to secure prestigious collections for sale. There were auctions such as the property of Lady Blessington at Gore House, where the Albert Hall now stands in Kensington Gore. William Thackeray attended the view, and objected to the mass of curious Londoners swirling about the rooms in which so many delicate society intrigues had bloomed. He wrote in his diary, 'Gore House full of snobs . . . brutes keeping their hats on in the kind old drawing room. I longed to knock some of them off and say "Sir, be civil in a lady's house".'[5] The sale only totalled £12,000, a trivial sum beside Lady Blessington's debts. The Marquis of Hertford bore away her portrait by Lawrence and it is still in the Wallace Collection; the Marquis had been in her Ladyship's old set and bought the splendid portrait cheaply, no doubt moved by artistic rather than sentimental reasons. Other Phillips sales included Lord Northwick's collection in 1858, numbering amongst its buyers the Dukes of Buccleuch, Hamilton, Cleveland and Newcastle and totalling £95,725.

In 1879 the firm belatedly changed its name to 'Messrs Phillips and Son', and then in 1882 William Augustus Phillips took his son-in-law into the business and the firm was registered as 'Phillips, Son and Neale', as which it remained until 1971, when it reverted to the traditional 'Phillips', adopting the present slogan 'Phillips the Auction People'. Although there are no Phillipses left in the business and so it cannot be called a family firm in the same way as Bonham's can, it nevertheless maintains much of the quality of a family firm, influenced to some degree no doubt by the fact that the partners have refused limited liability and proudly hold themselves and their families personally responsible for each others' debts as well as for those of the firm.

In the last quarter of the nineteenth century, Phillips suffered a decline which continued well into this century. Sale number 12,000 at Phillips in 1931 totalled no more than £353 whereas just less than a century earlier at sale number 3,000 a single lot, 'The Celebrated Idol's Eye Diamond of Extraordinary Size and Perfection',[6] was sold for £385. The necessary infusion of new blood arrived in 1937, when the Lisson Grove auctioneer G. Hawkings purchased Phillips, bringing with him a great deal more energy than finesse and indicating that there was nothing to be gained from auctioneers behaving like faded gentry and attempting to trade on the illustrious past. Hawkings almost immediately suffered the loss by fire of the premises at 73 New Bond Street, but, ever resilient, he promptly moved into Blenstock House in Blenheim Street, missing only one sale in the process. The well-established coin auctioneers, Glendining and Co, joined the company in its new premises immediately after the war; and in 1954 there was a further take-over, of Puttick and Simpson. Until recently all four firms continued to operate comparatively independently of one another, the Lisson Grove premises trading as G. Hawkings and Son until the late '60s, and Puttick and Simpson's experts mounting their own specialized sales of Baxter prints, Stevengraphs and other subjects until 1971. During this period things developed slowly, and Christopher Weston, the present chairman, remembers clerking sales for his predecessor Robert Hawkings which frequently totalled little more than £1,000.

Until 1967 there was no positive indication of the great increase in business that was to follow; indeed it was only in this year that Phillips moved on to the first floor of Blenstock House, adding three sale-rooms and extensive offices to its cramped quarters in the basement and on the ground floor. By 1974 they had taken over the remaining two floors of Blenstock House, giving them a total working area of over 6,000 square feet, in which over 500 auctions are mounted every year, comprising well over 100,000 lots. Phillips's first truly international publicity also came in 1967 with the sale at Cliveden House, the home of the late Viscount Astor and centre of activities for the notorious 'Cliveden set'. Curiosity about the Duke of Windsor's home-away-from-home, and some aggressive publicity by Phillips, brought the television cameras down to Maidenhead, and a sale that began as an ordinary country-house disposal of over 2,000 items of household furniture and effects became a national event. Fifteen hundred people attended the first of the five days of sales, and prices regularly exceeded pre-sale estimates tenfold, taking the final sale total to £156,654.

The Phillips potential indicated by the Cliveden House sale did not escape the notice of Christopher Weston, who had first started working for the firm at the age of thirteen during his school holidays from Lancing, and had become chairman at the age of thirty-five in April 1972. Although very different in style and temperament from Wilson of Sotheby's, Weston has begun to do for Phillips what Wilson did for Sotheby's in the late '50s and early '60s—to transform the fortunes of his firm simply by the force of personal leadership and through confidence in the timing of his drive for expansion. Weston sounds and appears at first sight like a relatively modest figure, but on his own admittance nothing is done at Phillips without his approval, all important decisions being made at his desk before 8.30 every morning. Indeed, all new employees other than the porters are still interviewed by him before confirmation of their appointment. Phillips have in Weston a leader of great ambition, who can proudly recall the days when he walked to work from Victoria Station to save the bus-fare and prepared himself for later responsibilities by gaining accountancy qualifications through evening-classes.

Almost everything Weston does is calculated to emphasize the differences between Phillips and its London rivals. Weston was the organizer and first chairman of the Society of Fine Art Auctioneers, of which the two biggest fine art auctioneers in the world—Christie's and Sotheby's—are not members. Where Sotheby's strengthens its auctions in Hong Kong and Christie's finally founds a major auction house in New York, Phillips broadens its nets in England, taking over four major provincial auctioneers whose loyalty has already been assured through membership of SOFAA. Their rivals have traditionally protected the genteel anonymity of their experts, even after their regular television appearances on 'Going for a Song'; whereas Phillips had more colour photographs of their directors and experts in the 1975 *Years Auctions* than they did of works of art. Where Christie's and Sotheby's project the modern sophistication of their company organizations, Phillips proudly emphasizes the importance of its having a staff canteen at Blenstock House where new members of staff are encouraged to feel as much at home as the head porter Bishop, who joined Phillips at the age of fifteen and at fifty-seven looks good for another twenty years' service with the firm. And Phillips was the first to appreciate the value of popularizing the auction scene, realizing that many readers of *The Connoisseur* would discover about important sales for themselves, whereas more expensive advertising in the *Evening Standard* would reach an audience which would not normally have thought of attending an auction. Phillips is still the only one of the four main London auction houses to open every Saturday morning, allowing many private buyers who work during the week to view the sales.

Phillips's crucial show of independence came with the announcement in Summer 1975 by Christie's and Sotheby's that from the beginning of the following month they were to reduce their selling-commission to 10 per cent and impose a buyer's premium of 10 per cent on all purchases, thus raising the overall commission received by the auction house to 20 per cent on each lot. Bonham's was persuaded to follow suit, but Phillips immediately grasped the opportunity to drive a wedge between London dealers and the other auctioneers by announcing that they too would reduce their vendor's commission to 10 per cent but considered a buyer's premium to be at best greedy and at worst unjust. The dealers boycotted premium sales off and on for several months, and made certain that the Press informed the public that this new system was the equivalent of a vendor's commission of at least 20 per cent, since the dealers would naturally reduce their bids to cover the premium. Phillips's advertisements were still emblazoned 'No Premium' until introducing it themselves in Autumn 1978.

The effect on the intake of property for sale in Blenheim Street was electric. The 1976 turnover marked the extraordinary increase of nearly 50 per cent when Sotheby's London turnover actually dropped 1 per cent during the same period. Phillips had already proved that they too could secure millionaire prices for works of art when a Ming vase sold for £135,000 in the autumn of 1973. The vase had been brought in with five others by a London bank official who had inherited them from his mother, and who hoped to realize £100 or so. Five of them sold for a total of £188, but the sixth was recognized by Phillips's expert as dating from the early fifteenth century, and it sold against world-wide competition for this enormous sum. In Monte Carlo, Rome, Sydney and even in Paris, their own slogan 'Phillips the auction people' may seem like provincial bravado, but it is beginning to sound perfectly natural to many people in England.

Blenstock House looks as though it had thought of being a suburban cinema, the pastel brick-work and curved side-window (now filled with preview works of art) connecting it with countless 1930s Odeons. Inside there is, unfortunately, no sign of the Art Deco. The busy reception hall on the ground floor used to be ruled over by a chain-smoking curly-blonde who surveyed her growing empire with justifiable pride, directing the majority of enquiries to the lift serving the other floors, where all the experts other than those dealing with furniture, books and coins can be found. A friendly informal atmosphere always prevails, the walls are decorated with specially commissioned auction-room cartoons by the *Punch* artist Kenneth Mahood, and even when there are few customers around there is a feeling of constant activity, with the telephone switchboard in one corner and the counter-girls always busy with some extra task such as mailing catalogues. At one side an old-fashioned sloping shelf holds wired copies of the sale catalogues for visitors to thumb through; at the far end of the hall an archway leads through to the cashiers, where clients also receive a far more courteous service than they can find at most of the other auction houses. Perhaps this friendliness stems from the enthusiasm generated within the firm by its current successes; clients seldom leave with those vague feelings of resentment that sometimes result from visits to Christie's and Sotheby's, where self-confident young experts may be indistinguishable in manner and looks from the too-pointedly unservile counter-assistants. Phillips may also change once the continuous pressure of work begins to take toll.

The heart of Phillips always used to be down in the basement at the popular Monday sales in the Pink Room, where 300–400 amazingly varied lots of furniture and works of art were sold every week. Now that there are all the new specialist departments upstairs, the Pink Room sales have lost much of their character, and dealers and collectors miss that feeling of expectation in pushing through the glass-panelled doors at the bottom of the

5

stairs to view the sale on Friday afternoon or Saturday morning.
The place used to be crammed with goods, chairs hanging from
the hot-water pipes near the ceiling, every cabinet in the sale
stuffed with a medley of glass and porcelain and all the larger
pieces standing around on the tables. There is still a big enough
selection to allow visitors to admire the way in which the porters
unerringly direct them to a particular lot without even consulting
their heavily marked 'location' catalogues; but there can no
longer be the justified expectation of making some kind of discovery which drew the art-market pirates to Phillips in the late
1960s.

Although prices have gone up in the Pink Room and the
quality has evened out, these Monday sales still attract their own
particular group of regulars who range themselves across the rows
of balloon-backed dining-chairs and Chippendale reproduction
armchairs. Others wander about the back and sides of the low-
ceilinged room, reappearing from behind pillars to bid and/or
make last-minute inspections. Much of the buying is done by
laconic individuals lounging by the door, against other dealers
seated in the front rows; there are also generally a number of
Continental buyers who aim to fill up their containers on Monday
mornings at Phillips. Many of the names called out without
hesitation by the auctioneer are unknown in other auction rooms,
but there is also a good selection of familiar faces ducking in and
out of the Pink Room in the course of the sale, like a beginning-
of-the-week rollcall of the London trade. A number of well-
known independent dealers try to slip in at the back unnoticed,
hoping to pick up some rarity they have spotted while viewing the
week before or have been tipped off about by one of the porters.
These dealers seldom bid in the room themselves for fear of attracting the other dealers' attention to the particular lot, so the bid is
normally left with the sales-clerk or a porter. Only the smaller
pieces from the cabinets behind the rostrum are actually held up
for inspection, the remainder being indicated by a shout from one
or other of the porters as they pace about the room, 'Showing over
here, sir'. The porters also have commissions to execute on many
of the lots, and the bidding frequently passes back and forwards
across the room between the porters without a member of the

public joining in at all. After the hammer has fallen, a broad smile
and a wink from a West End dealer standing quietly at the back,
indicates that the successful porter's commission has come from
someone who has been there all the time.

Another distinctive quality is to be found at Phillips's smaller
specialist auctions, such as the regular Staffordshire pot lids and
fairings sales which were taken on with the Puttick and Simpson
merger in 1954. Christie's South Kensington and Sotheby's
Belgravia both mount similar sales now, but for many years
Phillips were the only auctioneers to take the subject seriously and
their auctions still seem like the meetings of a private club. They
were held in borrowed space, a corner of the first floor, little more
than a large landing with constant traffic at the back—secretaries
clutching luncheon vouchers and cups of coffee, porters bearing
dangerous-looking musical instrument cases, and clients on their
way to the silver department with their carefully wrapped
treasures. Collecting fairings is apparently a family activity, for
there are plenty of husband-and-wife teams following the proceedings with keen and expert interest. The cataloguer and
auctioneer, Paul Viney, often dresses up in a spotted bow-tie on
auction day, and his enthusiasm helps make the auction a special
occasion for the collectors who have visited London for the day.
There are now between ten and twelve of these sales every year,
and five or six of Baxter Prints and Stevengraphs. The fur sales
are also an interesting, though very different, experience, there
being about eight of these a year.

Nowadays Phillips has two sophisticated new sale-rooms on the
upper floors of Blenstock House—a picture sale-room with its
wire-mesh screen, and a new gallery, bright white with bold
architectural decoration in the contemporary style (plate 29).
However the real drama at Phillips has shifted to the old Green
Room at the back of the building on the ground floor. Auctions of
the better-quality furniture and works of art are held there every
Tuesday morning and the quality of these sales is gradually over-
taking that of the weekly furniture sales at Christie's and Sotheby's.
Phillips's auction room is considerably smaller than either of
theirs and the crowd often overflows into the passage at the back,
from which there emerges a fog of cigarette smoke and babble of

conversation. They are usually boisterous sales but the noise is
less of a distraction than usual because it comes from excited
participation rather than boredom. The Italian dealers, many of
whom live permanently in London, are always strongly represented and, unable always to see who is bidding in the crush of
people at the back of the room, they frequently find themselves
competing against each other in their eagerness, a confusion which
is followed by a sale-stopping crescendo of invective and arm-
waving.

Auctions at the Marylebone Rooms in Lisson Grove are a
different kind of thing altogether. Considerably bigger and somewhat smarter than Bonham's similar Burnaby Street Rooms,
Phillips's oldest secondary auction house sells anything of saleable
value which can be removed at a total house-clearance, and this
huge cross-section of goods is ranged across two floors every
Friday. The second-hand furniture is stacked to the ceiling in
rows, and eager buyers can be seen clambering about the stacks
trying to ascertain whether a television set lodged on a chair ten
feet off the ground actually works, or if a side-table somewhere
else has or hasn't a damaged top. Occasionally an ominous
creaking will be followed by a long series of crashes, as part of the
stack tumbles down on to the backs of the audience. The origins
of a group of ordinary but attractive Victorian furniture are
revealed by the owner's luggage labels, still tied to the property
and inscribed in an arthritic hand, 'The joint property of Sarah
and Francis Lottie', which conjures up pictures of devoted
spinster sisters giving tea to the Vicar.

A distinctly ominous, if enigmatic, notice in the catalogue
reads: 'All pictures sold for what they are';[7] and at the end of a
poor day, with nothing left other than chocolate-box reproductions and evening-class oils, a dealer ruefully crosses out 'for'
and inserts 'despite' in his catalogue.

The latest addition to the London auction scene is Phillips
West 2, which opened in September 1976 at Salem Road off
Queensway. This attractive and ambitious project is rumoured to
have cost £2,000,000 to develop since the purchase of the site in
1973, some of which will be recovered from the sale of terraced
houses at the back, which have been converted to look on to a

picturesque garden in the centre. Situated just behind the domed suburban splendour of Whiteley's store, Phillips West 2 used to be the Savory and Moore warehouse; it now houses two vast 4,000-square-foot sale-rooms where masses of attractive period furniture and other works of art are disposed of every Thursday. Specially designed and equipped to serve the demand for a quick-service auction house, Salem Road will no doubt soon establish itself as a natural centre for the middle-range London dealers and exporters.

Phillips has recently opened an office in New York at 867 Madison Avenue, which was previously occupied by Christie's. This new office is headed by Brian Cole who had been running Phillips's operations in the Midlands. Phillips held their first series of sales in the late autumn of 1977, but the principal activities of this office will be with valuations and in an advisory role. Phillips regular auctions in New York are now held at 525 East 72nd Street and call themselves Phillips, the international fine art auctioneers to accommodate the new policy of holding regular foreign sales in New York, Montreal and Amsterdam.

It has been seen that Phillips is undergoing rapid expansion, but many of the qualities of a small auction house—such as rapid payment of sale-proceeds—have been carried over into the larger organization. At the same time the chain of satellite auction houses across England becomes stronger and stronger. Phillips is entering a crucial stage in its history, a period in which its powerful chairman Christopher Weston will seek to consolidate the immense advances that have been made in recent years.

Bonham's. The Family Auctioneers

At a time when the other three leading London auctioneers are continuously involved in headline-making programmes of expansion and amalgamation, it is most refreshing to find that Bonham's has chosen to emphasize rather than hide the narrow family base of its organization. Despite persuasive overtures from its rivals and tempting cash offers from developers with an eye for their wholly-owned premises opposite Harrods, the Bonham family fiercely maintains its independence, and thus preserves the unique character of its London auction house.

The extent of the family's dominance is clearly revealed in the boardroom line-up, where the chairman, Leonard Bonham, is attended by his youngest son Nicholas as Managing Director, and by his wife, sister and daughter in three of the seven remaining seats—making a family majority of five against four. Now that the chairman's eldest son Toby has returned to the fold, to head the watercolour and print department, Bonham's has closed its ranks completely to fight off the challenge of the other big three who are investing more and more money in new premises at home and abroad. It is typical of Bonham's that when sales of fine furs were revived in December 1973, the new department was put in the hands of Eve Bonham, who mounted the rostrum for the first time with the confidence she normally displays in captaining her all-female ocean-racing crew; and that the model showing furs at the sale should be another member of the family, Toby's wife Jenny. Not that a female auctioneer was anything new for Bonham's, as Eve's aunt Helen Maddick took sales regularly from 1940 till 1972.

With the present tendency for a diminishing number of properties to pass through the London auction rooms, Bonham's policy of internal consolidation instead of diversification of resources may yet prove the most prudent in the long term.

Bonham's was founded in 1793 as a fine art auctioneering partnership between William Charles Bonham and George Jones, with premises in Leicester Square. In 1826 they moved to more imposing rooms in Oxford Street. Very little documentary information about Bonham's early history remains in the family's possession, as an oil incendiary bomb razed the premises to the ground in 1940 and almost all the records were destroyed; but related material of the period indicates that Bonham's were quite influential auctioneers of houses and antiques in the nineteenth century. In Victorian sale-room advertisements, the space devoted to Bonham's in the local London Press equals Christie's and Phillips, while Sotheby's announcements are hardly to be seen except in the specialist book-trade journals. The company's full name, W. and F. C. Bonham and Sons, was registered in 1877, two years before the brothers William and Frederic Charles were granted a fifty-year lease on the Oxford Street premises, later numbered 63 and 65. The firm has passed directly from father to son since then, the last partnership deeds before it became a limited company being those of 1933, between Albert Charles Bonham and his son Leonard (the present chairman) when the weekly salary for directors was fixed at eight pounds.

On the expiry of the Oxford Street lease, Bonham's moved to New Burlington Street, and after direct hits by bombs there (and, ten days later, on their secondary rooms at Whitfield Street), they passed the remainder of the war in Newman Street, where Helen Maddick ran the firm in her brother's absence, holding a sale every Thursday at 11 throughout the war. Mrs Maddick remembers one sale when a flying bomb was heard approaching them: the audience dived beneath the tables, leaving herself and the sales-clerk looking on unmoved from the high rostrum—the bomb having exploded a block away before they had had a chance to make their precarious descent. On returning from active service, Leonard searched for premises until he finally bought a site in Montpelier Street. After a two-year battle to obtain full planning permission, work began on their present premises. The first sale was held there in June 1956, the same year that they took over two other firms of auctioneers—Robinson and Foster, and Tooth and Tooth. In the past Bonham's had also operated from secondary premises, and in 1959 they acquired the Old Chelsea Galleries in Burnaby Street, thus completing the structure of the company as it now stands.

Partly due to Leonard Bonham's ill-health, Bonham's failed to take advantage of the increased power that Peter Wilson had manufactured for the auction rooms in the 1960s, and in the course of a decade they lost any claim, other than historical, to be considered in the same category as Christie's, Sotheby's and Phillips. Even in the boom season 1972/73, Bonham's turnover was only £3,178,400, but as this represented an increase of 52 per cent it was a sign that things were on the move again in Montpelier Street. Although still in their twenties at the time, the principal instigators of change were Eve Bonham (who had returned from abroad in 1971 to work full-time with the firm) and her brother Nicholas (who is now the leading auctioneer and Managing Director).

The most important project in the revitalization of the company involved the construction of a new floor at the top of the Montpelier Galleries, the radical redesign of the picture sale-room and the reorganization of two other viewing galleries. These alterations were essential in order to accommodate the increasing number of specialized sales which were planned to coincide with the employment of more expert cataloguers. Two experts left Sotheby's valuations department for Bonham's—Andrew Hawkins, in the furniture department, and Sebastian Pearson, who joined them in 1974 and has introduced many new ideas in the ceramics and works of art department. These catalogues are now divided into several different categories and are produced in a larger format, with attractive illustrations, the benefit of this specialist approach being demonstrated by the fact that in the difficult season of 1974/75, Pearson's department was the only one at Bonham's to record a substantial increase of business. Other departments followed this example, and they began to hold separate sales of clocks and watches, and of carpets and rugs, instead of crowding all these together in general furniture catalogues. Other departments, which had been closed down since the war, were reopened with newly appointed experts or consultants, notably the wine and the book departments; and with the temporary demise of the Sotheby Veteran Car department and a lessening of interest at Christie's, Nick Bonham decided to try his hand in this difficult field, with sales at Alexandra Palace. At the same time more space was created by the removal of the Valuations Department to separate premises round the corner in Cheval Place, under the energetic leadership of another young enthusiast, John Stancliffe, whose job has recently been taken over by Leslie Gillham.

Although Bonham's have no overriding ambition to rival Phillips's network of auction houses in the British Isles, or Sotheby's on the Continent, they have recently appointed representatives in the West Country, Nottinghamshire, East Anglia, Scotland and Geneva, whose task it is to secure property for sale in London or to arrange influential house-sales. When Sebastian Thewes moved up to Perth with his Scottish wife, he became Bonham's representative there, and settled down to organizing their opening sale in Scotland at Blair Drummond, where an excellent sale total of £201,000 was achieved.

At the same time a number of eye-catching sales were found for the London galleries, and these were advertised and promoted with a great deal more energy than previously. In recent seasons the telegrams which resulted in the capture of Dr Crippen understandably attracted more attention from the Press than any other single lot. These original documents included the series of Marconi hand-written messages from *Montrose*, the first one of which was sent on 31 July 1910 and began, 'Have strong suspicions that Crippen London cellar murderer and accomplice are amongst saloon passengers moustache taken off growing beard accomplice dressed as boy voice manner and build undoubtedly girl'.[1] These sold for £1,600 in July 1974. In the same season Bonham's also proved that they could sell Old Master pictures for record prices when a pair of architectural views by Charles Thevenin secured £39,000. The canvases were covered in a thick brown varnish and were quite severely ripped and rubbed—the kind of condition that would have frightened off all but real connoisseurs at a price of more than a few thousand. The achievement of such a competitive price enabled Bonham's to assure future clients that all the important dealers in London viewed or attended their sales.

In March 1974 Bonham's held the most valuable auction of their history, the sale of Mr and Mrs Fielding Marshall's collection of Old Master pictures which secured nearly £300,000. Not all of the wide Press coverage of this sale was favourable, as the collection had previously been exhibited at Sotheby's with a catalogue produced by the Marshalls to which a self-protecting insertion had been added by Sotheby's experts, stating that not all the pictures would subsequently be sold with the same attributions. As a result of this addendum the angry owners then handed the disposal of the whole collection over to Bonham's. The next season another interesting collection that would normally have gone to Christie's or Sotheby's was consigned to Bonham's because they were again able to satisfy the owner's requirements. This was the Baron Winesberg collection of New Guinea Primitive Art, which Bonham's sold in a single catalogue of 191 lots when their rivals had only wanted to sell the 30 best pieces.

Bonham's imposing square building, with its newly painted bright tan façade, stands out clearly on the right off Knightsbridge, beyond Harrods on the way to the Victoria and Albert Museum. At the top of a small flight of stairs at the entrance is the furniture sale-room, the doors flanked by a pair of large bronze *putti* and photographs of forthcoming sales and previous record prices. Apart from the tangerine and purple carpeting on the stairs, the atmosphere is quietly unpretentious and old-fashioned, the cashiers' and administrative offices opening direct from the main reception area, and looking slightly Dickensian in this 1950s building. Like Phillips, the galleries are not open all the time but only on the two days before the sale, though there is a furniture sale almost every week. As in all categories other than pictures, the quality of these sales is considerably lower than at Christie's and Sotheby's, with less concern for age and condition and very few lots that secure more than £1,000. The big difference at Bonham's is the scale of operations, because a visitor to Christie's or Sotheby's at midday on any day of the week will always find a sale in progress somewhere in the building; and amongst the three or four sales on view there will usually be one section of rare and expensive works of art. On many days at Bonham's there is no sale at all, and the only gallery open for viewing may be almost empty. Not that collectors object to this comparative peace, as there are always some useful and attractive pieces of furniture in each sale, and less experienced collectors are able to inspect items in their own time without being conscious of inquisitive glances from the stream of professional traffic passing through the Bond Street and King Street rooms. All the same, whenever a rare piece of furniture turns up, even if it has been lurking in apparent oblivion in a dark corner for the whole of the view, there will invariably be a noticeable swelling of the audience about ten lots before it is due to be sold, and the auctioneer's face will brighten visibly. Each specialist dealer has his own network of 'informers' across London and the home counties, it being impossible for one man to run a shop and view all the sales himself. At Bonham's furniture sales the porters, in their smart bottle-green coats, are particularly experienced; and when no one else was interested in a lot they often used to buy it themselves and then leave it on the premises, knowing that it was likely to secure its full value in a sale three or four weeks later. A year or two ago the porters used to double their weekly wages when profits from this reselling was added to their earnings on commission bids. The porters are still a useful source of information, although they are carefully discreet in their treatment of inquiries. In answer to a collector's doubting comments on the age of a bureau described in the catalogue as eighteenth-century, a porter knowingly replied, 'Well, I imagine the owner insists that it has been in the family for 200 years, sir. But family records can not always be relied on, can they?'

All the furniture sales used to be taken by Edward Dale, a dour auctioneer whose only attempt to liven up the proceedings was the regular, indiscriminate comment in a mechanical tone, 'That's rather nice.' Although Bonham's furniture auctions are therefore seldom entertaining in themselves, they are nevertheless well worth attending regularly, as in the course of three months a private buyer could certainly furnish a house in the antique style of his choice at as good value as anywhere in London.

Bonham's picture departments are on the first floor, and the firm's reputation has traditionally rested on the picture sales, which for many years have been the best in London after Christie's and Sotheby's. The smartly redesigned gallery has wall-to-wall carpeting and efficient overhead lighting, giving a clear view of all the pictures hung on screens standing in parallel lines the length of the room. The auctions themselves are always well-attended, relaxed affairs, the 'Strictly No Smoking' signs in four languages being blandly ignored before the sale by the band of long-haired young porters who are obviously there to acquire a basic grounding in pictures and the picture market as quickly as possible.

Alexander Meddowes, whose broad general knowledge and instinctive feeling for paintings commands considerable respect from the London trade, conducts the sales in an efficient but informal style, taking particular care of the large number of regulars with whom he enjoys some innocent badinage throughout the morning. This relaxed approach encourages people to come and go freely during the sale, to interrupt with queries when they have forgotten which lot is being sold or wonder whether the frame is included; and in all but the most important sales there is a continuous background of subdued conversation. The chatter is often about the particular lot being sold, as a dealer asks a colleague for a last-minute opinion before bidding; and Meddowes sticks to his leisurely pace knowing that many of the buyers have failed to view the sale properly and are seeing the paintings for the first time as they dart up to the easel for hurried scrutiny through a magnifying-glass. Others sit near the back of the room gossiping quietly, waiting for a particular lot to come up later in the sale. Some sales are worth attending just for the overheard conversations—like that of a couple of dealers of indeterminate age and sex who were heard in laconic discussion over two paintings hanging beside each other on the wall, one a portrait of a sophisticated Edwardian lady of fashion with her beautiful child, and the other of a large Victorian lap-dog. Their final conclusion was, that 'The trouble with painting the human face is that there is no disguising its inherent evil, especially in society women and avowedly innocent children, whereas the dog, you see, is always a transparently good and beautiful creature.'

Bonham's have suffered in the past from critics concerning the efficiency of the reception areas, particularly with regard to the availability of staff to answer queries. Nobody, however, could ever quarrel with the service itself which has always been wonderfully friendly. In this respect, and many others, Bonham's is not unlike a leading firm of provincial auctioneers run by an influential local family. With a little more crispness of service Bonham's could turn this characteristic to advantage, as the complex structure of their three rivals makes it increasingly difficult for them to give the genuine personal attention that the Bonham family offers.

Auctions at the New Chelsea Galleries in Lots Road are very different from those in Knightsbridge, the scene dominated by the gas works towering over this dilapidated area of red-brick artisans' houses which have not yet been seized upon by the young married insurance brokers who swarm about this part of Chelsea and Fulham. Hopes of finding Bonham's secondary rooms housed in an unaltered late-Victorian warehouse are dashed at the sight of a newly yellow-painted 1950s factory, and bargain-hunters wonder if they might not have done better to stop off at the more inviting Furniture Cave which they passed at the corner on turning off the New King's Road. Once inside the visitor has no regrets. The big warehouse is stacked to the ceiling with furniture, beds, fridges, garden ornaments, carpets, pictures, pottery, metalware and almost anything else imaginable. In a rectangular patch in front of the rostrum two rows of upholstered settees and chairs face each other, and in these the regulars are comfortably seated, thumbing through well-used catalogues and intervening with an occasional shouted bid or a nod of the head. Others stand about in groups or follow the porters up and down the stacks of furniture as the lots are indicated, executing bids with a single wave of the catalogue and that characteristic simultaneous turn on the heel away from the auctioneer. If the lot is not knocked down to them at this one carefully-timed bid, they look back at the auctioneer with feigned incredulity at the price, and shake their heads in apparent disgust.

The audience at Bonham's New Chelsea galleries really does have a distinctive quality, for a high proportion of the items they sell are the kind of things which used to be crowded into those dark

little 'antique' shops that proliferated on the outskirts of large
cities, before antique-dealing and collecting became the fashionable
hobby of the British bourgeoisie. It is different from Phillips in
Lisson Grove, which operates on a larger scale through three
floors, or Lots Road Auction Galleries just around the corner,
which has little other than second-hand furniture. Recent bargain
lots include a set of eight 'Spy' framed caricatures and six others,
all for £12, a pair of Georgian-style dining-chairs for a single bid
of £1, and four simulated-bamboo side-chairs plus stool and a
carved ebonized side-chair for the remarkable low price (in these
days of bamboo revival) of £3. Some buyers also wait eagerly for
the bran-tub lots, such as an unsorted crate of 'at least fifty' books,
or a miscellaneous basket of plates that could contain an unusual
piece of early nineteenth-century blue-and-white. The only lots
to be avoided completely are those with the ominous initials 'a.f.'
after the description. These stand for 'as found', a term reserved
for lots in an irredeemable state of disrepair.

It would be foolish to imagine that everything goes for bargain
prices, for there are thousands of antique dealers in London
constantly on the search for stock, and a remarkable number of
people pass through Lots Road on the single viewing day—
more, it often seems, than at the main galleries in Montpelier
Street. There are continuous disappointments, as a small group
of eighteenth-century samplers or an enormous Spanish cast-iron
coffer, which seem to be going for next to nothing, are bid up to
twice what they would have secured in the West End rooms
because each of the three porters has a commission bid. An
expert from one of the other auction houses may even be seen
burrowing into a pile of rugs, paying quickly at the desk, and
hurrying back to the West End with his discovery tucked firmly
under his arm.

The domestic appliances and second-hand furniture seem better
value here than elsewhere. There is naturally no guarantee that
the fridges and cookers are actually in working order, but the
porters can normally point out the ones that were originally
removed in working order from 'a good home'. As Bonham's give
a complete house-clearance service to their Knightsbridge clients,
all sorts of unusual modern things are likely to turn up; but it

takes either a gambler or an electrical engineer to be convinced that an impressive-looking colour television set for £48 is a bargain. Amongst the best things to buy is second-hand modern furniture originally purchased in expensive limited editions, by famous modern designers at Oscar Woollens or Zarach. Some of this will be sold in years to come as rare collectors' pieces, just as Art Deco furniture by Rhulmann and functionalist design by Le Corbusier now sells at specialist auctions for thousands of pounds.

Although Bonham's has introduced a buyer's premium, the firm still operates at a lower rate of selling-commission than any other established fine art auctioneers, and Bonham's can be relied upon to avoid any excessive ambition that might endanger the traditional functioning of this family company. Leonard Bonham, who still heads the firm he began working with over fifty years ago, is likely to see fulfilled his wish that Bonham's might maintain its record 'for many years to come . . . as the only firm of London auctioneers which has remained a family business'.[2]

6

Sotheby's Belgravia and Christie's South Kensington

When Sotheby's opened their new premises at 19 Motcomb Street in October 1971 and revealed that their secondary auction rooms were to specialize exclusively in the period 1830 to 1930, there were knowing sighs and raised eyebrows in the London antique trade. At that time the British Antique Dealers Association still refused to admit that anything made or painted after 1830 was even 'antique', much less a 'work of art'. Many art market critics felt that this project substantiated accusations against Sotheby's of over-emphasis on commercial considerations, for surely no one with taste could ever allow the desire for commercial gain to lure him into specialized sales of unacceptable 'Victoriana'. (The term 'Victoriana' was at this time pronounced with the same note of disdain as Lady Bracknell's '*A hand-bag!*' in *The Importance of Being Ernest*.)

There were indeed strong commercial arguments for opening Sotheby's Belgravia, the most forceful being that it had become physically impossible to hold many more sales at the Bond Street premises, so that the only way the business could grow was by operating another auction room. Also, the scarcity of works of art was forcing both dealers and collectors to look more seriously at the nineteenth century, and as the volume of trade increased dramatically in this area Sotheby's naturally wished to share in it. With the increased values of Victorian paintings, furniture and silver, a specialized auction house became financially viable, and in fact Sotheby's in Motcomb Street immediately cornered £2,000,000-worth of extra business, and established in the 1975/76 season a turnover of £3,700,000.

While the costs and possible profits of this venture were

naturally assessed in strictly financial terms, the Sotheby's directors also realized that Motcomb Street would be successful only if it were run by a group of enthusiasts with a genuine respect for the art and artefacts of the Victorian and Edwardian periods. It was assumed that exporters and commercial dealers would automatically attend the sales; the real test would be whether it could secure the respect and loyalty of that relatively small, but powerful, group of knowledgeable collectors who had been studying the period since the V & A's influential Exhibition in 1951, commemorating the centenary of the Great Exhibition. Sotheby's Belgravia did not create, or even exploit, the fashion for 'Victoriana'; in fact it handled very little of the period paraphernalia and bric-à-brac implied by this term. It merely offered a venue for the expert sale and purchase of nineteenth-century works of art, in the same way Bond Street did for earlier pieces.

The original idea for Sotheby's Belgravia came from Howard Ricketts, a young director whose specialist responsibility was antique firearms, *objets de vertu* and early bronzes, but whose secret passion was for the Victorian period, particularly early photographs and stereoscopic slides. A venture of this kind fitted in with the overall pattern of development at Sotheby's during the previous decade—greater departmental specialization and the mounting of an increasing number of medium-quality sales. The removal to another premises of all English paintings and works of art dated later than 1830 benefited both houses, because it prevented the stylistic disharmonies which occurred as more and more pieces of later date had filtered into Bond Street sales. It also created more physical space for the sales of earlier objects.

Sotheby's Belgravia was set up by Marcus Linell, who joined Sotheby's in 1956, and was made a director at the age of twenty-six just before leaving for New York to take charge of the works-of-art department at the recently purchased Parke Bernet. On returning to London he was given the job of creating and running Sotheby's Belgravia, the administrative and physical organization of which was in the hands of John Cann, who in 1974 became the first person to rise through the administrative ranks to a directorship of Sotheby's. Quite a number of technical changes were made in rebuilding Sotheby's Belgravia, the most important dealing with the clearing of purchases during the sale. As each lot (except the bulkiest pieces of furniture) is sold, it is taken down in the goods lift to the basement: simultaneously, the sales-clerk sends a list of the buyers' names and prices through a compressed-air tube to the cashier's office in the main hall. This makes it possible at any point in the sale for a buyer to leave the auction, pay his bill, and collect his purchases from the basement. Sotheby's Belgravia is the only auction house in London with such a system, and it is of great benefit to private buyers and collectors who come just for one particular section of the sale.

The other major administrative innovation involved locating the majority of expert departments on the open-plan top floor, all served by one reception counter. In order to create the space for this, all objects for sale are removed by the porters immediately they have been catalogued, and are stored in the basement warehouse awaiting sale—very different from Bond Street where most experts work in isolation in tiny offices, jealously guarding all their borrowed treasures from the moment they are brought in till the day they go on view. The Belgravia system not only makes better use of space, but reduces the risk of breakage or loss. More important than this, it encourages experts in different fields to share their knowledge and enthusiasm, relating stylistic similarities and identifying with each other's successes.

Marcus Linell also brought about changes in the style and design of catalogues, changes that were again influenced equally by commercial and aesthetic considerations. One of the largest overheads at Sotheby's is the printing and postage of catalogues, and at Bond Street the method chosen to reduce expenses appeared to be producing smaller unillustrated catalogues on inferior paper for minor sales. At Sotheby's Belgravia a far more imaginative solution was found. The overall length of the catalogue text was reduced (by printing shorter descriptions on three-column pages) to make space for more illustrations. The logic for this was that the greater the number of small black-and-white illustrations in a catalogue, the cheaper the cost to the seller and the higher the recovery of printing-costs to Sotheby's Belgravia through the profit on sale of photographic prints. It has also been proved beyond doubt that the illustrated lots attract five or six times as many commission bids as the unillustrated lots, however detailed the description—thus justifying the extra charge to the owner of £8–£30, depending on the size of the block. These illustrated Belgravia catalogues also acted as apologists for the Victorian period, as they were dispatched via the Bond Street subscriber-lists into the homes of eighteenth-century devotees. Belgravia catalogues have become essential to the collector as works of reference and record, and have proved that it is financially feasible to produce attractive colour-printed catalogues for sales totalling no more than £30,000, whereas at Bond Street even single lots worth £30,000 are frequently denied colour illustration.

Another useful Belgravia innovation, which in this case was adopted in both Bond Street and King Street, was the inclusion of printed estimate sheets for distribution with the catalogues. Previously clients had found it necessary to lay systematic siege to the reception counters in order to obtain pre-sale estimate sheets; and even then all the important lots tended to be inscribed 'refer department', involving another series of frustrating telephone-calls in order to track down elusive experts. Some experts apparently suffer a paranoid fear that an object will fetch twice their estimate, and that they will subsequently be accused of having failed to appreciate the full quality or rarity of the piece. But providing both buyers and sellers are aware of the fact that printed estimates should not be taken as statements of value, but merely as educated guesses at a likely auction price, then their publication can only be to everyone's advantage. There would be fewer art-market disappointments if more people realized that virtually no work of art has an intrinsic value, and that an object is 'worth' whatever someone cares to pay for it in a particular place at a particular time—regardless of what a similar piece might have secured under completely different circumstances elsewhere.

Number 19 Motcomb Street has a history well suited to its use by Sotheby's as specialist Victorian auction rooms. This fluted Doric-columned building was the original Pantechnicon. The name is now used to describe large furniture-vans, but was coined by Seth Smith and his architect Joseph Jopling for this building which was designed for the 'sale and warehousing of carriages, works of art, and wines'.[1] An advertising leaflet issued towards the end of the first year of operations indicated that almost 500 carriages could be viewed at the Pantechnicon by potential purchasers, and that the 'Salon of Arts' contained 'a large collection of paintings etc. by the first masters . . . worthy of the highest patronage'.[2] Seth Smith even ran an omnibus 'for the accommodation of ladies and gentry coming out of the City to the Pantechnicon'.[3] The Pantechnicon charged a commission of 5 per cent on the sale of works of art; it proudly announced that the fire engine was always kept in order on the premises and that 'any servant in the Establishment receiving a gratuity will be immediately dismissed'.[4]

Sotheby's restored the façade, entrance hall and ground floor offices to their original condition: this was of the date 1831 and was particularly appropriate, being the earliest date of origin of the works of art that would be sold in the revived 'Pan'. Seth Smith had been the first of his family of West Country builders to enter the trade in Belgravia and was an important contributor in the construction of 'Cubittopolis' from 1824 onwards, when he was awarded the contract to build the south side of Eaton Square. In fact Seth Smith failed to finish this project but he did complete the imaginative construction of the Pantechnicon, and what is now called the Halkin Arcade which was built as a two-storey covered market linked by bridges on the first floor. The Pantechnicon survived two devastating fires. One, in 1874, devoured amongst a wealth of treasures a large proportion of Sir Richard Wallace's collection of armour, and Charles Dickens's daughter's collection of the author's letters. In 1939 the other large fire was quenched by a team of firemen led by Tim Clarke, until recently a senior director at Sotheby's. On returning the next morning he found three of his firemen sitting in the debris reading the unexpurgated edition of *The Arabian Nights*.

When the premises were rebuilt after the war, Commander Seth-Smith (as the family had become known) also mounted auction sales at the Pan under the name of the Motcomb Galleries. A high percentage of the lots in these sales was of property stored in the warehouse, which was sold either on behalf of the Pantechnicon itself, to recover bad debts, or on behalf of owners who realized that they and their families were never again to return to the grandeur of ten-bedroomed houses in Belgravia and could therefore never use the magnificent furniture that the Seth-Smiths had been storing for years. Because of the treasure-chest nature of many of the goods, wonderful discoveries were made by the knowledgeable at the Motcomb Galleries auctions in the '50s and '60s. But the Grosvenor Estate eventually decided to develop its land at the back of Motcomb Street. The Seth-Smith warehouses were removed to Chiswick, and the remaining part of the lease was sold to Sotheby's, there being a building use and protection order on the Motcomb Street block itself. The days of the old 'Pan' were finally numbered when Sotheby's Belgravia sold for Seth-Smith, in June 1973, Thomas Stuart Burnett's larger-than-life size marble statue of Rob Roy, which had stood for many years in the entrance hall.

From the very beginning Sotheby's Belgravia displayed a special quality that distinguished it from its more austere progenitor in Bond Street. The friendly, happy atmosphere had two main origins. Firstly, the expert staff at Sotheby's Belgravia were all young and therefore anxious to prove themselves in a field that had no history within the auction rooms. It was essential to make the dealers and collectors feel welcome, so that they would want to spend time viewing and attending sales at yet another London sale-room. In achieving this the gallery (plate 25) and the warehouse porters at Sotheby's Belgravia contributed as much as the experts, for they quickly established a reputation for being the most helpful and efficient porters in London. Secondly, the majority of owners bringing their Victorian heirlooms to Sotheby's Belgravia did not come with any preconceived ideas that these were necessarily of great value; they also knew that, apart from the Phillips sales of pot-lids, fairings and Baxter prints, no other auction rooms in London held specialized sales in these fields. Indeed, even the journalists were favourably disposed towards a venture that relieved the boredom of endless sales of ordinary Georgian furniture on the one hand and unreal multi-million-pound collections on the other. The public were therefore prepared to enjoy themselves and hoped to be impressed, and the staff were prepared to prove themselves and to give a first-class personal service to all their visitors.

Each type of sale at Sotheby's Belgravia has its own following, with many more private buyers attending the sales than at Bond Street, where on average more than 85 per cent of the lots are bought by dealers. Sales of photographs and photographic equipment at Belgravia are especially dominated by private collectors, who fly in from all over the world to compete for the rarities at rapidly escalating prices. Early photographs have been publicly acclaimed in London ever since Richard Cork's article in the *Evening Standard* in October 1973 produced a critical uproar that persuaded the Royal Academy to withdraw their Hill/Adamson volumes a day before the Belgravia sale. People began digging in hidden laundry-baskets and clearing out store-cupboards to produce early albums that could suddenly be worth thousands of pounds, the record price[5] in London for a single lot of photographs being a Cameron album for £52,000 sold in October 1974. Much of the time clients brought in valueless daguerrotypes of ancestors, or one of these endless volumes of Bombay views in the 1890s, but occasionally a hopeful caller would turn out to be a distant relative of one of the important early photographers and possessor of a unique album. Such was the album of Cameron photographs, which the owners spent feverish months trying to find at home after the first publicity had reminded them of their long-forgotten family heirloom. The rooms are normally quiet and concentrated during photographic sales, apart from the occasional 'Yipee' from Dr Burnside of Vermont and the buzz of approval and shaking of congratulatory hands at a particularly important purchase. One French lady delightedly blew the auctioneer a kiss on finally making a successful bid.

Other sales, such as the Allen Funt collection of Alma-Tadema paintings in November 1973, bring a number of the Bond Street buyers down to Belgravia. Funt, the American television director and originator of *Candid Camera*, only started collecting Alma-Tadema in 1967 when a London dealer showed him a painting by 'the worst artist that ever lived'.[6] From then on he made a single-minded effort to acquire all the best paintings by that artist which came on the market. He ended up with thirty-five Alma-Tademas, which because of a cash crisis caused by his accountant's embezzlement of over $1,000,000, were all included in a single-owner sale at Sotheby's Belgravia.

Sir Lawrence Alma-Tadema (1836–1912) had sold a relatively large number of paintings direct to America during his lifetime, including *A Reading from Homer*, which at $30,000 was the highest-priced painting of the 1903 season. Soon after his death, Tadema paintings dropped completely out of fashion: even as late as 1960 a major work such as *The Roses of Heliogabalus* sold for only £105 when it had originally been commissioned in 1888 at a cost of £4,000. At the Belgravia Funt sale in 1973 it sold for £28,000. It is not known exactly what Funt himself paid for the picture but it is unlikely to have been more than £10,000, even though by the late 1960s Tademas were enjoying a revival of interest and a well-known collector like Funt would have been forced to pay some dramatic prices. The sale total in 1973 of $425,000 was therefore particularly impressive as it is normally difficult to resell works of art that have recently been on the market.

Amongst other specialist auctions which always produce a fascinating crowd of knowledgeable fanatics are the 'collectors sales', a nebulous title given to a category that includes everything which does not quite fit into any other sale—often things that are seldom handled at all by the general antique trade. The sales are an amazing mélange of model steam-locomotives, phonographs and polyphons, toys, cigarette cards and postcards, automata, model soldiers, car mascots and almost anything for which there might be an esoteric collector's market. At first it was difficult for Sotheby's to find anyone in the firm who actually knew anything about these strange subjects, and in the early days the sales were produced by the furniture department, largely with straightforward descriptions of the physical appearance of objects and little information on points of interest to collectors.

There were thus some surprises, particularly from amongst a mass of material removed from the Nizam of Hyderabad's palaces in India which included unopened Art Nouveau boxes of Parisian perfumes and soaps, painted papier-mâché 'snake charmer' boxes, and assorted Edwardian toys. Immediately the viewing of this particular sale began, the Sotheby cataloguers realized that this first-ever collection of painted tin clockwork toys really was something special, as crowds of previously unknown enthusiasts from Paris and Munich, as well as from all over England, turned up to admire them. The remarkable thing about the collection was its condition, for the toys were found untouched in their original boxes and were thought to have been part of an automatic special delivery from the factory in Germany to the young Indian princes, who had never even opened some of them. Middle-aged toy fanatics competed mercilessly against each other for some of the early motor-car models and, much to the amazement of the auctioneer, the bidding went up to as much as £500 for individual toys.

For collectors sales, Sotheby's Belgravia normally opens on Saturdays for special viewing. Collectors and their families come for a morning's romp amongst the 400 or so fascinating lots; and radio interviewers record the strangest cacophony, composed of 1920s romantic ballads played on a wheezy polyphon, the whirr of clockwork toys, perhaps the cackle of a laughing clown automaton, the clatter of a model railway and the refined tones of a mandolin cylinder musical-box. The sales are now produced by a team of budding experts who have developed an interest in particular fields, the chief cashier cataloguing the cigarette cards, the picture department administrator cataloguing the posters and advertising material, and an ex-sales-clerk's ex-boyfriend cataloguing the phonographs. Now that the collectors sales produce a turnover of about £600,000 a year, Hilary Kay works fulltime in this field, marshalling her troupe of helpers to add to her own specialist knowledge of toys, advertising material, typewriters, and other mechanical devices.

As a result of another young cashier's involvement with the Magic Circle, Sotheby's Belgravia even produced a sale which included a specialized section of 'Magical Effects and Related Material', and for several days before the sale their Press officer was continually posing for photographs in the throes of decapitation by 'A large head-chopper, once the property of the Great Levante'. An antiquarian magician could also have bought at this sale 'A hand of bananas and a diminishing billiard ball' for £8, three Sorcar the Great posters for £16, or 'A large cabinet as used in Will, the Witch and the Watchman' for a £10 bid. (The auctioneer apparently considered offering an 'invisible lot' which would be magically revealed if a price of more than £100 was paid.) Since this successful sale, the magical cashier has not needed to advertise his connections by wearing that large red-spotted bow-tie which in a flash lit up and twirled around like a propeller, frightening old ladies in the lift.

Slightly off the dealers' normal beat, Sotheby's Belgravia has nevertheless established itself as a favourite haunt for devotees of the nineteenth century, who not only appreciate its expertise but also enjoy the friendly companiable atmosphere.

Christie's South Kensington is an even more recent foundation, its first sale having been held in February 1975. At first it was assumed that Christie's new venture was intended directly to rival Sotheby's Belgravia; but it soon became apparent that a completely different set of criteria applied. Where Sotheby's argued that Sotheby's Belgravia, far from being a secondary sale-room, instead extended the specialized Bond Street treatment to a wider range of works of art, Christie's South Kensington openly concentrated on 'works of art in the lower price ranges',[7] which would be offered for sale within two or three weeks of their consignment rather than the two or three months at King Street. In admitting the necessity of finding ways to sell less expensive works of art at a quicker pace, Christie's could not have acknowledged more clearly the growing threat of Phillips; and the remarkable success of Christie's South Kensington has shown how lucrative the bottom end of the antiques market can be.

Christie's new auction rooms are located in the premises of Debenham and Coe, whose managing director Bill Brooks became joint managing director of Christie's South Kensington with Paul Whitfield from Christie's furniture department. Debenham and Coe had itself been the result of an amalgamation in the late 1960s of the Covent Garden auctioneers Debenham Storr, founded in 1813, with Coe's, which had begun trading earlier this century. A number of elements from the old partnership were carried into the new company, notably the sales of modern costume jewellery, watches and gems which had always been Debenham Storr's speciality. Although Christie's have re-decorated the premises, the jewellery sale-room has changed little and the same highly professional audience of East End jewellers gathers there for the weekly sales. It is still just as bewildering for a private bystander, as the dozen or so dealers comprising the average audience look on with apparent disinterest as handfuls of rings, watches or necklaces are knocked down at a great rate to an unidentifiable 'Mr P.B.' for what appear to be extraordinarily low prices. Occasionally an otherwise indistinguishable lot may produce some aggressive shouted bidding from the back of the room and a flurry of activity in the front two rows, leading to a price of a couple of hundred pounds or so, indicating that all the previous glittering prizes were mere imitation. During the first year of operation, Christie's South Kensington sold over 18,000 lots of jewellery, more lots than were sold by any other department.

Christie's also made certain that the cavalier qualities of Bill Brooks as auctioneer were utilized in the new premises, although his assimilation into the 'establishment auctioneers' seems to have taken some of the cutting edge from his auctioneering technique. In Debenham and Coe days spectators used to attend sales just to applaud Brooks's witticisms from the rostrum, especially as actual bidding involved the risk of attracting public attention as a result of comments from the rostrum. The best protection was to use the pseudonym 'Brooks', because that usually provoked the friendly comment, 'Ah, what a very good name.' The most dangerous thing was to venture an uninvited interruption of Brooks in full swing, as happened on one occasion when a West End carpet-dealer called out a bid of £420 after Brooks had asked for £450. Brooks responded cuttingly, 'You obviously don't want this lot but do come to one of my evening parties; I give them every Saturday and you can learn how to be generous.' Brooks used to exhort his audience the whole time, threatening to turn on the fire-extinguishing sprinklers if people would not wake up and start bidding more quickly; and most of the time announcing the lots in a deep, rolling, music-hall voice, emphasizing the wrong syllables of such words as 'epidiascope' so as to make it sound like a character from Dickens. With the smart new lighting and fashionable repainting of the Christie's régime, Bill Brooks is denied the pleasure of remarking over the top of his quarter-spectacles, 'Sold to the bidder in the gerloooom, which might possibly be Mr Stern.'

Regulars also miss the basement sales of second-hand furniture which included office desks, fridges, modern suites, indeed almost anything which Coe's was asked to sell. This part of the business passed on to Lots Road Auction Rooms which now attracts the old Debenham and Coe customers, an odd combination of chain-smoking Cockney landladies picking up three or four Dralon-covered suites every week for £50–60 each and harrassed young Chelsea mothers hoping to buy a Victorian mirror or Windsor chair for a few pounds.

The impact of the Christie's management is clearly demonstrated by the improvement in turnover, from Debenham and Coe's annual average of £750,000 to the £2,250,000 turnover during Christie's South Kensington's first year. Despite the expenses of the initial purchase and the structural alterations, Christie's announced a small operating profit during this first year; and with double the turnover in the second year and a negligible increase in staff and overheads, the project immediately justified itself with sizeable profits. Certain specialized sales, such as costumes, textiles and fans, mechanical music, and photographic images, were moved to South Kensington from King Street, and there is little change in the structure of these sales which produce a substantial income. In most of the other categories (of which there are eighteen in all, producing over 250 catalogues a year), the material sold at Christie's South Kensington would not previously have been handled by Christie's at all; and the average price per lot is under £50. It is interesting to note that Christie's do not apply the buyer's premium in their new premises, which still operates under the old commission structure with a selling-commission of 15 per cent and, unlike Bonham's and Phillips, with no minimum charge per lot. This structure is popular with the dealers, who strongly objected to paying the 10 per cent buyer's premium to the auctioneer, especially for the lower quality goods where the profit margins are narrower. The removal of a minimum charge is equally attractive to both buyer and seller, as it means that individual lots can sell at only a pound or two without creating a net loss for the owner.

The main attraction at South Kensington to both private and professional seller is the speed of turn-around, and even Christie's admit that 'quite a number are insisting on having their pieces sold at South Kensington'[8] rather than at King Street. Most items are sold within three weeks of consignment, and payment of sale-proceeds is normally made no more than ten days after that. It is a refreshing change from the sometimes exhausting procedure of selling at Christie's King Street, or at Sotheby's, where the owner frequently has to work hard to secure even an estimate within three or four weeks, while the sale itself may be three or four months after that, by which time the expert may have changed his mind about the value of the object in question and may be suggesting a reduced reserve. At times the frustrated vendor cannot help feeling that the minimum of a month between the date of sale and payment of sale-proceeds simply gives the auctioneer an interest-free loan. The gap of only three weeks between the consignment and sale at Christie's South Kensington inevitably means that the majority of catalogues are unillustrated and cannot circulate to advantage outside the South of England, thus relying almost entirely on the London dealers for buyers; however, sellers find this theoretical disadvantage is more than compensated for by the speed of payment, and by the attraction to buyers of there being no buyer's premium.

While emphasizing the difference between South Kensington and King Street, it is nevertheless immediately apparent on entering the new Brompton Road premises that the two are part of the same firm. The same 'Sloane Ranger' secretaries and assistants answer queries on both premises, and with the increase of staff and turnover Christie's South Kensington has lost some of the qualities of the erstwhile Debenham and Coe, where all the porters seemed to know the answer to every question without reference to an expert or to a voluminous central registry. There is now a professional quality about the catalogues, and bargain-hunters can no longer hope to find many unspotted rarities, as the whole of Christie's international expertise is on hand for consultation.

Christie's is always thought of as the most traditional of auctioneering houses, but this imaginative takeover of Debenham and Coe and unhesitating entry into the more commercial end of the auction business shows that Christie's Board has no intention of merely relying on its established reputation. It is particularly interesting to note that in its second year Christie's South Kensington's turnover exceeded that of Sotheby's Belgravia, which had been operating for over five years on a similar staff of about forty. Perhaps the age-old adage that Christie's are gentlemen trying to be entrepreneurs and Sotheby's are entrepreneurs trying to be gentlemen, should actually be reversed.

7

The Specialist Auctioneers

There used to be many more specialist auctioneers in London than there are now, and even in the 1960s there were still totally independent auctioneers of wine, ivory, antiquarian books, arms and armour, and jewellery. The hardiest survivors amongst the specialist auctioneers seem to be Edward Barber and Son[1] who auction brushes and bristles; and the Tea Brokers Association[2] which still hustles through 300 lots an hour every Monday morning. These City auctions are most entertaining for any auction buff, but neither tea nor bristles quite fall within the category of collectable works of art. Specialist auctioneers in this category have mostly been ousted by the big four fine art auction houses, who regularly split the antique atom into ever smaller specialist sales. All the same there are three areas—stamps, carpets, and printed ephemera, including cigarette cards and postcards— where the small specialist auctioneers still dominate the London market.

The silver and ceramics collector tends to forget about the massive international market that has grown up in stamps, many of which are in every sense of the word 'works of art' as well as being technically 'antique'. The first adhesive stamp appeared in England in 1840 and stamps began to be collected in the 1850s, but postal history itself goes far further back and stamp auctions now even include antiquities such as Babylonian seals which were arguably a kind of postage stamp. Now that the leading London stamp auctioneers, **Robson Lowe** of Pall Mall, have a yearly turnover in excess of £5,000,000, Sotheby's must regret its failure to take advantage of the precedent it set in 1872 in holding the first-ever stamp auction in London. Regret may have been tempered with despair when in 1968 Robson Lowe announced an official association with the Christie organization.

Robbie Lowe himself is the doyen of stamp auctioneers, a man whose constant good humour and still boyish enthusiasm for collecting stamps brings him into personal contact with other enthusiasts throughout the world. It is a purely personal triumph that even though Robson Lowe publicly vilifies the 'investor' in stamps as opposed to the 'student collector', and charges one of the highest commissions in London, the firm is still the fastest growing in the stamp world.

Robbie Lowe began serious trading in stamps while still at school, making a record £150 profit during his last term which encouraged him to go straight into business on his own in 1920. By 1926 Robson Lowe Ltd had become a registered company, and six years later the first of Robbie Lowe's many and valuable publications appeared. The first auction by the firm in 1936 broke completely new ground, for it was devoted to postal history, a collecting subject which had in effect been created by Robson Lowe himself. Indeed the title was actually patented by him and he is still the most knowledgeable expert in the world on the intricate histories of the private postal services and curiosities of the eighteenth and early nineteenth centuries. His wife's favourite reply to incessant telephone callers is, 'I am afraid I can't disturb him now, he's upstairs playing with his hussies.'[3] Hussy, as many will know, had his own private issue of postage stamps and Robbie Lowe has a large collection of these.

The move to Pall Mall in 1940 was followed in 1948 by his purchase of Bournemouth Stamp Auctioneers which for many years, until the auctions in Basle were fully established in the early 1970s, remained the backbone of his expanding business. Robson Lowe admits to the wicked wish, during the first week of August every year, that it might rain so that holidaymaking fathers could slip off and introduce their sons to his special summer stamp auctions. With further offices now in Italy, Bermuda, and Australia, and with representatives in thirteen other countries, Robson Lowe supplies a service in the stamp field which is unparalleled. Apart from extensive activity in publications, other special services supplied by Robson Lowe include the Trustee Auction Service, which involves the appointment of a particular expert within the firm to look after and advise the owners or trustees of important collections; and the Busy Buyers Service, which sends cuttings and auction references to subscribers on specific topics. Robson Lowe International Ltd has the distinction of never having been involved in the purchase of stamps on its own account; and also of advising against investing in stamps unless the buyers have already established a genuine collecting interest. In the stamp auction world, as in the fine art auction market too, most auctioneers are constantly called on for investment advice, and most other stamp auctioneers are also constantly involved in the purchase and sale of stamps on their own account or for subsidiary companies.

Stamp auctions themselves are conducted in a very similar manner in all the London auction rooms, and they present to the outsider an unusual combination of professional speed and efficiency, together with a surprisingly informal relationship between auctioneer and bidders. Everyone entering the auction room is obliged to register his name and address beside an individual number in the visitors' book, and as the auctioneer speeds through at least 150 lots an hour the buyers are referred to by this number. The dealers and collectors remain relatively subdued, concentrating on making careful pencil notes of all the prices and occasionally reaching into their large briefcases to pick out a reference book to check their strategy for an approaching lot. The auctioneers at Robson Lowe (plate 33), as at many of the other stamp auction rooms, know almost every buyer by name. Indeed they seem to be on Christian-name terms with most of the 300 registered stamp-dealers in London, often making comments from the rostrum like, 'Are you through, Fred?' or encouraging the bidders by saying, as happened recently, 'Come on, someone, say something sensible and save my breath', at which a dealer obligingly called out '£35', and the auctioneer replied, 'Bless you, Bill'.

A stamp auction catalogue is fully comprehensible only to a collector, even though the glossary and instructions are often printed in a number of languages. The amateur's confusion arises

Plate 23

Sotheby's flair for creating news-worthy events is evident at this sale of costumes and sets from the Diaghilev and de Basil Foundation at the Scala Theatre, 1968. The backdrop is Picasso's design for Cocteau's *Le Train Bleu*

4

by's modern
ss approach is
k contrast to
mises, where
sical instru-
expert still
in an old-
ed *ambience*

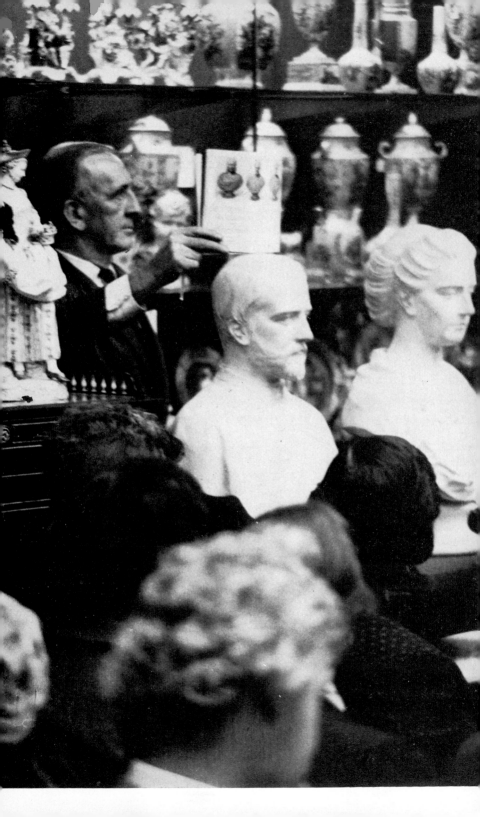

(*Opposite*) A porter indicates the lot being sold at Sotheby's Belgravia,   *Plate 25*
which specializes in the period 1830–1930

(*Above*) Sotheby's front counter, where people can bring their   *Plate 26*
treasures to be valued free of charge. In the foreground – Julia Clarke,
the young *objets de vertu* expert, with a client

Plate 27

The frontispiece of an early Phillips catalogue

A
CATALOGUE
OF

The capital, genuine, and valuable Collection

OF

PICTURES,

The PROPERTY of

Sir Joshua Reynolds, Bart. dec

LATE PRESIDENT OF THE ROYAL ACADEMY;

COMPRISING SEVERAL FINE SPECIMENS OF THE WORKS OF

TENIERS, VANDYCK, RUBENS, POUSSIN, REMBRANDT,
BASSAN, TITIAN, CASTIGLIONE, &c. &c.

WHICH, BY ORDER OF THE EXECUTORS,

Will be SOLD *by* AUCTION,

By Mr. H. PHILLIPS

At his Great Room, 67, *New Bond-Street,*

On TUESDAY, MAY 8, 1798,

AND FOLLOWING DAY,

At ONE *o'Clock each Day.*

May be viewed by Catalogues (at ONE SHILLING each) to be had as above: of
LLOYD, Bookseller, Harley-Street; Mr. VARLEY, York Hotel, Bridge-St
Blackfriars: and of Mr. PHILLIPS, at his House, No. 22, BURY-STRE
St. James's.

Plate 28

Portrait of Harry Phillips, one of James Christie's clerks who founded his own auction house in 179

Plate 29

(*Opposite above*) The new galleries at Phillips's main premises in Blenheim Street, off Bond Street

Plate 30

(*Opposite below*) One of the two enormous new sale-rooms at Phillips's premises in Salem Road, off Queensway, W2

Bonham's façade in Montpelier Street, near Harrods, after the recent addition of an extra floor

Plate 3

Nick Bonham, Managing Director of the family firm, in aggressive mood in the rostrum

Plate 3

A recent auction sale in progress at Robson Lowe, the largest firm of
stamps auctioneers in England, now associated with Christie's

Plate 33

Plate 34

Stanley Gibbons's
premises in the Strand, to
which the firm moved
in 1893

Plate 35

Cataloguers at work in the
basement of Hodgson's
Rooms in Chancery Lane,
taken over by Sotheby's
in 1968

not so much from the fact that the descriptions are full of abbreviations and jargon such as f.a.c. (forwarding agent's cachet), c.d.s. (circular date stamp), traffic light block, *tête-bêche* or phosphor-graphite sets, but from the sheer complexity of a subject that makes so many subtle distinctions and boasts so many different categories. The newcomer is grateful for the precise single-figure estimates printed beside each lot, but these are so often wildly and inexplicably exceeded that stamp-valuing these days seems to be no easier than valuing pictures or furniture.

Of all the different specialist sales, the most interesting for outsiders are the postal history auctions which are now mounted by all the auctioneers, following Robson Lowe's pioneering work in this field. The expert description of these much-travelled letters or envelopes of the early nineteenth century gives a marvellous sense of times past. Some of them have passed through countries at war or in civil rebellion; others have enjoyed the honour of a maiden voyage on a new steamship or locomotive. All the varied histories are recorded in stamps, dyes and cancellations. All the same, no item of postal history has quite the romantic attraction of the British Guiana 1856 one cent penny black on magenta stamp, fondly billed as the most valuable stamp in the world; the only known example is in an anonymous collection in America, at a theoretical valuation of £200,000. This locally printed stamp was found by an English schoolboy on a visit to British Guiana in 1873 and sold to a local collector for six shillings; it last appeared at public auction in the Ferrary sale in Paris in 1922, when it was bought by Arthur Hind for £7,300.

As a result of the famous catalogue which has appeared without a break since its first publication in 1865, the best-known name in the stamp business is **Stanley Gibbons**, but the firm's entrance into the auctioneering of stamps is a fairly recent event, first in partnership with Harmer Rooke from 1958, and then in 1968 with the joint reconstruction of the company under the name of Stanley Gibbons Auctions Ltd, in Russell Street, Covent Garden. Harmer Rooke had held their first auctions in 1901, but Stanley Gibbons himself started trading stamps at a desk in his father's pharmacy in 1856. Edward Stanley Gibbons was born in 1840, an auspicious year for the birth of a future stamp-trading magnate,

6

for it was this same year that Rowland Hill initiated his Uniform Penny Postage scheme to be paid for by the world's first adhesive postage stamps, the Penny Black and the Twopenny Blue. One of the young Gibbons's early trading *coups* was the purchase from two sailors in 1863 of a sackful of triangular Capes for only £5. The sailors had apparently won the stamps at a raffle in Cape Town, and included in the haul were the rarest examples in mistaken colours, such as Penny Blues and Fourpenny Reds. These are now worth thousands of pounds each, and Stanley Gibbons was forced to sell them in sheets of a dozen at three shillings a sheet. Even at these bargain prices, Gibbons still succeeded in disposing of the sailors' £5 sack for nearly £500.

By 1874, when Stanley Gibbons moved to London, he had set up an efficient source of supply of stamps from all over the world, and there is an amusing record of his receiving a letter from a West Indian postmaster denying the existence of a stamp Gibbons had asked for, but pre-paying his courteous reply with a specimen of the stamp in question. With successes like these behind him, it is hardly surprising that on retirement in 1890 Stanley Gibbons was able to sell the business to the Phillips family for £25,000 plus 6 per cent debentures; three years later the new company, Stanley Gibbons Limited, moved into 391, the Strand (plate 34) premises that are still at the centre of its international trading.

The business advanced rapidly with the foundation of a number of new publications, as well as foreign offices such as the Buenos Aires branch which Frank Phillips was shipped off to run in 1910. His principal discovery was the South African stamp collection of Miguel Gambin, at a purchase price of £6,000. This was a considerable amount of money when compared with the price of £6,160 which was paid in New York in 1910 for Rubens's *Ixion Deceived by Juno*, now in the Louvre; or £945, for which Christie's auctioned a perfectly genuine Canaletto of the Doge's Palace in the same year. Another member of the Phillips family, Ernest, son of the Managing Director C. J. Phillips, started in the same year the business of selling those packages of stamps which still delight the schoolboy collector. After retiring, the founder spent his time travelling around all those countries in the world which could boast a postal service of sorts, and some account of his travels appeared periodically in the *Monthly Journal*, including details of the occasion when he bought up the complete stock of a provisional stamp at the Post Office in Wadi Halfa on the edge of the Sudan, at that time under Anglo-Egyptian jurisdiction and therefore within reach of the Imperial Postal Service. Stanley Gibbons died in 1913, the year before the firm was honoured by being appointed Royal Warrant holders to the 'Philatelist King, George V, an enthusiastic collector and student of stamps of all countries that composed the vast Empire over which he reigned.'4

Stanley Gibbons Stamp Auctions continues the parent company's tradition of regular development of new commercial outlets, and some of its experts are now available for consultation on such fringe subjects as postcards and cigarette cards. A number of lots to interest ephemerists now appear in postal history catalogues. In May 1976 the firm held an auction of militaria at the Imperial War Museum in Lambeth, and proved themselves to be highly competent in cataloguing medals and maps—as well as items within their traditional line of expertise, such as an envelope addressed to a British trooper who was killed at Custer's Last Stand. This empty envelope might have been a sad disappointment to an expert in the manuscripts department at Sotheby's, but to the postal-history fanatic it was worth £750 because of its various postage stamps and inscriptions, including the original franking from Margate on 30 July 1876, the re-addressing to the Bighorn Expedition, and the final inscription 'Dead'. On the back of the envelope there is a further inscription from 'the Dead Letter Office', reading 'To be returned to writer:— John S. Hiley was killed in Battle of Little Big Horn River Mt. June 25 76'.5 There was also the date stamp of Fort Abraham Lincoln, sending the letter on its way back to the dead man's relative in Margate.

In December 1974 Stanley Gibbons Auctions poached on the preserve of its rival Robson Lowe by holding an auction of reproduction 'die' proofs of the sensational forger Jean de Sperati. Robson Lowe himself had done much of the original research in identifying Sperati's fakes, had secured Sperati's stock for the British Philatelic Association, and had published a catalogue of his work in 1955 shortly before Sperati's death. At

a yearly sale total of about £5,000,000 auctions now account
for 20 per cent of the Stanley Gibbons Group turnover. The
auctioneers can also pride themselves on having sold a single
stamp for £50,000—the Bermuda 1854 Postmaster's Provisional
Penny Red on a complete letter. The only other known example
of this is in the Queen's collection.

The two oldest extant firms of stamp auctioneers in the country
are **Plumridge and Co** of Adam Street, the Strand, founded in
1898; and **H. R. Harmer Ltd** of New Bond Street, which was
founded in 1919 when Henry Harmer broke away from his
brother. Plumridge's, although the oldest, is the smallest of the
four main London stamp auctioneers but its expert staff of four
produce ten good auctions a year, which are held in the Strand
Palace Hotel. Harmer's hold as many as seventy sales a year, with
a turnover of over £2,500,000 in the 1977/78 season excluding
the auctions in Sydney and New York. A most refreshing feature
of their London auctions is the provision of mid-morning tea for
thirsty bidders; while the auction remains in progress the tea is
handed round in Apsley Pellett white pottery cups decorated
with the Harmer emblem in blue.

The collecting of coins requires a similar kind of dedicated
attention to variations of date and detail as the collecting of
stamps, but it naturally has a far older collecting history as ancient
coins were eagerly studied and collected in the Renaissance period.
The first regular coin auctions in London were started at Sotheby's
in the 1820s and Sotheby's experts were pre-eminent in this
specialized auction field for a hundred years after that. However
as Sotheby's began to concentrate more on wresting control of
auctions in the fine arts from Christie's, the firm of **Glendining**
was able to establish the lead in coin auctions that it maintains
today. Although Glendining has technically been part of the
Phillips organization since soon after the War, it still operates
almost entirely independently of its benevolent owners. The
Glendining rooms, tucked in on the ground floor of Phillips's
Blenheim Street premises, are a peaceful haven from the constant
toing and froing of the rest of the firm.

Cigarette cards, less exalted in origins than the Roman Imperial coinage, are nevertheless collected with equal enthusiasm and expertise. The established literature on the collecting of cigarette cards shows that there is a greater complexity in the variations of title, lettering and date than the casual observer could ever imagine; and up and down the country enthusiasts are to be found devoting years of research to the production of final, definitive lists of certain pre-1918 sets, particularly the legendary Taddy's series. The vast increase over the last two years in the collecting of postcards suggests that this subject will also soon have a literature to match that of cigarette cards; and both fields are already served by specialist auctioneers in London—Ken Lawson of the **Middlesex Collectors Centre** for postcards; and the **London Cigarette Card Company** and **Murray Cards (International) Ltd**, for cigarette and other trade cards. All three hold auctions in the York Chambers of Caxton Hall, Westminster, and an observer at these sales sees considerably more of the real qualities of collecting than are any longer apparent at many West End auctions, where concern for 'investment' often entirely overwhelms the natural pleasures of collecting.

Caxton Hall is one of the Londoner's favourite venues for civil weddings, so the Saturday morning viewer of cigarette-card auctions often finds that on windy days he must first contend with a tornado of confetti whipping around the corner of Caxton Street, and must then circumnavigate an unruly family photograph group that sways on the steps beneath the Edwardian portico. It is a day for the exchange of expertise at the long trestle-tables set out with 400–500 lots, as respected collectors from all over the West of England gather in London for the auction. The room divides into constantly changing groups of collectors in eager discussion; from time to time collectors halt in their rounds to consult heavily thumbed notebooks full of detailed numerical lists, the bones of their collection. The atmosphere is of course completely different from the art dealers' palaces in the West End. Here woollen cardigans replace pin-striped suits and flasks of tea and sandwiches are produced instead of mock champagne and canapés. But there is the same, if not a greater, air of excitement, the same mystique of expertise, and the same steely edge of cut-throat competition beneath the surface camaraderie. This too is an hierarchical world in which two or three venerable collectors give audience to a stream of young acolytes, seeking the benefit of their experience.

Cigarette-card auctions are fraught with danger to the amateur. First, at the view there is the problem of returning a set of fifty cards to the tight cellophane band from which it was so casually removed. With an embarrassed grunt the novice hands them over to a frowning attendant, who slips them back instantly with a practised hand. Then follows the auction—and the temptation to bid recklessly on anything below £10, especially after a paper-bag from a Taddy's tobacconist sells for over £4, making one's purchase of a whole set of Ogden's 'Birds of Paradise' seem extremely cheap at £8·50. Not so, apparently, as a stage-whisper three rows back announces, 'Good Lord, that's nearly twice the catalogue price.' Too late one learns that, as at Stanley Gibbons with stamps, the London Cigarette Card Company produce a detailed priced catalogue of their stock which has become the standard price-reference work. The newcomer should also be warned that an enjoyable afternoon, with what seems at the time like the occasional bid of a pound or two, can easily end up with the shock of a bill of over £50. Listen to the voice of experience.

The London Cigarette Card Company was founded in 1933 by Colonel Charles Lane Bagnall, DSO, MC, TD, who also produced in 1950 the first catalogue of *British Cigarette Card Issues 1888–1919*. For the last ten years of his life the Colonel was unable to take an active part in his professional hobby and the company was controlled by his formidable daughter, the doyenne of the card world, Dorothy Bagnall, who has recently appointed Ian Laker to a directorship of the LCCC and made him, in effect, her heir-elect. Until recently Miss Bagnall still took most of the sales (see page 26), very much the benevolent monarch and given to using the oldfashioned auctioneer's phrase 'Going, going, gone', which is heard so seldom these days.

It is important to remember that neither the LCCC nor Martin Murray's auctions, nor indeed Ken Lawson's postcard sales, are strictly open auctions, for all three are principally dealers in their fields, and a high percentage of the lots in each auction is actually from their own stock. As auctioneers they are scrupulously honest and never take advantage of the many inexperienced bidders who recklessly stick their hands in the air and leave them there until after the hammer falls. All the same, the auctioneer-dealer's stock necessarily has protected values, and this often annoys other dealers who feel that the minimum figures may be unrealistically high and that many private buyers may be unaware that these are not strictly free auctions. However a high proportion of the lots in cigarette-card auctions are always sold, often below the printed estimates, and the sales are conducted with an openness that clearly precludes deception. Martin Murray is particularly forthright about his dealing status, admitting that this is the principal part of the business, and even advertising in his auction catalogues for particularly rare issues which he wishes to purchase privately. At the time of writing, the two highest recorded auction prices for one complete set of cigarette cards are £2,000 and £1,900, which were paid for different sets of Taddy's Clowns at Martin Murray and Sotheby's Belgravia respectively. A single card has been sold at auction in Preston for £105, a rare example from Wills Advertising series.

The Middlesex Collectors' Centre postcard auctions also take place in the York Hall, but they are normally held on Monday evenings so that customers avoid the Saturday crowds of football match policemen clambering in and out of coaches outside New Scotland Yard—as well as the wedding receptions. These auctions are also presented in finely detailed catalogues with realistic estimates. With the interest in postcards growing daily, the pattern of the auctions changes all the time; but at a typical sale in September 1976 503 lots were knocked down in three and a half hours for a total of £3,450. The sale was attended by over 100 collectors and dealers, but more than half of the first hundred lots were sold to postal bids, often without a single bid from the room, while only seven or eight lots failed to sell. In fact over the whole sale there were only sixty separate buyers in the room, and 100 different postal buyers, making the auction itself rather dull from the point of view of spectator-sport. With rumours that a single card has been sold in the trade for as much as £500, and the record at Sotheby's Belgravia of one Mucha postcard securing £75, my purchase at this MCC/SPA auction of nine novelty cards for only £4 seemed relatively cheap. This novelty lot included a large cut-out of a mackerel which opened up to a concertina of small views of the seaside; attached to it by string was a mini-luggage label for the address, captioned 'An O-fish-al Souvenir of Folkstone'. Another one bore the label, 'The latest catch from Garelochhead'.

The first **Ephemera Society** auction does not strictly qualify for inclusion in a book on the London auction rooms, for it was held in a rose garden in Hampshire on a Sunday afternoon in the middle of the 1976 summer heatwave. The most prominent sale-room notice warned the audience to beware of the bees in one corner of the garden, and the most important sale-room announcement reminded people not to leave their modern paper ephemera lying around but to put it in the wastepaper baskets. But since then the society has held a number of sales at various venues in London, including a sale of posters at Sotheby's Belgravia which, unlike many of the others, was also open to non-members. Its inclusion here amongst specialist London auctioneers can therefore be justified.

The first sale was a tremendous event, comprising nearly 250 lots of ephemera of all kinds, including such items as a French firearms permit of 1832; the first number of the *Wipers Times*, only 100 of which were issued; 'Grocer's wrapping-paper Lincolnshire circa 1910';[6] a broadside sheet announcing the services of a stallion in 1843; and a railway timetable of the Baltimore to Potomac line in 1878. All the lots had been consigned by members of the society and were immaculately displayed during the morning in the ballroom of a member's house. At lunch-time everyone dispersed to various corners of the garden and adjoining wheatfields for picnics, reassembling at 2.30 in the rose garden for the auction. The auctioneer, a member of the Ephemera Society who normally wields his ivory hammer in Sotheby's rostrum, was seated at a card-table on top of a kitchen-table placed in the shade of a yew tree. The audience found it less easy to keep in the shade, and the bidders were consequently dotted about the garden, recumbent in long grass or deck-chaired in the shade of the potting-shed sixty yards away. Halfway through the sale a Portobello book-dealer reminded the auctioneer of his presence by raising an arm from the middle of an azalea hedge, and the lot was 'sold to the gentleman behind the bush'. A little later parrots in a cage at the end of the garden began whistling to attract the attention of their captive audience, but mercifully refrained from breaking into speech and confusing the auctioneer even more. Several junior members of the Society were there, one boy bidding confidently for the trade letterheads by replying to the auctioneer's questioning glance 'Yes, all right', 'Yes, all right'. The enjoyable thing about such occasions is not just the auction itself but the gathering together of a group of enthusiasts from all over the South of England, who spend the day in excited discussion of their extraordinary collections, exchanging addresses with new-found contacts. It is always possible at such meetings to find a sympathetic ear for any problem, even that of one lady in satisfactorily displaying her massive collection of printed paper napkins.

London carpet auctions, despite the appearance of being sophisticated social gatherings, do not serve a wide public and are really just an elaborate form of direct trading. The auction has proved itself to be a highly successful way of disposing of works of art, and for this reason several carpet-trading organizations regularly employ this method for selling their stock. While carpet auctions, especially those of Lefevre and Partners, are interesting to attend, it is important to realize that these auctions differ from those of the independent auctioneers on two significant points. Firstly, a high percentage of or even all the lots can belong to the auctioneer himself; secondly, substantially less than 50 per cent of the lots are normally sold to bidders in the room. There have even been London carpet auctions at which more than 70 per cent of the lots have failed to find any buyers at all, and yet the auctioneer-dealer presumably manages to make profits sufficient to cover the not-inconsiderable overheads of mounting auctions.

Potential buyers at specialist carpet auctions in London should approach these sales as though they were in a shop, because there is normally a minimal amount of genuine competitive bidding, except from commissions. Carpets are seldom sold at much less than the bargaining retail price, and often at rather more because of the apparent auction competition. Another unusual feature in many of these sales is the auctioneer's announcement that all lots are sold without reserve, but that he has the right to withdraw any lot which does not realize a 'realistic' price. This happens quite frequently in certain sales, as the auctioneer finds it impossible to manufacture fictitious buyers lot after lot and has openly to 'withdraw' one or two carpets at prices just below the published 'estimates'.

The important sales at **Lefevre and Partners**, previously the Persian Carpet Galleries, are a delight to view for the connoisseur—or anyone who enjoys seeing fine carpets. The catalogues, with sentences like 'the extraordinary flourish of artistic endeavours . . . stands as a tribute to the great artistry and craftsmanship of the Moors',[7] and with frequent quotations from the embullient Arthur Upham-Pope, may seem a little exaggerated compared with the sombre tones of Christie's and Sotheby's, but the rugs and carpets are described with an accuracy of date and attribution that has not yet been consistently achieved by any of the big four fine art auctioneers.[8] Lefevre catalogues are not only beautifully illustrated and presented, they are also full of all the information that a carpet collector could require, particularly as regards a detailed assessment of the state of repair and condition of the rare early carpets in which they specialize. For example, even in a comparatively ordinary sale in 1974 an attractive little Yomut prayer-rug was dated clearly to the mid-nineteenth century, its form and colour described in recognized terms, and its condition openly acknowledged with the printed description, 'the pile is a little low in parts and the selvedge has been replaced.'[9] Oriental carpets and rugs are notoriously difficult subjects for the European to master, and expertise of this quality is of inestimable value to the collector.

Rippon Boswell is an old-established firm tracing its foundation to the year 1884, and the London office is now at the head of an influential carpet auctioneering and importing company with offices or associates in Frankfurt, Basle, Sydney, Hong Kong, Nassau, New York, Paris, Tokyo, Rotterdam, Singapore and Toronto. The company has wide-ranging contacts and has been directly involved in many novel projects in the international carpet trade, including an organization called 'The Union of Association Brotherhood and Guild of Persian Knotting' which showed films of the tribal weaver in Iran and was said to be selling directly on behalf of the weavers themselves. Most of Rippon Boswell's auctions are held in the ballroom of the Hyde Park Hotel in Knightsbridge, and the various auctioneers, sipping gin and tonic through the sale and launching into German or French to satisfy foreign clients, fit smoothly into their surroundings. Each rug is introduced with a dissertation on its qualities, and the porters are frequently required to turn the carpets around to show the silent audience the closeness of the knotting. The particular stylistic characteristic of one rug was described, somewhat confusingly, as 'making this even more unique' and about another lot the auctioneer warned the audience that 'this might be the last Brussa you'll ever see'.

David Hansford's auctions of contemporary carpets and rugs are mounted in a similar style in various London hotels, and the announcements in the Press normally carry an eye-catching slogan such as 'A delayed export consignment ordered for immediate disposal in this country . . . this unusual auction represents a unique opportunity to acquire beautiful and valuable Oriental rugs . . .'[10] Again the auctioneer can be carried away by his own persuasive rhetoric into making statements such as 'a unique Quoom . . . a Quoom like this with the background is really quite unusual'; or 'an exquisite investment the Gold Daloutabad, some sort of unique item, you don't see them very often'. Unlike Lefevre, who supplies a certificate for each purchase confirming the catalogue description, Hansford has the identical confusing conditions of sale as Rippon Boswell. Condition 6 reads 'The vendors guarantee that all items offered are authentic, genuine and handmade', and is largely gainsaid by condition 7, 'The Auctioneer and Vendor accept no responsibility for the correct description of any item, and are not responsible for . . .

any statement made as to origin, date, age, provenance or condition . . .'[11]

Hodgson's Rooms in Chancery Lane have been part of Sotheby's since 1968, but they maintain their own highly individual style and they merit inclusion in this chapter as the only auction room remaining in London which specializes exclusively in books. Most of the auctions are taken by W. B. Hodgson, a direct descendant of one of the founding partners. Hodgson is still addressed by the older retainers as 'Mr Wilfred' and until quite recently the experts were summoned from the cellars (plate 35) by the sale-clerk's sharp stamp on the hessian-matted floor. Robert Saunders set up the firm in 1807, and was well enough established by 1823 to be entrusted with the sale of Garrick's library. Edmund Hodgson was taken as partner in 1826 and two years later the firm moved to larger premises at the corner of Fleet Street and Chancery Lane. By 1863 the firm had transferred a few doors up the street into the building which it still occupies, with the traditional floor-to-ceiling shelves along the two long sides of the room crammed with books, which can range from sixty-four volumes of the transactions of the Ophthalmological Society to a collection of George Orwell first editions. Unlike at any other Sotheby auction room, the dealers at Chancery Lane are allowed to smoke during the sale and they sit there in the light, airy, rectangular room puffing on their pipes while making gruff offers for selected lots.

None of these specialist auctioneers ever enjoyed quite the same reputation as **Steven's Rooms** in Covent Garden, founded in 1776 as a book auction house but specializing after 1830 in botanical and zoological specimens under the inspiration of J. C. Stevens.[12] Some wonderful sales are recorded, such as the 1855 disposal of the animals from the Surrey Zoological Garden at which it was possible to pick up an elephant for £336 and a pelican for £18 10s. J. C. Stevens died while mounting the rostrum to take a sale of orchids, which were always a speciality of the firm, especially during its most prosperous period from 1870 until its closing sale in 1939.

With the London auction houses growing bigger and bigger, and the regular threat of an amalgamation between Christie's and Sotheby's, Phillips and Bonham's or any combination of the four, there is a great anti-monopolistic need for the survival of the old specialist auctioneers.

8

The Smaller Auctioneers

The local auction is a typically English institution. Played at its best, the auction game requires that exaggerated degree of phlegmatism, which comes naturally only to an Englishman. Of course there are numerous auctioneers on the Continent and in America, but the basic quality is different as a Frenchman really looks on the disposal of household effects in public as a little coarse; the Italian finds it a suspiciously straightforward way of doing business and therefore suspects the worst of everyone involved; and the American turns every auction into a public carnival. In England, the auction is a standard feature of town and country life, the local estate agent and auctioneer taking his place in the community alongside the local solicitor and doctor. It is rather different in Central London, as the specialist auctioneers as well as the big four fine art auction houses with their international clientele serve a broader commercial purpose; but London is also full of smaller auction houses that sell anything and everything, and largely serve the residents of their locality.

In the last few years, several of the favourite haunts of bargain hunters in Central London have closed down due to the inexorable rise of rates and rents—Druce's of Baker Street, Knight Frank and Rutley, and the Army and Navy being the most notable casualties. Now that Debenham and Coe has amalgamated with Christie's, Harrods is the only old-fashioned secondary auction house of this kind remaining. However, on venturing out of Central London the picture is quite different, and there are almost as many auctioneers as there are Underground stations. All these auctioneers mount regular sales of household effects, second-hand commercial goods and miscellaneous properties consigned by order of the liquidator or local magistrates' courts; and each has its own character and charm. Many of them also occasionally offer highly respectable antique furniture and works of art. It is not possible to describe here every such firm and a few have been selected to give an overall impression of the local auctioneer, from Hounslow to Barking, from Tooting to Cockfosters, from Watford to Bromley.

For dealers and collectors living in Fulham or Chelsea, and especially for foreigners, a visit to one of these smaller auction houses has the quality of a long journey even if it is actually only a mile or two outside the City. The effect of distance is heightened by using the Underground, which summarily ejects the adventurer into completely new surroundings, where the first thing noticed is the fact that the station itself, instead of being just a dark hole in the base of a vast office block, is a detached building dominating the immediate neighbourhood. The recent aesthetic rehabilitation of the 1920s and '30s means that the geometric patterned brickwork, thin steel-framed windows, and pastel ceramic tiles of outlying tube stations now demands as much serious appreciation as private villas in the Sessionist suburbs of Antwerp or Brussels.

One local High Street is much like another, with many of the same shops, the same crowds of housewives pushing prams loaded with packaged food, the same streams of traffic circulating endlessly through the over-populated South-East of England—a similarity and familiarity that is frightening in many ways. The local auction rooms also differ very little from each other in appearance, and each is filled with its own very similar, but totally new, group of habitués who wander about chatting to each other and the porters as though in an isolated village instead of Greater London. Even though the visitor's presence is seldom acknowledged by anything more than the occasional questioning glance of the auctioneer, he invariably feels as conspicuous and intrusive as a Christian in Mecca.

Any sense of being alien soon retreats before the more confident hope of making a discovery amongst the bric-à-brac and broken furniture. Even at the auctions devoted entirely to office equipment and second-hand furniture, the enthusiast lives in the hope of finding a Mies van der Rohe chair or one of Ringo Starr's limited-edition polished steel tables removed from the suburban palace of a bankrupt property speculator. A collector accustomed to the measured tones of a Christie's catalogue may need a little practice before being able to sort out the jargon of the secondary rooms, having to wait till the lot is called to discover that 'a walnut BRS' is a bedroom suite and has nothing to do with British Railways. Other unfamiliar cataloguese includes 'Qty sundries in box', 'three rolls of ditto', 'SP dish', 'a modern-style signed watercolour' and the explicit 'two old cups and saucers',[1] which is precisely what some of the more elaborate West End descriptions of 'enamelled decoration in Sèvres style' or 'of classical form indistinctly marked', are really saying. The most important abbreviation to be learned is the omnipresent 'a.f.' ('as found') which normally means that the piece is so badly damaged as to be irreparable. The tentative 'slightly a.f.' which is occasionally seen defies interpretation.

One of the most exciting, but by no means most typical, of the secondary rooms is **Forrest's** of Cobbold Road, Leytonstone, where there is a mammoth whole day sale of 'Antiques and Objets d'Art'[2] about every six weeks. Cobbold Road is just off Wanstead Flats in the East End, a large expanse of fields which used to be part of the marsh leading to the Thames Estuary but which is now a favourite training-ground for greyhounds and aspiring professional footballers. It is the kind of place where the bus conductress knows most of the customers on the midday bus and passes the current gossip from one East End enclave to the next. The auction room itself is beneath the arches of a viaduct over which the trains rush, leaving the crowd of auction-goers breathless with the noise and vibration. Inside it is all artificial light, the large auction gallery as wide as it is long. Smaller rooms at the side have arched ceilings, and one has for several months been the stall for an enormous stuffed moose standing two or three feet taller than a man. To the left of the entrance is the office, and to the right a tea and sausage-roll counter which sustains the professional through the 700–800-lot sales.

'Now this is rather exquisite,' calls the auctioneer about a lot tantalizingly described as 'Pair of oil paintings on canvas, sea-scapes signed and dated 1873',[3] which are pointed out on the wall near the front by one of the porters standing on the long dais. Several dealers begin to push through the crowd of a couple of hundred or so people, but the pictures are knocked down long before they can get to the front to read the signatures. The dealers grimace, again regretting their failure to come in the day before to view the many interesting lots, which seem to go quite cheaply to the regulars comfortably ensconced in deep, discarded, armchairs with their heavily marked catalogues. 'Now this is an important lot', enthuses the auctioneer, who constantly reproaches the audience for not bidding more aggressively and then delays the proceedings himself by forgetting everyone's name. The bidding opens at £5 and several familiar faces from the West End finish up bidding spiritedly against each other for some Art Deco glass. Perhaps bargains are not so easy to come by as one imagines.

Maxwell Miel's auction house in Palmer's Green is more typical of the suburban auction scene, with curious shoppers stopping in the High Street to peer in through the plate-glass window at the small crowded room. The auctioneer is seated at the principal lot of the morning, a Regency mahogany work-table, which is placed on top of a kitchen-table giving him a dominant view of his regulars. Like most Chartered Auctioneers—as opposed to the West End fine art auctioneers—he calls out the next bid before it has been offered, 'At six pounds then, six pounds? Sold then for five, Mr Jackson.' Maxwell Miel FSVS, FIBA, FRSH, FInst, PLA, runs a flourishing and extremely efficient business, with estate office branches in Edmonton, Southgate and Winchmore Hill; but in the traditional manner of the local auctioneer he cultivates a plaintive style from the rostrum, shaking his head in apparent disbelief at most of the prices and, with a wry smile, congratulating a regular for deciding to start the bidding at half the initial asking-price. The auctioneers at Miel's are also drawn irresistibly to making caricature comments on objects, such as 'a double-barrelled percussion shotgun'[4] which was introduced as 'an ideal birthday present for the mother-in-law'. Jewellery always commands competitive bidding at Miel's, with rings and necklaces securing £70 or £100 in quick succession, after a series of lots of porcelain and pottery at no more than £10—£15 a lot. Auctions at Camden Goods Depot (**Highgate Auctions**) are a particularly entertaining way of spending a Sunday afternoon, as one of the auctioneers, sustained by a glass of beer at hand and the occasional cigarette, excels in auction repartee of the traditional kind. A 'Newhall Chamberpot with Kingfisher Design'[5] is 'recommended for the morning cup of tea', and on selling 'five assorted necklaces'[6] for only 50p he remarks, 'I don't think you'll lose on that, Mr Collins, unless you trip yourself up.' The auction room itself used to be at the side of the Fairlight Hotel but the sales are now held in an old warehouse just above Camden Lock, conveniently near the Sunday market. On many afternoons now it is difficult even to squeeze in at the door, and prices have improved—despite the music-hall misprints in the catalogue. 'SP conjection dish and fork'[7]—'A what dish?' says the auctioneer.

In April 1976 Rosan's, the Croydon auctioneers, opened another premises in Covent Garden, the seventeenth- and eighteenth-century centre of the auction trade, but later in 1976 the auction house was purchased by Richard Duboff, Rosan's partner, who renamed the rooms **Harvey's Auctions Ltd.** Although the removal of the fruit and vegetable market from old Covent Garden has been accompanied by carefully controlled developments, there is no longer a true local community which Harvey's could serve, and the auction house relies on trade and litigation properties to fill this deep warehouse which has been converted into the Long Acre auction rooms. Auctions of some sort are held every other week and almost anything can turn up there, although a particular speciality is the regular section of antiquarian books.

Peter Bainbridge of **West London Auctions** in Ealing and Hounslow is the most ambitious of the local London auctioneers, with his Sunday collectors sales bidding for the custom of the ever-increasing bands of collectors of postcards, cigarette cards, coins, badges, photographs and ephemera. Bainbridge and his staff spend much of the week chasing around London for properties to improve the quality of the increasing number of sales, and with their immensely hard-working attitude to the normally unambitious life of the local auctioneer, and with their determined salesmanship, West London Auctions have a good-looking future.

The Hounslow auction room is on the flight path into London

Airport, and the three palm trees in the middle of Hounslow High Street near the auctioneers seem to have dropped from some much-travelled jumbo jet. The new premises in Ealing are distinguishable from those of less successful rivals by the greater density of walnut and mahogany furniture amongst the stacks, and by the relentlessly familiar repartee of the auctioneer at his perch in the high rostrum.

The king of the local London auctioneers, however, is still **Harrods Estate Offices** with its fortnightly three-day sessions of antique and modern furniture, pictures, prints, works of art, books, silver, jewellery and the 'Secondary Sale of Household Effects', all of which (except the last) are attended or viewed by a high percentage of the middle-range of London dealers. Harrods sales are the only survivals from the days when the Pantechnicon and the Army and Navy used to hold regular disposals of properties from their large depositories. Harrods sales continue to disgorge forgotten oddities from their warehouses—furniture and works of art which families have hoped one day to reclaim, but are finally obliged to sell merely to settle the mounting storage bill.

A trip to Arundel Terrace for the Harrods sales solves a problem that vexes many who listen to the Oxford and Cambridge Boat Race on the radio, and are amazed at how the crews shoot so quickly underneath Hammersmith Bridge after passing Harrods. The commentators are referring not to the Knightsbridge store itself, but to its Depository standing on the south bank of the river hard by the Bridge. The Depository is a vast, imposing, red-brick building whose twin terracotta turrets, elegant factory fenestration and monumental ceramic lettering above the château-esque main entrance would be strongly defended by the Victorian Society at any hint of alteration. It was built on the site of the Cowan Soap Works, its opening in 1894 being celebrated by a combined fête, festival and carnival, at which the varied entertainments included 'the Merry Mummers and their Seismic sensation the Earthquake', 'the refined music of the Criterion Hand Bell Ringers and Glee Singers', and 'Miss Taylor's most artistic groups of living statuary'.[8] In the evening a grand Ball was held, for which the riverside promenade was illuminated with thousands of lanterns and an elaborate early electric-lighting system. The handsome terracotta façade facing the river was originally intended to extend all the way to Hammersmith Bridge, which was opened in 1887 by Prince Albert Victor.

Harrods first regular auction sales were recorded in 1922 at Trevor Place, and a number of high prices were noted there before the war, particularly the 5,500 guineas for a Chippendale commode and 1,600 guineas for a Herat carpet. After the Trevor Place premises were directly hit by a flying bomb, the auctions were moved to Stackhouse Street where the government's post-war price-controls forced the auctioneer to halt the bidding once a certain figure was reached on a particular object, and to leave the final choice of purchaser to a draw of cards amongst the remaining bidders. The final move of the Auction Galleries to their present location at the Depository took place in 1968.

The visitor will be impressed by the uniformed security guard at the iron gates on Arundel Terrace leading on to the open parking-space with a flotilla of Harrods removal vans at one end. The auction takes place in three or four large rooms on the ground floor of the central warehouse, the auctioneer moving his pitch every time a particular section is finished. The three-day jamboree can amount to over 1,000 lots, and it is certainly well worth reserving a couple of hours on the Monday or Tuesday to view the sale. A typical sale early in May 1974 contained 1,030 lots catalogued in detail proportionate to the quality of the lot, varying from the studied expertise of 'A French 19th Century Provençal walnutwood cabinet, the top half having carved cornice with cupboards under fluted and turned columns, the lower half fitted drawers and cupboards, and having applied cornucopia, foliate scrolls and ribbons, 4ft 7in wide,' to the simple truth of 'Twelve cotton sheets'.[9] The Harrods auctioneers work under considerable pressure, for there are only 5 or 6 cataloguers together with the occasional outside consultant. The catalogue is produced between Monday morning and Wednesday afternoon when it goes to the printers; is posted to subscribers on Friday, and the furniture and works of art go on view on the Monday, two days before the sale. Given the fact that this fortnightly cycle goes on throughout the year, the quality of the cataloguing is extremely high.

The audience is highly professional and many dealers will have left commissions with the porters. The spaciousness of the ground floor of the Depository is a great attraction after the cramped quarters of most of Harrod's rivals, and even though the 'buyer's attention is drawn to the fact that Lots in this room cannot be viewed while the sale is in progress',[10] it is nevertheless still possible to steal a good look at most of the lots as they come up. Although this blind bidding may add to the drama of the auction room, it is extremely frustrating not to be absolutely certain whether a Wedgwood basalt figure is early- or mid-nineteenth century, the date being neither in the catalogue nor precisely discernible by scrutiny from three yards away behind the buyer's barrier.

Another group of smaller auctioneers concentrates almost entirely on second-hand domestic goods and property from the liquidator. **Henry Lewis and Co** of Kilburn advertise as exclusive auctioneers of liquidated property, with a special bent for clearing up unsuccessful dress manufacturers and boutiques. Henry Lewis takes most of the sales himself and gives a virtuoso performance of the forceful auctioneer, even when there are only half a dozen regulars in the room who have heard it all before. His auctions begin promptly, 'Right, let's get on with it, there'll be no mucking about here,' and for the first few lots he concentrates on getting his audience into the mood. Sometimes he instructs the porter to open up one of the packaged blouses 'because some of you are not accustomed to seeing quality'. 'There'll be a lot more people here soon, so don't think you'll have it all your own way,' he says to the six people in the auction room. Sure enough there soon arrives a posse of buyers led by a broad-shouldered character in a wide-brimmed trilby and expensive overcoat. The newcomer has obviously not been to the rooms for some time, for he is greeted effusively by the auctioneer. However the pleasantries do not last long and Lewis then reverts to his normal more aggressive style. At one stage he even threatens to leave the rostrum altogether and close the sale, saying he could sell 'the large and important range of ladies' quality day, evening and casual wear in exclusive fine-quality fabrics and styling'[11] far better 'down the Lane' on a Sunday morning. 'I'm stopping soon actually', he says and then leans over confidentially to the porter to tell him in a stage whisper, 'If they can't be bothered to bid then I'm not wasting my time here.'

Henry Lewis and Co do only liquidated property, but there are a number of auctioneers in Soho who include such property along with their normal trade—for example **A. Stewart McCracken**, who specializes in catering equipment, or **Frank Bowen** who handles almost anything but generally has a good line in office equipment. Bowen's is in the very middle of Soho and customers make their way from Oxford Street or Regent Street past 24-hour strip joints and rows of lighted bell-pushes with provocative notices. For the last half-hour of viewing, before the sale begins at 2 o'clock, the rooms are crowded with a variety of buyers. A Sikh in a raspberry silk turban sensibly test-feeds a calculating machine with sums to which he knows the correct answers, while less mechanically-minded buyers abstractedly press the keys of typewriters and teleprinters in the hope that the machine will mysteriously reveal whether it works or not.

The sale starts with a number of motor-cars belonging to bankrupt companies, and a well-fed Persian student tries to persuade the porter to guarantee the condition of the Receiver's Rover Saloons and Alfa Romeos at the garage in Bethnal Green. Near the end of a recent sale there were a few lots sold 'By order of the Trustee Re: P.L.M., deceased in bankruptcy',[12] which marked the sad end of a smart young man who had owned thirteen suits, nineteen pairs of size 10 shoes and a seemingly endless supply of freshly laundered shirts. Most poignantly reminiscent of past glories were the cricket and golf bags which contained a number of sporting trophies, several of them inscribed with the young man's name which was so carefully concealed in the catalogue.

Dowell Lloyd and Co Ltd operates from smart blue-and-white-painted premises facing Putney Bridge on the corner of the High Street, and sells both second-hand manufactured goods and a certain amount of furniture and works of art. The auctions are all held in the basement, and the furniture and household effects are ranged through a labyrinth of cellars with progressively lower coved ceilings, ending in a dank pile of broken divans and wardrobes suffering from the cellars' proximity to the Thames. The **Lots Road Auction Galleries** are located towards the end of the King's Road, just round the corner from Bonham's secondary rooms, and have a similar turnover to Dowell Lloyd, but on a larger scale. Although the Galleries were founded recently, in 1975, they have already become a favourite hunting-ground for collectors of 1940s cocktail cabinets—as well as the army of landlords with furnished flats, who constantly replace crockery, beds, fridges and almost every kind of household appliance from the fortnightly Tuesday evening sales.

For the sale-room fanatic, every auction has an irresistible fascination, whatever is being sold. Within 15, or even 5, miles of Marble Arch there are more than enough auctions every week to satisfy even the most dedicated auction-goer, and each one has its own special character and charm.

9

A Guide to the London Auction Rooms
for Buyers and Sellers

The individual qualities and characteristics of the London auction houses have been described in detail in the preceding chapters, where the professionalism, honesty, expertise and world-wide influence of the London fine art auction market is acknowledged. The following general advice on the practice of buying and selling at auction, and the detailed information about the individual services, rates of commission and operation of the different firms, is here presented in note form for easy reference. The commission structure of the major rooms has recently been altered, and is therefore likely to remain stable for several years; but other information in the guide may be subject to change. The public galleries of all the London auction rooms are open free of charge, both during sales and during views, to all members of the public.

General Advice for Sellers

1. It is advisable to insist that important and valuable works of art are included in specialized sales with other items of quality, which will receive world-wide publicity. The time of year of the sale does not matter, merely its quality.
2. For items of low value, notice should be taken of the minimum selling-commission per lot charged by some auctioneers, which can sometimes be a high percentage of the item's value.
3. For important collections or single masterpieces the seller is in a strong negotiating position, as all the London auctioneers compete for these properties and will often be prepared to make considerable reductions in the selling-commission. It is worth remembering that many auctioneers make an automatic reduction in selling-commission to dealers.

4. Sellers should always enquire carefully into the various charges that may be levied in addition to the commission, such as photographic charges, insurance, carriage, etc.
5. Make sure that a sensible protective reserve is placed on every lot sold at auction, and where possible seek an outside opinion as to value before fixing the reserve.
6. It should be remembered that the paintings and works of art which regularly secure the most competitive prices are those which have been in private hands for many years, and it is extremely damaging to the subsequent auction-prospects of a work of art if it has previously been offered privately to a number of people in the trade, or if it fails to find a buyer at auction because of an excessive reserve. Many auction houses charge a substantial commission on lots which fail to reach their reserve.
7. All auction houses recover VAT charges on their commission.
8. Before delivering large pieces check the day, time and place of acceptance. Also secure an approximate estimate of sale-room value (via photographs) before going to the expense of engaging a removal firm.
9. Try to attend the pre-auction view, in order to ascertain that your property is still in good condition and is well placed on the view.
10. There is no direct taxation at time of sale, but private sellers who are British residents are liable to capital gains on single lots selling at net price of £2,000 or more.

General Advice for Buyers
1. Before leaving commission bids try to view the sale, or ask for specific information about condition as this is seldom printed in the catalogues.
2. Beware of bidding solely against high reserve prices or, as happens occasionally, against the owner bidding in the room. On valuable pieces it is advisable to conceal any interest you may have in it. If a large commission bid is to be left, then it is safest to communicate this direct to the sales-clerks, commission box, or to a personal contact within the firm.
3. Remember that a buyer's commission (up to 10%) is charged

by many auction rooms and there can also be VAT charged on the hammer price of lots as indicated in the catalogues, these lots being sold by antique dealers who are not operating the special scheme.

4. Try to clear furniture and large works of art promptly, as a storage charge is often levied on delayed collections.

5. Many auction houses automatically charge interest on lots unpaid for after a certain date. Credit arrangements are always possible for major purchases, but it is advisable to discuss these with the Managing Director or Finance Director before the sale.

6. The experts are available on request for detailed discussion about any item in forthcoming sales. Regular buyers at auction should cultivate a relationship with the experts at the auction houses in their particular fields.

7. Care should be taken to discover whether the auctioneer has a personal interest in the items being sold, or indeed is the outright owner. This need not necessarily be a disadvantage to buyers but it does alter the complexion of the sale.

8. Very few of the London auction houses actually give a binding guarantee of authenticity but all the major fine art and specialist auctioneers will, in order to protect their reputation, cancel the sale of a work of art that was radically miscatalogued, even though their conditions of sale disclaim all responsibility. It should be pointed out, however, that it is often difficult to secure expert agreement on matters of authenticity and attribution.

9. Catalogue subscriptions to specialized categories of sale are usually available.

10. Bidders should remember that lots can be re-offered immediately after the hammer has fallen, and if the auctioneer has failed to notice a bidder he should not hesitate to intervene. Also, if a lot is mistakenly knocked down to someone who is not bidding, he should immediately contest this on the fall of the hammer, and the lot can be re-offered.

11. Buyers of pictures, sculpture and other attributable works of art should take careful note of the glossary of terms in the front of the catalogue, as there is an established convention by

which the major auction houses indicate the firmness of their attribution to a particular artist. The convention normally adopted is that firm attributions have been ascribed only to those paintings, sculpture, etc, where the artist's surname, titles and Christian names, are printed *in full*. Thus the description of painting as by 'Rubens' in fact means that the cataloguer believes that the picture is definitely *not* by Rubens, indeed is not even of the same period, but is merely a later pastiche. The smaller sale-rooms also have their own catalogue jargon which should be learnt.

12. After-sale price lists are produced by many auction houses and on some of these lists (notably Sotheby's) lots which failed to sell are not included.

General Characteristics of the Four Principal Fine Art Auctioneers

1. Most lots are sold with some kind of protective reserve, but this is an entirely confidential matter between the seller and the relevant expert. Estimates are either printed with the catalogue or are available on enquiry.

2. All four of the major auctioneers either employ or have access to specialist experts in all fields, and their services in London are backed by international organizations.

3. Transport and shipping can be arranged, as can restoration and insurance valuation.

4. Anyone can bring any work of art in at any time for free advice about its disposal at auction, including its identification and verbal valuation.

5. Forthcoming sales are usually announced in the *Daily Telegraph* on Monday and *The Times* on Tuesday; they will also often be advertised in *Apollo*, *The Connoisseur*, the *Burlington Magazine*, *Art and Antiques Weekly*, *Collectors' Guide*, the *Antiques Trade Gazette* and many other journals and specialist magazines.

6. Commission bids are accepted without charge.

7. The auctioneers act as agents only and do not buy or sell works of art on their own account. The one partial exception to this rule is Sotheby's, which occasionally purchases works of art from clients when all other methods of securing the sale

have failed; some goods also revert to the ownership of Sotheby's when a special guaranteed price is not reached, and these goods would subsequently be sold at auction in the name of Sotheby's.

8. Inspection visits to clients' homes are made by all the auction houses, and although small charges are theoretically made for this, in practice this is supplied free to anyone whom the experts assess may have important works of art to sell.

9. The conditions of sale are similar for all four houses, with full protective disclaimers against all disagreements from buyers and sellers, and categorical assertions that all descriptions are to be taken as opinions and not as facts—that is, the accuracy of attributions is not guaranteed. All four major auctioneers will cancel the sale of a 'deliberate forgery', but Sotheby's is the only firm that offers an official five-year guarantee of authenticity. The auctioneer reserves the right to refuse bids or to accept certain properties for sale at will.

10. House-contents sales—all four have periodic house-sales.

CHRISTIE'S

Main sale-room:
Christie, Manson and Woods Ltd
8 King Street, St James's
London SW1Y 6QT
Telephone 839 9060
Telex 916429

Secondary sale-room:
Christie's South Kensington Ltd
85 Old Brompton Road
London SW7 3JS
Telephone 581 2231

I. *Opening times:* open 9.30 to 5.00 p.m. Monday to Friday. No sales in August or September, but open for receipt of goods.

II. *Types of sales:* specialist sales in all areas of the fine and decorative arts including such peripheral subjects as wine, veteran cars, model steam-engines (sales held at the Brighton and Hove Engineereum, Holdstone Pumping Station, Neville Road, Hove). All the major sales are held in King Street; the sales of less important material are at Christie's South Kensington, including certain specialist fields such as costume, Staffordshire pottery, and mechanical music. Christie's wine department's offices are at 15 King Street. All stamps are sold by Christie's associates, Robson Lowe of 50 Pall Mall, London SW1Y 5JZ, telephone 839 4034, telex 915410.

III. *Number of sales:* approximately 350 a season at King Street and 250 at Christie's South Kensington.

IV. *Turnover:* season 1976-77 £66,414,000 sold
(internationally, including unsold lots)
season 1977-78 £89,106,000 sold
(internationally, including unsold lots)

V. *Staff:* about 250 in London, some 70 of whom are employed in an expert capacity. Two outside consultants are regularly used.

VI. *Offices and agents in the British Isles:* exclusive agents in Edinburgh, Glasgow, Argyll, Limerick, York, Kirkby Lonsdale, Bridgnorth, Templecombe, Downpatrick, Corbridge and St. Austell.

VII. *Foreign offices:* permanent foreign offices or agents in 13 other countries; auctions held regularly in Geneva, Rome, Amsterdam, and Australia; large auction rooms opened in New York in May 1977.

VIII. *Company structure and affiliated companies:* in 1973 Christie's became a public company and Christie, Manson and Woods Ltd, under the chairmanship of J. A. Floyd, now wholly owned by Christie's International Limited. The first chairman was I. O. Chance. Subsidiary companies include White Bros who print the Christie catalogues, and

Christie's Contemporary Art which produces and markets
contemporary prints. Christie, Manson and Woods
Ltd has 35 directors, all in full-time employment, and
the majority of them are senior experts in specialized fields
of the arts.

IX. *For Sellers at Christie's*
   (a) *Delivery:* everything except furniture and large bulky
   collections should be delivered to relevant auction room
   during normal opening hours; appointment not necessary but advisable if particular expert required for on-
   the-spot estimation. All furniture and carpets to be
   delivered Monday to Friday (but Monday to Wednesday preferred) to Hudson's Depository, No 1 Building,
   Victoria Station Approach, Wilton Road, London SW1.
   No furniture to be delivered without prior arrangement
   with the furniture department in King Street.
   (b) *Inspections:* expert staff available to call on owners and
   advise with a view to sale. There is no standard charge
   for this service and it is normally supplied free in
   London if the client will agree to pay for the expenses;
   and at a negotiable fee plus expenses for visits outside
   London. Fees are refunded if goods received for sale
   within one year total over £1,000.
   (c) *Seller's commission and charges:* 10% of the hammer
   price, except for wines, coins and medals which are
   15%. A charge of 5% of the hammer price is paid on
   all lots failing to reach their reserve (2½% above £500).
   The selling-commission at Christie's South Kensington
   is 15% and a charge of 10% of the approximate value is
   made for goods withdrawn before the auction. In
   practice, the vendor's commission is negotiable on
   important properties and trade terms of 6% are
   offered to all dealers. The only extra charge is for
   insurance, which is not at a fixed rate. For an experimental period there are no catalogue illustration charges
   or advertising charges. (NB. *There is a buyer's premium
   of 10% at King Street, but not at South Kensington.*)

(d) *Sales procedure:* items are normally included in a sale 10 to 12 weeks after their receipt, and client is informed by catalogue of forthcoming sale. Sales advice notice is sent immediately after the sale and payment of sales-proceeds within a month. At Christie's South Kensington items are normally included in sales within 2 or 3 weeks of delivery, a catalogue is sent to owners 3 days before the sale, and payment is made within 14 days of the sale, providing the buyer has settled his account.

X. *For Buyers at Christie's*

(a) *Sales programme:* auctions are held Monday to Friday, October to July, and they normally begin at 11.00 a.m. Monday—European or Oriental pottery and porcelain, and Oriental works of art; Tuesday—*objets de vertu,* coins, watches and scientific instruments, antiquities, and watercolours, prints and drawings; Wednesday—silver and jewellery, books and manuscripts; Thursday—furniture, clocks, bronzes, rugs and carpets, and wine; Friday—pictures. (This is the normal programme, though there are variations and there is by no means a sale in every category every week.) The lots are on view for at least 3 working days prior to the sale. Christie's is not open for viewing on Saturday, but every week-day from 9.30 to 5.00.

(b) *Buyer's premium:* in King Street sales a buyer's premium of 10% of the hammer price is charged to all buyers (no premium on wine, coins or medals). At Christie's South Kensington there is no buyer's premium.

(c) *Payment and clearance of purchases:* no lots can be cleared during the sale, and all pictures and furniture not paid for and cleared by the Wednesday week following the sale are taken to Hudson's Depository, No 1 Building, Victoria Station Approach, London SW1, and a charge of £1 per lot is made for transport and a further £1 per month or part-month for storage.

At Christie's South Kensington a charge of £1 per lot per day is charged on furniture and pictures not collected within 3 days of the sale. Christie's reserve the right to charge interest of 2% above the bank-rate on all lots not paid for within 2 days of the sale, and to resell any lot not paid for within 6 months of the sale. New buyers are requested to make themselves known before the sale.

(d) *Catalogues:* all catalogues can be obtained on yearly subscription. They are divided into 58 categories for King Street (all catalogues £509), 12 categories for South Kensington (all catalogues £295), and 13 categories for Overseas. For detailed lists, apply to Catalogue Subscription Department, White Brothers Printers Ltd., Offley Works, Prima Road, London SW9 ONB. Every catalogue subscriber receives a free copy of the monthly *Forthcoming Sales* pamphlet. The catalogues are normally printed one month in advance of the sale.

(e) *Commission bids:* bids may be placed by telephone but should officially be confirmed in writing or by telex. These bids are normally executed by the auctioneer or the sales clerks and there is no charge.

XI. *Further services at Christie's*

(a) *Valuations for insurance, Probate or Family Division:* detailed inventories, produced at a charge of 1½% up to £10,000, 1% from £10,000 to £100,000, ½% from £100,000 to £200,000, and ¼% thereafter. Minimum charge of £10 in London and £20 outside. Living expenses also charged at £5 per day plus travelling expenses.

(b) *Estate duty and Capital Gains Tax advice:* Christie's have one director specializing full-time in this field.

(c) *Introductory commission:* a commission of 4% is payable to those dealers introducing property for sale to Christie's.

SOTHEBY'S

Main sale-room:
Sotheby Parke Bernet and Co
34–35 New Bond Street
London W1A 2AA
Telephone 493 8080
Telex 24454

Sale-room specializing in period 1830 to 1930:
Sotheby's Belgravia
19 Motcomb Street
London SW1X 8LB
Telephone 235 4311

Sale-room specializing in books:
Sotheby Parke Bernet and Co
Hodgson's Rooms
115 Chancery Lane
London WC2A 1PX
Telephone 405 7238

I. *Opening times:* Open 9.00 to 4.30 Monday to Friday.
No sales in August but open for receipt of goods.

II. *Types of sales:* Specialist sales in all areas of the fine and decorative arts, including stamps (in the US) and veteran cars. The same specialized sales as Christie's. All lesser-quality or badly damaged goods are passed by arrangement to another London auction house for sale (at the time of writing, the Sotheby association is with Harvey's of Covent Garden). All paintings and works of art dated after 1830, except Continental, modern British and contemporary paintings, prints, drawings and sculpture, and jewellery, coins, medals, arms, armour, books and manuscripts, are sold at Sotheby's Belgravia.

III. *Number of sales:* Approximately 340 a season in Bond Street, 90 at Motcomb Street and 20 at Chancery Lane.

7

IV. *Turnover:* season 1976-77 £123,937,000 sold net
(internationally)
season 1977-78 £161,097,000 sold net
(internationally)

V. *Staff:* about 460 in London, 110 of whom are departmental experts. 13 outside consultants are engaged on a
regular basis.

VI. *Offices and agents in the British Isles:* full-time repre-
sentatives in Edinburgh and Dublin. Associations with
Sotheby-Bearne in Torquay, Devon and Sotheby Beresford
Adams in Chester.

VII. *Foreign offices:* the US organization of Sotheby Parke
Bernet is about the same size as the London branch of the
firm, and sales are held regularly in New York, Los
Angeles and Toronto, with offices in Texas, Massachusetts,
Florida and Virginia. There are permanent Sotheby offices
and agents in 14 other countries, and auctions are held
regularly in Monaco, Hong Kong, Amsterdam (at Mak van
Waay, wholly owned by Sotheby's), Florence, Zurich,
Frankfurt, Johannesburg and Madrid (at Saskia Sotheby,
part ownership of Sotheby's).

VIII. *Company structure and affiliated companies:* in June 1977
Sotheby Parke Bernet Group Ltd became a publicly quoted
company, the principle subsidiaries of which are Sotheby
Parke Bernet and Co (Sotheby's in London) and Sotheby
Parke Bernet Incorporated (Parke Bernet in New York).
Sotheby's, the London company, has, at the time of
writing, 48 directors, 16 assistant directors and 4 Associates,
the majority of whom are art experts, under the chairmanship of Peter Wilson CBE, who is also chairman of the
parent public company.

IX. *For sellers at Sotheby's*
(a) *Delivery:* all porcelain, bronzes, carpets, works of art,
paintings, books, etc to be delivered to Bond Street
(or Motcomb Street if dated later than 1830) between

9.30 and 4.30, Monday to Friday. Furniture to be consigned to Sotheby's Warehouse, 21 Lillie Road, London SW6 1RS (385 2306) Monday to Wednesday 8.00 to 4.30 (closed 1 to 2); it should be noted that furniture will not be accepted on Thursday or Friday as other furniture is being collected for the weekly sales, and appointments should be made for the delivery of a large consignment on the other days.

(b) *Inspections:* experts will visit clients in their homes at a charge of £6 within 2 miles of the London office, £12 up to 100 miles from London, £15 between 100 and 200 miles, and £20 over 200 miles; plus travel and subsistence expenses. These fees are refunded if £1,000-worth of property is received within 3 months of the visit.

(c) *Seller's commission and charges:* the commission is 10% of the hammer price, with the exception of wine, coins and medals. For wine it is 15%, and there is a minimum charge per lot of £7·50 for coins and medals. Unsold lots are charged buying-in commission of 5% of the final hammer price. Other charges include insurance at 50p per £100, illustration in the catalogue (from £200 for a colour plate to £8 for a small black-and-white plate), and special advertising on agreement. (NB: *there is a buyer's premium of 10%.*)

(d) *Special commissions:* Sotheby's openly acknowledge that the commission is negotiable on important properties, particularly with regard to including all the expenses and buying-in charges in a standard rate of commission. Further than that, it has been possible to negotiate a guaranteed price with a higher rate of commission if this price is exceeded, and even an outright purchase agreement. Sotheby's is also willing to find a private buyer for direct sale if requested. All property sold by dealers is offered at a reduced vendor's commission of 6%.

(e) *Sales procedure:* the same system is employed at all three of Sotheby's London auction rooms, items being

included in a sale from $2\frac{1}{2}$ to 5 months after arrival
(catalogues go to the printers exactly 2 calendar months
before the sale). A pre-sale advice note, and then a
catalogue under separate cover, are sent to each owner,
about 3 weeks before the sale. Sale-proceeds are paid
exactly 30 days after the sale, although the company
reserves the right to withhold payment if the purchaser
has not paid. Currency can be brought forward the day
after the sale if requested.

X. *For buyers at Sotheby's*
   (a) *Sales programme:* auctions are held Monday to Friday,
   September to July, and they normally begin at
   11.00 a.m. The sales schedule for Bond Street is
   Monday—books and manuscripts, antiquities, eth-
   nographical, glass, *objets de vertu*; Tuesday—European
   or Oriental pottery and porcelain, Oriental works of
   art, arms and armour, Old Master drawings; Wednesday—pictures, wine; Thursday—silver, jewels, watercolours and prints; Friday—furniture, clocks, bronzes,
   rugs and carpets. At Sotheby's Belgravia, Tuesdays—
   pictures; Wednesdays—furniture; Thursdays—silver,
   pottery, porcelain, glass and Oriental works of art;
   Fridays—Art Nouveau and Art Deco, and photographs.
   Chancery Lane book sales on Thursdays. Each sale
   will be on view for at least 3 days, and viewing is from
   9.00 till 4.30.
   (b) *Buyer's premium:* in all Sotheby's London sales a
   buyer's premium of 10% is charged (except for wine,
   coins and medals).
   (c) *Payment and clearance of purchases:* usually at Bond
   Street, and always at Sotheby's Belgravia, lots can be
   paid for and cleared during the sale (at Bond Street
   payment to the sales-clerk in the auction room; at
   Belgravia to the cashier and collection from the basement). All furniture not collected immediately after the
   sale will be removed to Evan Cook Limited at 404
   North End Road, Fulham, S.W.6. No charge for

collection before Thursday following the sale, thereafter charge of £4 for the first week and 30p per lot per week after that (lots are not insured at Evan Cook and can only be released on production of a note of authority or payment-receipt from Sotheby's). Sotheby's reserve the right to charge interest not exceeding 0·05% per day for lots not paid for within 7 days, and automatically charge interest at 2% above the bank rate on all lots not paid for within 30 days of the sale. New buyers must either make prior arrangements or wait 5 working days for the clearance of their cheques before being allowed to remove purchases. Credit arrangements can be made available.

(d) *Catalogues:* catalogues are normally printed 3 weeks in advance of the sale and are available on yearly subscription divided into 45 categories for Bond Street (all catalogues £442) and 9 categories at Sotheby's Belgravia (all catalogues £92). *Preview,* a monthly illustrated brochure of forthcoming sales, can be sent on subscription of £5 per season. For application form, contact Catalogue Subscription Department at the Bond Street address.

(e) *Commission bids:* these can be placed by telephone or telex and should be confirmed in writing. No member of Sotheby's staff is allowed to bid personally in the rooms; all commission bids are executed by the auctioneer or the sales-clerks, and there is no charge.

XI. *Further Services at Sotheby's*

(a) *Valuations for insurance, Probate or Family Division:* full descriptive inventories at charge of 1½% up to £10,000, 1% from £10,000 to £100,000, and ½% thereafter. Revaluations at half the standard charge. Minimum fees of £10 for items brought into the office, £15 for those in Greater London, £20 for those in the country; plus travel and subsistence expenses.

(b) *Taxation and investment advice:* the tax experts at Sotheby Minet Financial Services Ltd are available for discussion on all matters relating to art and taxation. Sotheby's also act in an expert advisory role to the British Rail Pension Fund, in the purchase of works of art for long-term investment.

(c) *Introductory commission:* a commission of 40% of the net commission earned from the vendor is payable to antique dealers, estate agents and auctioneers, banks and official advisers for the introduction of property for sale at Sotheby's.

(d) *Works of art course:* Sotheby's runs a 9-month course for 50 students every year, 3 to 5 of whom normally join Sotheby's staff and another 20 of whom secure work in the art trade. The course covers every subject handled by Sotheby's, and currently costs £1,500. Application forms are available from the counters and should be returned marked for the attention of Derek Shrub, before the end of April. The course starts in October.

(e) *Packaging and forwarding:* a comprehensive service is internationally available through the subsidiary company James Bourlet and Sons Ltd.

(f) *Picture framing and conservation:* available through another wholly owned subsidiary, J. J. Patrickson and Sons Ltd.

(g) *American Real Estate:* Sotheby's founded a company in New York in 1971 to handle the sale of American real estate, and the company became active in the market early in 1976.

PHILLIPS

Main auction room:
Phillips
Blenstock House
Blenheim Street
London W1 OYAS
Telephone 629 6602
Telex 28604 ref 302

Secondary rooms:
Phillips West 2
10 Salem Road
London W2 2BU
Telephone 221 5303

Household Goods, etc:
Marylebone Auction Rooms
Hayes Place
Lisson Grove
London NW1
Telephone 723 2647

I. *Opening times:* 8.30 to 5.00 Monday to Friday (but certain departments closed for lunch), and 8.30 to 12.00 Saturday. Sales all the year round.

II. *Types of sales:* in their 3 auction rooms, Phillips have the facilities to handle all types of works of art and household effects. At Blenheim Street there are specialist sales of all kinds of pictures, paintings and works of art; at Salem Road weekly sales of less important furniture and works of art, specializing particularly in furniture; at Lisson Grove second-hand furniture and household effects. Phillips are proprietors of Glendining, the coin auction specialists who operate from the Blenheim Street premises.

III. *Number of sales:* approximately 500 a year at Blenheim Street, 50 at Salem Road and 80 at Lisson Grove.

IV. *Turnover:* season 1976-77 £21,506,908 sold in London
season 1977-78 £23,865,505 sold in London

V. *Staff:* according to information supplied by Phillips they employ about 120 people in London, 60 of whom are specialists; and they have 3 regular consultants.

VI. *Offices and agents in the British Isles:* Phillips have a comprehensive network of associated or wholly owned auction houses throughout the British Isles, Phillips in Knowle, Hepper House in Leeds, Phillips in Edinburgh and Glasgow and in Dublin, and Jollys of Bath.

VII. *Foreign offices:* offices and sales in Montreal, Geneva, New York, Toronto, Ottowa, Boston and Amsterdam.

VIII. *Company structure and affiliated companies:* still a private partnership with unlimited liability, under the chairmanship of Christopher Weston, with 5 other directors and 2 associates.

IX. *For sellers at Phillips*

(a) *Delivery:* all period items to Blenheim Street, with prior warning requested for delivery of large consignments of furniture. On goods delivered without sufficient sales instructions, Phillips reserve the right to a minimum warehousing charge of 25p per day, and goods not collected within 3 weeks of request for notification can be sold to defray costs. Other deliveries to Salem Road and Lisson Grove.

(b) *Inspections:* experts from London and provincial offices are available for selection visits. There are no fixed charges, but these are normally about £10 plus expenses in the London area, and the fee is refunded if it leads to a sale of more than £1,000 within 3 months.

(c) *Seller's commission and charges:* vendor's commission is a uniform 10%, with a minimum charge of £4 per lot whether sold or bought in. Other charges—50p per £100 for insurance. Phillips do not normally charge for advertising or illustration in the catalogue but the client 'is invited to contribute to costs'. Trade terms are offered and the commission is negotiable for important properties.

(d) *Sales procedure:* items for the weekly sales (furniture and works of art, silver, paintings, ceramics) are sold within 2 to 3 weeks, and for other sales within 4 to 8 weeks. Seller is sent a notification of each sale his goods are included in. Sale-proceeds paid 14 days after the sale, although Phillips reserve the right to withhold payment if there is a danger that purchaser may default.

X. *For buyers at Phillips*

(a) *Sales programme:* auctions are held Monday to Friday at 11.00 a.m. and 2.00 p.m., viewing 9.30 to 4.30 at least two days previously. Phillips West 2 open 9.00 to 7.00 the day before the sale. The precise sales schedule is announced to the public a year in advance, and the normal days are, Monday—paintings, and secondary furniture and works of art; Tuesday—furniture, carpets, clocks, bronzes, etc; Wednesday—ceramics, glass, and Oriental works of art; Thursday—furniture and works of art at Salem Road; Friday—silver, and household goods at Lisson Grove.

(b) In all Phillips London sales a buyer's premium of 10% is now charged (except for wine, coins and medals)

(c) *Payment and clearance of purchases:* purchases can be paid for and cleared immediately after the sale, and the auctioneers reserve the right to charge 25p per day on all lots not cleared within 2 days of the sale.

(d) *Catalogues:* catalogues for Lisson Grove and Salem Road are printed 5 days in advance, and for specialized sales at Blenheim Street up to 4 weeks in advance. All catalogues are available on yearly subscriptions in 34 categories, applications to Blenstock House.

(e) *Commission bids:* can be placed with the porters as well as the auctioneer or sales-clerk, and it is normal to give the porter a small gratuity on successful bids.

XI. *Further services at Phillips*

(a) *Valuations for Insurance, Probate or Family Division:* Full service supplied throughout the British Isles and abroad, charge 1½% up to £10,000 and 1% thereafter, plus expenses and VAT.

(b) *Introductory commission:* a commission normally amounting to 20% of commission earned by the auctioneers is payable to recognized professional firms and certain dealers for introduction of property for sale.

BONHAM'S

Main auction rooms:
W. & F. C. Bonham and Sons Ltd
Montpelier Galleries
Montpelier Street
London SW7 1HH
Telephone 584 9161/9
Telex 916477
      916341

Secondary auction rooms:
New Chelsea Galleries
65-69 Lots Road
London SW10
Telephone 352 0466

   I. *Opening times:* 9.00 to 5.30 (Lots Road 8.30 to 5.00) Monday to Friday throughout the year.

  II. *Types of sales:* at the Montpelier Galleries, regular sales of books, arms, armour, carpets, ceramics and works of art, clocks, furniture, furs, pictures, silver, jewellery, cars, and wine; and lesser items of all sorts including household effects at Lots Road.

 III. *Number of Sales:* about 260 a year at Montpelier Street and 90 at Lots Road.

  IV. *Turnover:* season 1976-77 £6,033,190
              season 1977-78 £7,541,400

   V. *Staff:* about 75 in London, 20 of whom are cataloguers.

  VI. *Offices and agents in the British Isles:* offices or agents in Scotland (Perth), East Anglia (King's Lynn), Nottinghamshire (Langwith), the West Country (Cheltenham) and the South West (Axminster).

 VII. *Foreign offices:* Bonham's have an office in Geneva and in the past have announced plans to open one in New York.

VIII. *Company structure:* Bonham's is still a family firm, 5 of the 9 directors being directly related to the chairman Leonard Bonham. The Managing Director is Nick Bonham.

IX. *For sellers at Bonham's*
(a) *Delivery:* small properties can be brought to Montpelier Street for inspection any time between 9.00 and 5.30, and at Burnaby Street between 9.00 and 4.00, except on Tuesdays. Clients are advised not to bring ceramics, works of art or watercolours on Wednesdays or oil paintings on Thursdays, as the experts are normally busy at the auctions.
Consignments of antique furniture are accepted at the basement warehouse (Cheval Place) of the Montpelier Galleries between 9.00 and 5.00 on Wednesdays, and small consignments also on Thursdays and Fridays.
(b) *Inspections:* fee for inspection visits, £6 in London, £12 plus expenses within 30 miles, £18 plus expenses for up to 100 miles from London, and by arrangement thereafter. The fee is refunded if it leads to a sale totalling more than £1,000 within 3 months. Bonham's have their own van which is available for collections in the London area at a small fee.
(c) *Seller's commission and charges:* vendor's commission is 10% at Montpelier Street (except for furs and costumes which are 12½%) and 12½% at Lots Road. Vendor's commission for dealers is 5%. There is a minimum charge per lot at Montpelier Street of £4 and at Lots Road of £2. Any lot not reaching a reserve suggested by Bonham's is charged for at £2, or 3% if the reserve is placed by the client. All items valued at less than £5 are insured free of charge, the remainder at a charge of 50p per £100, minimum charge of 13p. There are no other charges except statutory VAT on the commission. (NB: *There is a buyer's premium of 10% on everything but wine and furs.*)

(d) *Sales procedure:* property is normally included in a

sale within 3 to 5 weeks of its consignment (6 to 7 weeks for paintings). Every owner is sent a catalogue about 10 to 14 days before the sale, and sale proceeds are paid 3 to 4 weeks after the date of sale.

X. *For buyers at Bonham's*

(a) *Sales programme:* the viewing galleries close at 3.00 p.m. the day before the sale, viewing during normal working hours the day before that (late night viewing Tuesday to 7.00 p.m.) Sales throughout the year, normally at 11.00 a.m., Tuesday—silver and jewellery; Wednesday—watercolours, furs, prints, books; Thursday—furniture, paintings; Friday—ceramics and works of art. Lots Road sales are held on Tuesdays every week for furniture, works of art and household effects; every other week there is a section of pictures; every third week a section of carpets and rugs.

(b) *Buyer's premium:* 10% is charged to the buyer on all lots.

(c) *Payment and clearance of purchases:* purchases are normally paid for and cleared the day of the sale, and items left for longer than a week can be charged 50p per lot per weekday (i.e. £2.50 per week) storage. The Bonham's van is available for delivery, and official warehousing can be arranged.

(d) *Catalogues:* important sale catalogues are circulated 3 weeks in advance and the minimum advance notice is 9 days. Catalogues on subscription in 22 categories (total charge £153 per annum). They can be taken on a 6-monthly or yearly basis on application to Montpelier Galleries.

(e) *Commission bids:* can be placed with any member of the firm including the porters, who normally receive a tip.

XI. *Further services at Bonham's*

(a) *Valuations for insurance, Probate or Family Division:* detailed valuations for insurance at 1½% up to £10,000, 1% on the balance up to £50,000, ½% on the balance thereafter. For Probate or Family Division, 5% up to

£500, 2% on the balance up to £10,000, 1% on the balance thereafter. Minimum charge at Gallery of £10; elsewhere £15, plus expenses. For any items included on such inventories which are sold at Bonham's within a year, a 50% reduction in the valuation fee is credited.

(b) *Introductory commission:* an 'introductory commission is paid (2½% of the hammer price) to anyone (usually Estate Agents) introducing business'.

(c) *Charity auctions:* Bonham's hold many charity auctions in London.

The Specialist Auctioneers

(It should be noted that the four leading fine art auctioneers also hold regular specialized sales in many of these fields.)

STAMPS

The four main specialist stamp auctioneers in London all conduct their sales on a similar basis. Although the conditions of sale state clearly that all statements should be taken as statements of opinion and not of fact, a certain period is allowed (maximum 3 months) in which the authenticity can be tested by outside experts and the sale cancelled if an error be proven. Buyers are required to register their names and addresses with the auctioneers before each sale; commission bids can be left without charge. Estimates are normally printed in the catalogue beside the description of each lot. The delivery of lots for sale, and the collection or dispatch of purchases, pose no problems. It should be noted that Robson Lowe and Harmer's are the exception in the stamp-auction world in as far as they are not involved in the purchase and sale of stamps on their own account, nor on account of their associated companies. Foreign sellers should note that VAT must be paid on lots less than 100 years old.

1. *Stanley Gibbons Auctions Ltd*
Drury House
Russell Street
London WC2B 5HD
Telephone 836 8444
Telex 28883

Opening times: Open for the delivery and inspection of stamps for sale from 9.30 to 4.30, Monday to Friday, and for the inspection of sales from 10.00 to 4.30 (view normally the 3 days prior to sale) and 10.00 to 12.00 on the day of the sale.

Auction procedure for buyers and sellers: specialized sales on a regular basis of all philatelic goods, divided into numerous categories; and of paper currency, of medals, and of maps. The auctions themselves are normally held almost every week on Wednesday, Thursday and Friday, at 1.30 p.m., from September to mid-July. It normally takes 3 months for a consignment to be included in a sale, and payment is one calendar month after the sale (although the buyer can, on application within 7 days, secure a maximum 3 months' extension to satisfy himself as to the authenticity of a stamp). Otherwise the purchaser is required to settle his account within 7 days (14 for foreign purchasers) after which time the auctioneer reserves the authority to resell the lot or to charge interest on the debt.

Selling-commission: From April 1979 vendor's commission of 10% and a buyer's premium of 10%. Lots withdrawn before the auction are charged normal commission on the estimate. No insurance charge; cost-price charge for illustrations in colour in the catalogue.

Catalogue subscriptions: there are about 40 sales a season, the catalogues are produced approximately 6 weeks in advance and the yearly subscription is currently £6 (special airmail edition £8.50).

Turnover: In excess of £5,000,000 season 1977-78.

Inspections and valuations: valuations are undertaken at a charge of $2\frac{1}{2}$% plus out-of-pocket expenses. Fee refunded if property sold at Stanley Gibbons within a year.

Other services
(a) *Sale by private treaty:* sale by private treaty can be negotiated at no cost to the vendor.

(b) *Investment:* advice occasionally given but only as a matter of private opinion by an individual director.

(c) *Publications:* Stanley Gibbons publications are widely distributed.

Staff: 30, 5 of whom are regular expert cataloguers.

Other Offices: permanent offices in Germany, and auctions held in South Africa, Hong Kong, Australia and Japan.

Company structure and affiliated companies: Stanley Gibbons Auctions Ltd is part of Stanley Gibbons International Ltd, comprising about 20% of the turnover. The principal business of Stanley Gibbons International Ltd is the direct sale of stamps, coins and maps, and publishing philatelic works.

2. *Robson Lowe Ltd*
50 Pall Mall
London SW1Y 5JZ
Telephone 839 4034
Telex 915410

Opening Times: for the delivery of property Monday to Friday 9.00 to 5.30, and for the viewing of sales 10.00 to 5.00 in the week prior to the sale (no viewing on the day of sale).

Auction procedure for buyers and sellers: specialized sales of all philatelic goods with particular emphasis on postal history, a subject invented by Robson Lowe. The sales normally start at 10.30 and are held on 4 days a week once a month. No sales in London in August. It takes approximately 4 months for a collection to be offered for sale, and settlement is made 4 weeks after the sale unless the purchaser has requested an extension (up to 60 days). If neither payment nor notification of extension is received within 7 days of the sale (for foreign buyers within 7 days of receipt of goods), the auctioneers reserve the right to charge interest up to $1\frac{1}{2}$% for the first month or part of month, and 1% thereafter (the exact figure depends on the prevailing bank rate). Buyers paying in foreign currency must allow 1% extra to cover bank charges.

Selling-commission: up to £100—20%; £100 to £500—17½%; £500 to £1,000—15%; £1,000 to £2,000—12½%; over £2,000—10%. Minimum charge £4 per lot (£5 per lot of pre-adhesive covers or postal history). Unsold charges are respectively £2 and £3, but additional charges are made if the reserve is more than 80% of the estimate. Withdrawal fee up to 75% of the commission that would have been earned if sold for estimate. No additional charges, as these are all covered by the commission.

Catalogue subscriptions: average 55 to 60 sales a season. Catalogues available on subscription about 6 weeks in advance. The annual subscription for England to all sales in London, Bournemouth and Overseas is £14 at present.

Turnover: 1976-77 £5,300,000 (internationally)

Inspections and valuations: inspection fee depends on amount of work and distance from London, but fee is refunded if leading to a sale within a year amounting to more than £1,000. Written valuations are at a minimum of £5 in the office, and £10 outside or 2% up to £500, 1½% from £500 to £5,000, and 1% thereafter. All these fees are refunded if instructions are received to sell within one year.

Other services
(a) *Sale by private treaty:* considerable business in this field, commission same as auction.
(b) *Tax advice:* detailed advice from Mr Robson Lowe.
(c) *The Trustee Auction Service:* in association with the auctioneers Fox and Sons of Brighton, the TAS looks after a Trust property of any kind including works of art.
(d) *Publications:* Robson Lowe have an extensive list of books and magazines published under their supervision.
(e) *Busy Buyer's Service:* this informs a collector about stamps to be offered for sale in his particular field of interest.
(f) *Introductory commission:* not more than 2% of hammer price.

Staff: about 20 in London, 4 of whom are stamp experts, but all the cataloguing is done in the Bournemouth office.

Other offices: Robson Lowe has a large office in Bournemouth where regular auctions are held, as they are in Basle, Bermuda, Stockholm and Geneva. In addition there are offices in Italy and Australia. Robson Lowe have agents in 11 other countries and 5 different agents in the USA.

Company structure and affiliated companies: Robson Lowe is associated with Christie's. It is also a member of the Uncommon Market with Jacques Robineau of France, J. L. van Dieten of Holland, Paul von Gunten of Switzerland and Adriano Landini of Italy.

3. *H. R. Harmer Ltd*
41 New Bond Street
London W1A 4EH
Telephone 629 0218
Telex 268312

Opening times: for the receipt of property, 9.15 to 5.15, Monday to Friday; sale viewing 10.00 to 4.00 on the Wednesday, Thursday and Friday prior to the sale, and on the day of the sale until 1.00 p.m.

Auction procedure for buyers and sellers: auctions of postage stamps and postal history are held in London on Monday, Tuesday and Wednesday every fortnight, starting at 1.30. It takes 3 to 4 months for a property to be included in a sale, and settlement is made 30 days after the sale. Purchasers are required to pay or give notice of the intention to question the authenticity of a lot, within 7 days (foreign purchasers 'within a reasonable time'). An extension of 30 days is allowed from date of sale to test authenticity, and all outstanding debts after that date are liable to an interest charge of 2% per month.

Selling-commission: 20% up to £1,000, 15% thereafter, 12½% for single lots over £500. There are not normally official reserves, as all lots are automatically protected at ⅔ to ¾ of the estimate, and the unsold charge is therefore only £1 per lot. Lots withdrawn after being catalogued can be charged full selling-commission on estimated price.

Catalogue subscriptions: there are 60 to 70 sessions of auctions a season, and annual subscription is £8 in England.

Turnover: 1976-77 £1,936,597 (London only excluding private treaty)

1977-78 £2,514,915 (London only excluding private treaty)

Inspections and valuations: charge for inspection visits is a £5 minimum, plus valuation fee if client does not agree to sell. Charge for official written valuation is between 1% and 2½% depending on the work involved, and this is refunded if property is sold within 2 years.

Other services
(a) *Sale by private treaty:* 15% up to £1,000, 10% thereafter.
(b) *Postal viewing:* if requested far enough in advance, lots can be sent to a collector unable to come to London to view.
(c) *Lloyds stamp insurance:* a special scheme with Harmer's.
(d) *Introductory commission:* 10% of auctioneer's commission.

Staff: about 25, including 8 resident experts. There are 2 regular outside consultants at present time.

Other offices: regular sales are held at Harmer's New York and Sydney offices.

Company structure and affiliated companies: a family-run business with Cyril Harmer as President, Bernard Harmer as Chairman, and five other Directors.

4. *Plumridge and Co*
6 Adam Street
Strand
London WC2N 6AA
Telephone 836 0939
836 8694

Opening times: 9.00 to 4.45 Monday to Friday. Viewing of sales is by appointment once the catalogue is printed (about 2 months before the sale).

Auction procedure for buyers and sellers: stamp auctions are held every month at the Bonnington Hotel, from October to July. Property is included in a sale within 2 to 3 months of arrival, and proceeds are paid one week after the sale unless there is a dispute.

Selling-commission: basic rate of 15%. 10% for single lots over £250. Unsold lots charged 25p a lot. No further charges.

Catalogue supply: there are 10 sales a year and the catalogues are obtained individually on application, free of charge. About 800 are sent out automatically by the auctioneers.

Inspections and valuations: no charge for sellers, but otherwise up to $2\frac{1}{2}\%$.

Other services: introductory commission is paid of $2\frac{1}{2}\%$.

Staff and structure of company: private partnership of A. N. Zinopoulos, A. Walford and C. M. Zinopoulos, all on permanent expert staff. Total staff of 5, plus 2 part-time and one consultant.

CARPETS AND RUGS
In all three specialized carpet auction houses the catalogue description is not guaranteed and there are protection clauses in the conditions of sale; however sales will be cancelled if purchases are proved not to be authentic. No buyer's premium or any charge on commission bids. Turnover figures not available for any of these auctioneers. Buyers at carpet auctions should remember that the auctioneers are often substantial owners in the sales, and that a relatively high percentage of the lots do not reach their reserves.

1. *Rippon Boswell and Company*
The Arcade
South Kensington Station
London SW7 2NA
Telephone 589 4242

Opening times: 9.30 to 4.30 Monday to Friday, appointment advisable. Viewing of the goods usually from 9.30 a.m. at the Hyde Park Hotel on the day of the sale.

Auction procedure for buyers and sellers: specialized sales of antique Oriental carpets and rugs, weavings, embroideries and

any other textiles, normally held at 11.30 on a Saturday morning
at the Hyde Park Hotel, Knightsbridge. Entries are required a
minimum of 8 weeks in advance, and settlement is within 3 weeks
of the auction, provided the purchaser has paid. 25% or more of
the purchase price must be paid at the end of the sale, and 11%
per month is charged on debts outstanding 3 weeks after the sale.
Storage of goods free for 2 weeks after the sale and delivery in
London free.

Selling-commission: the 20% commission rate includes all expenses
such as valuation, insurance, advertising, illustration, etc. No
commission on unsold lots. Commission negotiable on property
with total reserve price in excess of £10,000.

Catalogue subscription: there are at least 4 sales a year and subscription is £5 per annum in the UK.

Inspection and valuation: inspection visits are made at a cost of £10
per carpet plus travelling expenses. This is the standard charge
for a written valuation.

Other services: include detailed investment consultancy, which is
already supplied on a permanent basis to 17 companies; publications and lectures. Modern carpets are passed to David Hansford
and Co for sale.

Company organization: Rippon Boswell was established in 1884
and is now a subsidiary of The General Consultants Group Ltd
of Jersey. In London there are 5 senior expert consultants and 2
specialist cataloguers. Rippon Boswell has offices in Frankfurt
and Basle, and agents in Sydney, Hong Kong, Nassau, New York,
Paris, Rotterdam, Singapore, Toronto and Tokyo. According to
information supplied by the auctioneers, 40–50% of the lots sold
at auction are owned by themselves or associated companies.

2. *David Hansford and Company*
302–4 Old Marylebone Road
London NW1
Telephone 262 6628

Specialists exclusively in hand-made contemporary Oriental

carpets and textiles. Five to eight sales held a year, normally in a West End hotel on a Saturday at 11.00, viewing from 9.00. Potential buyers can be put on a regular mailing list and sales are announced extensively in the Press.

3. *Lefevre and Partners*
152 Brompton Road
London SW3 1HX
Telephone 584 5516

Opening times: as the company also sells carpets directly, the gallery is open during normal working-hours. Viewing of the sales on the Saturday prior to auction, from 10.00 to 4.00, and Monday to Thursday 10.00 to 6.00 (late closing on Wednesday at 7.00).

Auction procedure for buyers and sellers: auctions specialize entirely in Oriental rugs, carpets and textiles, and are held on the premises at 11.00 on Fridays. Lots must be cleared within 6 days of the sale, and each item will be supplied with a certificate stating the catalogue details and including a colour photograph.

Selling-commission: standard selling-commission of 20%, but a surcharge of 5% on all lots with a reserve in excess of £1,500. Commission includes valuation, insurance, and normal advertising expenses, but there is an extra charge for illustration in colour in the catalogue, and for cleaning and repair which is often insisted on. Unsold lots charged expenses and not commission.

Catalogue subscription: there are between 5 and 10 auctions a year, and catalogues can be obtained on subscription (including price lists) at £3 a year in the UK.

Other services: Colour photographs of lots can be sent to interested buyers, at a charge of 50p each.

Company organization: until 1975 the company operated under the name of the Persian Carpet Galleries, but no details are available about the present structure. Outside consultants are acknowledged in the catalogues.

CIGARETTE CARDS, POSTCARDS, AND OTHER PRINTED EPHEMERA
All three specialists (excluding the Ephemera Society) are full-time dealers, and the major part of their business is in direct sale. They are all active in production of specialist publications. It is normal practice for goods to be paid for and cleared at the sale.

1. *M. A. Murray*
Cigarette and Trade Cards
76 Barnet Way
Mill Hill
London NW7 3AN
Telephone 959 4039

Goods handled and opening times: specialist in cigarette and trade cards but also handles other ephemera of all kinds. Open by appointment from 9.00 a.m. to 9.00 p.m.

Auction procedure for buyers and sellers: the auctions are held at Caxton Hall, Westminster, on Saturday at 1.30 p.m., viewing from 11.00. Collections must be delivered 8 to 10 weeks before the sale and proceeds are paid about 2 weeks after the sale. Buyers are requested to pay within 2 days, commission bidders are informed by sending price list and must settle within 7 days of notification. Every effort is made to ensure the accuracy of descriptions, but any lot can be returned within 5 days if authenticity is doubted.

Selling-commission: 20% inclusive of all charges. Lots failing to sell are charged full commission of the reserve price. Calls are made to inspect interesting properties at no extra charge.

Catalogue subscriptions: there are an increasing number of sales a year, between 6 and 10 at present, and subscription charges vary (currently £1·20 per annum). The reserve price is listed for each lot, together with a condition report. Catalogues printed 5 weeks in advance of sale.

Other services: valuations at $1\frac{1}{2}$%. Publication of trade catalogues, etc.

2. *The London Cigarette Card Company Ltd*
34 Wellesley Road
London W4 4BP
Telephone 994 2346

Goods handled and opening times: the company auctions cigarette
and trade cards and other cartophilic items. Receipt of goods by
appointment, or on day of auction for a subsequent auction.

Auction procedure for buyers and sellers: auctions are held at Caxton
Hall on a Saturday, normally at 2.15, viewing from 11.00.
Property sold between 2 and 8 eight months from delivery. Postal
bidders informed within 7 days and must pay within 7 days from
then, and purchases sent by post. Proceeds not paid until purchaser has paid. If there is any challenge to the catalogue
description, purchases must be returned to the auctioneer within
10 days.

Selling-commission: 20%; minimum charge of 75p for unsold lots
or 5% of reserve price. No calls can be made for inspection.

Catalogue subscriptions: there are 4 to 6 sales a year and they are
circulated free of charge, to between 2,000 and 2,500 collectors
and dealers. Estimates and condition of each lot are listed. No
postal bids under 75p accepted.

Other services: investment advice offered on application. Postal
auctions are occasionally held. Extensive publications include the
monthly *Cigarette Card News* and *Trade Card Chronicle.*

3. *Middlesex Collectors Centre*
(Specialized Postcard Auction Department)
24 Watford Road
Wembley HAo 3EP
Telephone 908 2636 (Wed–Frid only)

Goods handled and opening times: specializes in pre-1930 postcards,
cigarette cards, ephemera and associated material. Open Wednesday to Friday 10.30 to 1.00, and 2.30 to 7.00.

Auction procedure for buyers and sellers: the auctions are held at
Caxton Hall on Monday evenings at 6.00 or 6.30, depending on

the length of the sale. Viewing at the Middlesex Collectors Centre the previous Wednesday, Thursday and Friday, at normal opening times and 12.00 to 6.00 at Caxton Hall on the day of the sale. Purchases cleared at end of sale or sent by mail after payment is received. Collections sold within 6 weeks of consignment.

Selling-commission: 20% under £50 per lot, 15% thereafter. Large collection split into separate lots, special fee by arrangement. Otherwise, minimum charge £1 per lot; unsold lots 50p; withdrawal from the sale 5% of reserve, which is generally at the auctioneer's discretion. Calls can be made to inspect property.

Catalogue subscriptions: presently 10 sales a year, with subscription fee of 85p per 5 sales, plus 65p for list of prices realized. Catalogues printed at least 2 weeks in advance, each catalogue has at least 36 illustrations and estimates on all lots.

Other services: valuations by arrangement. Investment advice from Ken Lawson, the proprietor and sole permanent employee at present time.

4. *The Ephemera Society*
Paper Point
10 Fitzroy Square
London W1P 5AH
Telephone 387 7723
(Private membership auctions, information from secretary.)

BOOKS

Sotheby Parke Bernet and Co
(Hodgson's Rooms)
115 Chancery Lane
London WC2A 1PX
Telephone 405 7238

Goods handled and opening times: sales are held approximately once a fortnight on Thursdays and Fridays at 1.00 p.m., viewing at least 2 days before, during normal opening hours from 9.30 to

4.30. Auctions post-1830 books, letters and manuscripts. Specialized sales include children's books, Broadsides, pamphlets, playbills, art reference books, travel books, law books, first editions, presentation copies, etc.

Further information: see the section on Sotheby's.

COINS AND MEDALS

Glendining & Co Ltd
Blenstock House
7 Blenheim Street
London W1Y OA5
Telephone 493 2445

General information: Glendining's holds about 20 sales a year devoted entirely to coins. The sale-room and offices are located at the back of Phillips's premises and exactly the same opening times and terms of sale apply. Glendining's became part of the Phillips organization soon after the Second World War, but still functions very much as a separate entity.

THE SMALLER AUCTION ROOMS
There are a large number of smaller auctions held every week in the Greater London area, many of them by the local estate agents, and the list below (in alphabetical order) is by no means comprehensive, as it concentrates on those most accessible to Central London. Only brief information is supplied in most cases and further enquiries should be made direct to the auctioneers. Sellers should note the minimum charges levied by most auctioneers, as in some cases, given the cost of transport, it can be better to sell low-value household effects for an agreed price to a house-clearer. Before doing this, it is vital to take professional advice. Most of the firms listed below have qualified auctioneers on the staff (unlike the four main fine art auctioneers) and, in accordance with standard conditions of sale, do not offer any guarantee of authenticity. It is normal practice for commission bids to be left with the porters, the payment for this service being at the discretion of the bidder. Few of these auctioneers publish estimates, but these can often be obtained from the porters.

1. *Allen of Lee Ltd*
Lewisham Auction Rooms
165 Lee High Road
London SE13
Telephone 852 3145

Goods sold: mixed sales of liquidation stocks, second-hand goods and furniture.
General information: sales every one to two weeks on Saturdays. The firm is also active in the removal and storage business.

2. *Bermondsey Auctions Ltd*
175 Bermondsey Street
Newhams Row
London SE1
Telephone 403 2065

Goods sold: Miscellaneous antiques relating to trade in Bermondsey market.
General information: sales every week on Fridays at 11.30, market day at Bermondsey Square

3. *Borough Auctions*
6 Park Street (off Storey Street)
Borough Market
London Bridge
London SE1
Telephone 407 9577

Goods sold: Antiques, second hand and reproduction.
General information: sales almost every week on Sundays at 2.30.

4. *Frank G. Bowen Ltd*
15 Greek Street
Shaftesbury Avenue
London W1
Telephone 437 3244/5

Goods sold: all kinds of office furniture, some household effects, and liquidated property, including motor-cars.

General information: auctions every 2 to 4 weeks on Thursdays at 10.30 and 2.00, viewing whole of the day before. Motor vehicles sold at Hadleigh Street Garage, Malcolm Road, E1. Firm also sells houses and flats.

5. *Bowyer and Bowyer*
8-10 Silver Street
Enfield Town
Middlesex
Telephone 363 8531

Goods sold: Antiques and Household effects.
General information: Sales every other Tuesday at 10.30

6. *Camden Auctions Ltd*
c/o 14 Arlow Road
London N21
Telephone 886 1445

Goods sold: All kinds of antiques.
General information: Sales held monthly on Mondays at 6.30 in The Old Town Hall on Haverstock Hill.

7. *A. Douch*
63/65 Crotched Friar
London EC3
Telephone 642 3772/2502

General information: occasional auctions of silver and jewellery at Caxton Hall.

8. *Dowell Lloyd and Co Ltd*
Putney Bridge Auction Rooms
4, 6 & 8 High Street
Putney
London SW15 1SL
Telephone 788 7777/8/9

Goods sold: all kinds of second-hand and some antique furniture, and mixed selection of consumer goods.

General information: furniture etc sold every fortnight or so on Thursdays; general sales every 3 weeks on Mondays. Standard selling-commission for furniture and works of art $17\frac{1}{2}\%$, but reduced to 15% for quantity. Minimum charge of 25p on unsold lots.

9. *Forrest and Co*
79/85 Cobbold Road
Leytonstone
London E11
Telephone 534 2931

Opening times and acceptance of consignments: delivery Monday to Friday 9.30 to 5.00, except sale days and viewing days. Visits for inspection free of charge. All kinds of antiques and works of art sold, as well as liquidated stock, household effects, etc.

Auction procedure: sales at 11.00 every other Thursday. Every third sale specializes in antiques and works of art. Viewing day before sale, 10.00 to 8.00.

Commission structure: normal selling-commission of 15%, with 5% if item fails to sell on owner's reserve. No minimum charge at present, but 5p per lot catalogue charge.

10. *Fuller Horsey Sons and Cassell*
52 Bow Lane
London EC4
Telephone 248 7954

Goods sold: general household effects.

General information: auctions held at Great Danes Hotel, Ashford, Kent.

11. *General Auctions Ltd*
53/65 Garrat Lane
London SW18
Telephone 870 3909

Goods sold: all kinds of household and second-hand goods, also liquidation stock and bicycles from the Metropolitan Police; separate sales of motor vehicles.

General information: sales every Monday at 10.00, viewing Fridays 9.00 to 12.30 and 1.30 to 5.00. Selling-commission is 12½% for household goods (minimum charge per lot £1) and 7½% for vehicles.

12. *R. F. Greasby (London) Ltd*
211 Longley Road
London SW17
Telephone 672 1100
            672 2972

Goods sold: all kinds of second-hand goods, as well as London Transport Lost Property.

General information: auctions every Monday at 10.30, viewing on the previous Saturday. Selling-commission of 15%.

13. *Great Metropolitan Auction Sales*
115 Lower Clapton Road
London E5
Telephone 985 1579

Goods sold: largely trade auctions of 'seconds', of all kinds of manufactured goods.

General information: sales on Tuesdays at 1.30, viewing on Mondays. Sales on Saturdays at 11, viewing from 10.

14. *Harrods Estate Offices*
Auction Galleries
Arundel Terrace
London SW13
Telephone 748-2739

Opening times and acceptance of consignments: delivery of all properties by appointment, as the only official opening hours are 9.00 to 5.00 on the Monday and Tuesday of sale week. Visits for inspection made and carriage arranged (charge variable). All kinds of antiques and household effects, including specialized sales of furniture, silver and jewellery, wines, pictures, books, etc, as the occasion arises.

Auction procedure: a series of sales are held every fortnight, Wednesday for antique and reproduction furniture, Thursday for works of art, paintings and any specialized sales, and Friday for household effects. Viewing the Monday and Tuesday of that week 9.00. to 5.00. All sales start at 10.00 a.m., with luncheon breaks announced at particular places in the catalogue. Consignments are usually sold within one week of their arrival. Payment and clearance required according to conditions of sale within one day of the sale, thereafter a charge of £1 per lot per week, but in practice a fortnight is allowed for collection.

Commission structure: normal selling-commission is 12½%, with a minimum charge per consignment for all principal sales of £3 and for household properties of £6, or £1 per lot whichever is the greater. Unsold lots charged 2½% if auctioneers suggest the reserve, otherwise 5%. Only further expenses are special advertising and catalogue illustration at negotiated price if necessary (few catalogues illustrated). Payment of sale-proceeds normally within a fortnight. Charge of £3 per lot if withdrawn from the sale.

Catalogue subscription: there are over 100 sales a year and catalogues can be obtained on subscription.

Other services and information:
(a) The Auction Galleries are part of the Estate Office of the Knightsbridge store, and the premises are at their Depositories in Barnes. There are 6 full-time cataloguers and 3 or 4 freelance consultants for specialized sales.
(b) Transport and storage always available (also parking for 200 vehicles).
(c) Valuations undertaken, scale of fee on application.

15. *Harvey's Auctions Ltd*
22/23 Long Acre
London WC2
Telephone 240 1464/5/6/7

Opening times and acceptance of consignments: open Monday to Friday from 9.00 to 5.00 for delivery (without appointment) of all kinds of antique furniture and works of art and household effects, with specialized sections of antiquarian books, pictures, clocks and watches, wines, etc.

Auction procedure: auctions held every Wednesday at 10.30, viewing the previous day from 10.00 to 4.30. Consignments usually sold within 2 to 3 weeks of arrival. Purchases not cleared within one week of the sale are charged £1.25 per lot per week.

Commission structure: vendor's commission of 10%, and buyers' premium of 10%, £1 minimum charge per lot. Only other charges are insurance at 25p per £100. Payment of sale proceeds about 10 days after the sale, guaranteed within 14 days.

Catalogue subscriptions: current subscription charge at £15.00 per annum; catalogue printed one week in advance.

Other services and information:
(a) In August 1976 Harvey's took over Rosan's of Covent Garden which had been founded in April 1976 as an Associate of Rosan's of Croydon. There is a staff of 6 or 7, plus the directors. Harvey's is owned and run by Richard Duboff.
(b) Auctioneers and Bailiffs by appointment to various London Courts.

16. *Patrick Harvey Promotions*
United Reform Church
Streatham High Road
London SW16
Telephone 769 6762

Goods sold: Antiques and household effects.

General information: Every four to six weeks on Tuesdays at 10.30.

17. *Highgate Auctions*
Camden Goods Depot
Warehouse No. 8
Chalk Farm Road
London NW1
Telephone 267 2124

Goods sold: exclusively 'antique' furniture and works of art of all kinds.

General information: sales every 2 or 3 weeks on a Sunday at 2.30. Selling commission is 10% for all sellers (no minimum charge).

18. *Hollingsworth's Auction Rooms*
4 Burford Road
London E15
Telephone 534 1967 (Auction Rooms)
          839 2189 (office for all enquiries)

Goods sold: good selection of antique and second-hand furniture, works of art, and liquidated stock. Department of Environment sales of office furniture at India Pavilion Exhibition Grounds, Wembley, now taken over from Fuller Horsey.

General information: auctions every other Friday at 11.00, viewing Thursdays. Selling-commission of 10% for antiques and works of art sales; 12% for general sales (no minimum charge).

19. *Jarvis Auction Rooms Ltd*
263 Archway Railway Approach
High Road
Leytonstone
London E11
Telephone 539 1941

Goods sold: almost anything from liquidated stock of gaming clubs to antiques.

General information: firm established in 1880 and general sales on the last Wednesday of the month at 12.00; occasional antiques sales on Mondays.

20. *Henry Lewis and Co.*
258 Belsize Road
Kilburn
London NW6
Telephone 624 0151

Goods sold: firm specializes entirely in liquidated properties of all kinds (particularly clothes) and is therefore not open to private consignment.

General information: auctions normally at 10.30 on Wednesdays, about 20 a year fully advertised in national Press. Viewing 9.00 to 5.00 day before sale and from 9.00 on day of sale. Purchases to be cleared by 5.00 on the day following the sale, otherwise liable for the 'expenses of the sale and any loss thereon'. Catalogue subscriptions currently at £10 per annum.

21. *Lots Road Auction Galleries Ltd*
71–73 Lots Road
London SW10
Telephone 352 2349

Opening times and acceptance of consignments: open Monday to Friday 9.00 to 4.30, and warning should be given in advance of delivery of large loads during these hours. Goods sold include antique and modern furniture and general household effects. Inclusion in sale 2 to 3 weeks after arrival. Auctioneers reserve the right to refuse low-value goods or to arrange disposal at owner's expense.

Auction procedure: auctions held on Tuesdays at 7.00, viewing all day on the Mondays and on Tuesdays. Payment must be made within 48 hours and purchases cleared, or the auctioneers are 'entitled at their absolute discretion . . . to resell or store'. A 25% deposit is normally required.

Commission structure: selling-commission of 15%, minimum charge £1 per lot even if unsold (unsold lots 5% of the reserve price). Goods withdrawn prior to the auction, 10% of the approximate value. Only further charges are for insurance (£1 per £100) and removal charge if applicable. Payment of proceeds within 10 days (cash by arrangement) whether buyer has paid or not. Unsold lots must be removed within 3 days of the sale.

Other services and information:
(a) Valuations are carried out at 2½%, or by negotiation.
(b) An introductory commission of 2½%-5% is paid to certain clients.
(c) Lots Road auctions began in May 1975, has a staff of 5, 2 of whom are cataloguers, and a turnover during its first year of £18,000.

22. *Maxwell Miel*
109 Green Lanes
Palmers Green
London N13
Telephone 888 3535

Opening times and acceptance of consignments: open for delivery from 9.00 to 6.00 Monday to Friday, appointment advised for specialist items. Inspection visits arranged free of charge. Firm sells all kinds of specialist furniture and works of art, jewellery, watches, silver, paintings, etc.

Auction procedure: sales held every third Wednesday at 10.00, viewing the day before from 9.00 to 6.00. Consignments sold within maximum of 3 weeks of delivery. Payment and clearance of purchases requested by 4.30 the day after the sale, after which a storage charge can be applied at the auctioneer's discretion.

Commission structure: selling-commission 15%, and 7¼% for items failing to sell, minimum charge £1. No further charges. Proceeds paid within 3 days of the sale, providing the purchasers have paid.

Catalogue subscriptions: there are 12 to 15 sales a year. The catalogues are distributed but cannot be purchased on subscription.

Other information and services:
(a) Maxwell Miel have 4 Estate Offices in North London. The staff at Palmers Green comprises 8 people, 2 of whom are cataloguers, plus 2 consultants.
(b) Valuations undertaken in accordance with the normal scale of fees of the Incorporated Society of Valuers and Auctioneers.

23. *North West London Auctions*
Lodge House
9-17 Lodge Lane
Finchley
London N12
Telephone 445 9000

Goods sold: antiques, reproductions and 'shipping goods'.

General information: sales on Mondays at 6.00, viewing all day Sunday as well as day of the sale.

24. *Portobello Green Bicycle Auction*
Bay 49, Westway Flyover
Portobello Road
London W11
Telephone 221 7272

Goods sold: began in April 1978 merely with secondhand bicycles but expanding to hold regular sales of builders materials, tools, and secondhand furniture and household effects.

General information: sales every Saturday (Portobello market day) at midday.

25. *P. W. Silverstone*
210/212 Brick Lane
London E1 6SA
Telephone 739 3764/5

Opening times and acceptance of consignments: auctioneer of trade stocks, plant and machinery, grocery, confectionery and wines. Normal working hours; an appointment is advised.

Auction procedure: sales on Wednesdays· at 10.00, viewing from 9.30 to 4.30 the previous day. Consignments sold within 4 to 8 weeks.

Commission structure: commission depends on type and extent of the property, ranges from $7\frac{1}{2}\%$ to $12\frac{1}{2}\%$. No charges for unsold goods. Payment of proceeds when purchaser has paid.

Catalogue subscriptions: 20 to 30 sales a season, about 1,500 subscribers.

Other information and services:
(a) Staff of 10 with a turnover of approximately £200,000 per annum.
(b) Valuations at normal charges. Firm specializes also in property valuations.

26. *S. W. London Auctions*
Dennis Taylor
5 Falcon Grove
London SW11
Telephone 228 1375

Opening times and acceptance of consignments: open for pre-arranged delivery 8.00 to 1.00, and will sell all general household goods and jewellery but reserve right to dispose of goods delivered that have no value at auction, in any way, including dumping. Goods can be brought for inspection during sale-viewing time.

Auction procedure: auctions held at 10.00 every third Tuesday, viewing the previous Monday and Friday from 10.00 to 4.00 (sometimes Saturday as well). Consignments normally sold within 2 weeks of arrival. Payment and clearance required within 2 days, thereafter can be charged 'one shilling' per day storage.

Commission structure: 15% selling-commission, 25p minimum

charge. Unsold lots 5%. Only further charge is insurance at 25p per £100.

Catalogue subscriptions: currently 14 sales a year; catalogues available on subscription at £2 per annum, printed approximately one week in advance.

Other services and information:
(a) Introductory commission to estate agents, auctioneers and depositories of 2½% of the commission.
(b) Staff of 6, some part-time.
(c) Valuations at normal scale of fees.

27. *A. Stewart McCracken Ltd*
69 Dean Street
London W1
Telephone 437 8374/5

Goods sold: specialized sales entirely for the catering trade, but some equipment suitable for private houses.

General information: sales on Wednesdays at 2.00, viewing on the morning of the sale.

28. *West London Auctions*
Main Sale-room
Sandringham Mews
High Street
Ealing W5
Telephone 567 7096

Secondary Sale-room
295 High Street
Hounslow
Middlesex
Telephone 572 8070
          572 9005

Opening times and acceptance of consignments: delivery of goods accepted 9.00 to 6.00, Monday to Friday, and 9.30 to 12.00 Saturday. Prior arrangement necessary for large consignments (clients are advised to enquire as to suitability for sale before going to expense of transport). Items accepted include antique furniture and works of art, collectors' items, coins, medals and badges, office furniture at Ealing and general household goods at Hounslow. Charge for use of auction transit-van plus two men is £5 per hour.

Auction procedure: antiques are sold every other Wednesday in Ealing at 11.30. Delivery one to 2 weeks before sale; viewing 2.30 to 7.30 the day before and 9.30 to 11.30 on the day of the sale. Collectors' items are sold on Saturdays or Sundays in Ealing at 3.00 (viewing, day of sale from 10.30). Office furniture and equipment sold once a month in Ealing on Thursdays at 11.30 (sold within a minimum of 3 days after delivery, viewing day before sale 3.00 to 7.00, and day of sale from 9.30). General goods sold in Hounslow on Saturdays at 11.00 (sold from 2 days to 5 weeks after delivery, viewing day before sale 5.30 to 7.30, and day of sale from 9.30). Payment and clearance by noon on the day following the sale, or client is liable to storage and insurance charge of 50p per lot per day. Buyers may be required to deposit 50p per pound per lot. Commission bidders will receive notification directly and must pay and clear within 5 days.

Commission structure: it should be noted that there is a buyer's-commission of 25p per lot and a further 25p per lot for commission bidders. The selling-commission is $12\frac{1}{2}\%$, plus a lot charge of 50p per lot (25p per lot on coins, medals and collectors' items). Buying-in charge of $6\frac{1}{4}\%$ on owner's reserve, but lower if reserve placed on auctioneer's advice. Withdrawn lots only charged lot fee at present. Only other charges are insurance of $\frac{1}{2}\%$, for coverage 75% of agreed reserve, and £7 illustration charge where applicable. Settlement of sale proceeds within 2 weeks, but withheld if purchaser has not paid.

Catalogue subscription: at present 50 sales a year; catalogues 6 to 10 days in advance, obtainable on subscription to various categories (10 issues £2·50).

Other services and information:
(a) Valuations carried out by arrangement.
(b) Introductory commission seldom paid.
(c) Special or trade terms available for regular sellers.
(d) Company began in March 1976, is expanding rapidly having opened the new premises in Ealing in May 1977. There are at the moment 8 full-time employees, 2 of whom are directors and 4 of whom are cataloguers, plus 5 part-time, 8 occasional and 5 consultants.

Notes and Sources

1. *Auctions and Auctioneers*

1 Quoted Gerald Reitlinger, *The Economics of Taste*, 1960. This seminal work is the primary source for much of the information in this chapter
2. Alan B. Saarinen, *The Proud Possessors*, 1959
3. G. D. Hobson, *Some Thoughts on the Rebuilding of the Art Market after the War*, 1949
4. H. C. Marillier, *Christie's*, 1926
5. *The Year at Christie's*, 1927–28
6. Reitlinger, op. cit.
7. Quoted J. Carter, *Art at Auction*, 1970–71
8. The *Weekend Telegraph*, 31 May 1974
9. Ibid.
10. Quoted Marillier, op. cit.
11. Quoted G. D. Hobson, *Some Notes on the History of Sotheby's*, 1917
12. Quoted J. Russell, *Christie's Review of the Year*, 1965-66
13. Quoted Reitlinger, op. cit.
14. R. Wraight, *The Art Game*, 1965
15. *Art at Auction*, 1961–62
16. Wraight, op. cit.
17. A. C. R. Carter, *Let Me Tell You*, 1940
18. Wraight, op. cit.
19. *The Times*, 11 August 1976
20. Knight Frank and Rutley no longer hold auctions of antiques in London, having closed their Bond Street auction rooms in 1970 and amalgamated this part of their business with Christie's
21. *Sunday Times*, August 1966
22. Wraight, op. cit.
23. Ibid.

2. *Christie's*

1. John Herbert, interview with author 1975
2. *Christie's Season*, ed. A. C. R. Carter, 1928
3. Christie sale catalogue, December 1766
4. Ibid.

5. *Public Advertiser*, December 1768
6. Quoted H. C. Marillier, *Christie's 1776–1925*, 1926
7. Charles Jenner, *Town Eclogues*, 1772
8. John Taylor, *Records of my Life*, 1832
9. W. T. Whitley, *Artists and their Friends in England 1700–1799*
10. Ibid.
11. Quoted Marillier, op. cit.
12. Quoted P. Colson, *A Story of Christie's*, 1950
13. The Farington Diaries, 8 vols, 1922–28, ed. J. Grieg
14. Quoted Whitley, op. cit.
15. Quoted Marillier, op. cit.
16. Information supplied by H. Mallalieu
17. Quoted Marillier, op. cit.
18. Ibid.
19. Christie's sale catalogue, 1825
20. Quoted W. Roberts, *Memorials of Christie's*, 1897
21. Marillier, op. cit.
22. G. Reitlinger, *The Economics of Taste*, 3 vols, 1961–70
23. Mariller, op. cit.
24. Ibid.
25. Quoted Reitlinger, op. cit.
26. George Redford, *Art Sales*, 1888
27. Ibid.
28. Quoted A. C. R. Carter, *Let Me Tell You*, 1940
29. Ibid.
30. Ibid.
31. Reitlinger, op. cit.
32. Quoted Marillier, op. cit.
33. Carter, op. cit.
34. Quoted Reitlinger, op. cit.
35. *Christie's Season 1928*, op., cit.
36. Ibid.
37. Colson, op. cit.
38. *Christie's Review of the Year*, 1956
39. *Christie's Review of the Year*, 1958
40. *Christie's Review of the Year*, 1967
41. Ibid.
42. *Christie's Review of the Year*, 1968
43. Ibid.
44. T. S. Eliot, *Old Possum's Book of Practical Cats*, 1962
45. *Christie's Review of the Year*, 1972

46. Quoted Christie's sale catalogue, 2 July 1976
47. Ibid.
48. *Christie's Review of the Year*, 1973
49. Christie's sale catalogue, 27 June 1974

3. *Sotheby's*
1. A. C. R. Carter, *Let Me Tell You*, 1940
2. Lenore Coral, *Art at Auction*, 1969–70
3. Ibid.
4. Quoted *Art at Auction*, 1973–74
5. Quoted M. J. Webb, *Art at Auction*, 1964–65
6. *Art at Auction*, 1968–69
7. *Art at Auction*, 1970–71
8. A. C. R. Carter, op. cit.
9. *Art at Auction*, 1967–68
10. *Art at Auction*, 1968–69
11. Ibid.
12. *Art at Auction*, 1967–68
13. Ibid.
14. Ibid.
15. J. Carter, *Art at Auction*, 1970–71
16. Ibid.
17. Ibid.
18. The *Weekend Telegraph*, op. cit.
19. Quoted Pearsall and Webb, *Inside the Antique Trade*, 1974
20. Quoted G. D. Hobson, *Some Notes on the History of Sotheby's*, 1917
21. Quoted P. Cabanne, *The Great Collectors*, 1963
22. *Art at Auction*, 1970–71
23. Sotheby's catalogue, Horbilt Collection Part 1, 10 June 1974
24. Sotheby's catalogue, Plesch Collection Part 1, 16 June 1975
25. G. Brown, unpublished manuscript, 1975
26. Letter dated 5 December 1929, in the possession of C. Donaldson

4. *Phillips*
1. Phillips's auction catalogue, Thursday 11 August 1836
2. Ibid.
3. Quoted in *Twenty Thousand Sales at Phillips, 1796–1974*
4. Phillips's sale catalogue, 9 February 1798
5. Quoted in *Phillips*, op. cit.
6. Ibid.
7. Marylebone Rooms catalogue

5. *Bonham's*
1. *Bonham's Review*, 1973–74
2. Ibid.

6. *Sotheby's Belgravia and Christie's South Kensington*
1. Pantechnicon Advertising Leaflet, n.d.
2. Ibid.
3. H. Hobhouse, *Thomas Cubitt*, 1971
4. Leaflet, op. cit.
5. As at January 1977
6. R. Ash, *Art at Auction*, 1973–74
7. Christie's press release, February 1975
8. *Christie's Review of the Year*, 1974–75

7. *The Specialist Auctioneers*
1. Edward Barber and Son Ltd holds its sales about six times a year in Sir John Lyon House on Upper Thames Street. The cases of graded bristles usually come from India or Nepal, and the most sought-after seem to be 'Agmark Extra Stiff Certificate'.
2. The Tea Brokers Association auctions average £2,500,000–£3,500,000 every week at their headquarters in Sir John Lyon House. The technique is very different from the fine art auction houses, as each tea broker auctions his own tea, while the tea buyers for the big houses such as Brooke Bond call out their own bids, and even divide consignments during the sale. The auctions are fast–moving, noisy and exciting
3. Interview R. Lowe
4. *Stanley Gibbons 1856–1956*
5. Stanley Gibbons catalogue, 5 May 1976
6. Ephemera Society catalogue, July 1976
7. Lefevre catalogue, 2 April 1976
8. Jack Franses joined the staff of Sotheby's as carpet consultant in September 1976, (he is now a Director) and Sotheby's London catalogues of carpets immediately improved in quality and are building up to a high standard.
9. Lefevre catalogue, 17 May 1974
10. *Daily Telegraph*, 17 June 1974
11. Rippon Boswell catalogue, 7 June 1976
12. For a complete history of these unusual auctioneers, see Allingham, *The Romance of the Rostrum*, 1924

8. *The Smaller Auctioneers*

1. From assorted catalogues
2. Forrest catalogue, April 1976
3. Ibid.
4. Maxwell Miel catalogue, July 1976
5. Highgate Auctions catalogue, April 1976
6. Ibid.
7. Ibid.
8. Galbraith, *Harrods Estates Office 1922–1972*
9. Harrods catalogue, May 1974
10. Harrods sale catalogue notice
11. Henry Lewis and Co catalogue, March 1976
12. Frank Bowen catalogue, April 1976

Select Bibliography

ALLEN, F. L., *The Great Pierpont Morgan*, London, 1949
ALLINGHAM, E. G., *The Romance of the Rostrum*, Witherby, London, 1924
BEHRMAN, S. N., *Duveen*, Hamish Hamilton, London, 1973
BLANC, C., *Le Trésor de la Curiosité tiré des Catalogues des Ventes*, Paris, 1858
BURNHAM, B., *The Art Crisis*, Collins, London, 1975
CABANNE, P., *The Great Collectors*, Cassell, London, 1963
CARTER, A. C. R., *Let Me Tell You*, Hutchinson, London, 1940
CARTER, J. W., *Books and Book Collectors*, London, 1956
Connoisseur, The, London, 1903–
DUPLESSIS, G. V., *La Vente des Tableaux au Dix-huitième Siècle*, Paris, 1874
DUVEEN, J. H., *The Secrets of an Art Dealer*, London, 1937
ESTEROW, M., *The Art Stealers*, Weidenfeld and Nicolson, London, 1967
GETTY, J. P., and ELLEN LE VANE, *Collectors Choice*, London, 1955
GIMPEL, R., *Diary of a Picture Dealer*, Hodder and Stoughton, London, 1966
GRAVES, R., *Art Sales*, London, 1918–1921
HASKELL, F., *Rediscoveries in Art*, Phaidon, London, 1976
HELFT, J., *Treasure Hunt*, Faber, London, 1957
HERMANN, F., *The English as Collectors*, London, 1972
JEPPSON, L., *Fabulous Frauds*, 1970
KEEN, G., *The Sale of Works of Art*, Nelson, London, 1971
LUGT, F., *Repertoire des Catalogues de Vente 1600–1825*, 2 vols, Paris, 1938
MIDDLEMAS, K., *The Double Market*, Saxon House, London, 1975
REDFORD, G., *Art Sales*, London, 1889
REITLINGER, G., *The Economics of Taste*, Vol I 1961, Vol II 1963, Vol III 1970, Barrie, London
RHEIMS, M., *Art on the Market*, Plon, Paris, 1960
RUSH, R. H., *Antiques as Investment*, Prentice-Hall, New York, 1968
    Art as Investment, Prentice-Hall, New York, 1961
SAARINEN, A. B., *The Proud Possessors*, Random House, New York, 1958
SOWERBY, E. M., *Rare People and Rare Books*, London, 1967
STUART-PENROSE, B., *The Art Scene*, London, 1969

TAYLOR, J. R. and BROOKE, B., *The Art Dealers*, Hodder and Stoughton, London, 1969
The Year's Art, ed. A. C. R. Carter, London, 1882–1947
WHITLEY, W. T., *Artists and their Friends in England 1700–1799*, 2 vols, London, 1928
WRAIGHT, R., *The Art Game*, Leslie Frewin, London, 1965

Christie's
'A Chat about Christie's', *London Society*, 1871
Christie's Review of the Season, London, 1971–
Christie's Review of the Year, London, 1956–1970
Christie's Season, Constable, London, 1927–1931
COLSON, P., *A Story of Christie's*, Sampson Low, London, 1950
MARILLIER, H. C., *Christie's 1766–1925*, Constable, London, 1926
ROBERTS, W., *Memorials of Christie's*, London, 1897
SUTTON, D., *Christie's Since the War*, London, 1959
'The King of Epithets', D. Sutton on James Christie, *Apollo*, November 1966

Sotheby's
Art at Auction, London, 1966–
BOURLET, J., *The Works of the House of Bourlet*, London, 1959
HOBSON, G. D., *Some Notes on the History of Sotheby's*, London, 1917
Hodgson & Co, One Hundred Years of Book Productions, 1807–1908, London
Ivory Hammer, The, London, 1926–1966
KARSLAKE, F., *Notes from Sotheby's*, London, 1909
Sotheby's Season, London, 1957–1962
TOWNER, W., *The Elegant Auctioneers*, New York, 1971

Index